Contents

Foreword

John B. Cobb Jr.

As a group of progressive Christians the authors of this book find ourselves called not only to reform the world but also to resist much that we cannot reform. But what do we mean by calling ourselves "progressive" Christians, and what do we mean by "resistance"?

PROGRESSIVE CHRISTIANITY

We identify ourselves as "progressive Christians." This term has gained wide currency only in the last decade or two. We who now call ourselves progressives are liberals in the sense that we rethink our faith in the light of critical-historical study, especially that of the Scriptures, and we take into account in our thinking the well-established conclusions of the natural and social sciences. Furthermore, we are heirs of the North American "social gospel."

We are still "liberal Christians" in the sense that we have listened to criticism and found much of which to repent in our own ecclesiastical history. On the other hand, if to be "liberal" means to hold fast to positions that liberals adopted a century ago, or fifty years ago, or even ten years ago, then we are not liberal.

In particular we recognize that Protestant liberalism internalized the values of the eighteenth-century Enlightenment with much too little criticism. The Enlightenment affirmed the rights of the individual against oppressive societies. We continue that affirmation. But we now realize that the Enlightenment tended to understand societies only as aggregations of autonomous individuals and that many liberal Protestants also adopted this extreme individualism. Too many of us have accepted economic and political theories and practices that are based on this erroneous view. Too often we have regarded even the church as a voluntary aggregation of like-minded individuals. Against this we strive to recover Paul's understanding that we are members one of another. As community life has been eroded, we have come to appreciate its value and to repent of our acquiescence in its erosion.

We recognize that liberal Protestantism through its internalization of Enlightenment individualism often understood the human norm in terms of the Christian, or even the Protestant, European male. Its universalistic rhetoric actually supported contempt for the supposedly inferior cultures and races. Its missionary programs too often worked hand in hand with colonialism. At best it supported efforts to "raise" other people to "our" level and to integrate them into "our" society.

Within Christian societies, liberal Protestants long supported the continuation of patriarchy. In the social gospel, men often sought to protect women from extreme exploitation and abuse, but they assumed the difference of roles in ways that clearly left them in charge. It took strong action on the part of women to awaken liberal Christian men from their patriarchal slumber.

As heirs of the American social gospel, we have been deeply informed by Reinhold Niebuhr's critique of its naiveté and unrealistic optimism. Then in turn we have come to see the failure of Niebuhr to transcend a Euro-American perspective on world history. We now try to set our history in the context of the larger planetary one and our religious tradition in the broader context of the history of world religions.[1]

In the sixties we were inspired and reenergized by the civil rights movement of Martin Luther King Jr. In the seventies our assumptions about the normativity of the Anglo-Saxon Protestant person and culture were challenged by the Black Power movement and by black theology. During those decades we became more aware of the horrors we had inflicted on the indigenous inhabitants of this continent not only by obviously vicious theft of their land and near genocide but also by our efforts to assimilate them into our culture. We saw that the ideal of "integration" was itself damaging not only to blacks and Native Americans but also to Hispanics and Asians and even to various European groups. We began to shift from promoting integration into *our* society to trying to envisage and support a multicultural and multireligious one.

During the same period we also became aware of how traditional Christian teaching bore great responsibility for the genocide of the Jews in Europe. We discovered that the liberal form of Christianity was hardly less anti-Jewish in many of its formulations than was orthodoxy. We tried to change our theology to overcome Christianity's negative depiction of Judaism.[2] More recently we have realized that at times our effort to overcome the anti-Judaism of our tradition has heightened Christian opposition to Islam.[3]

In the seventies and eighties, we were informed and transformed by Latin American liberation theology. Prior to that time few of us took Latin America seriously enough to evaluate critically American policy toward it. Now our eyes were opened not only to the injustices and oppressions of a class society there but also to American involvement in its establishment and its maintenance, and to American exploitation of Latin American people and resources. The issues of class that had faded with the decline of the earlier social gospel once again were brought to the fore in our thinking. The third-world development programs we had been supporting and trying to expand no longer looked like an adequate, or even an appropriate, response to the real needs of much of the third world. We were also taught new ways of reading the Bible. Women and men from diverse American ethnic communities and from Latin America, Africa, Asia, and the Pacific, often inspired by black and Latin American theology, have been contributing their distinctive insights, and we have tried to learn from them.

During much the same period, we have realized that our Enlightenment heritage has been particularly harmful in its anthropocentrism and its dualistic understanding of humanity and nature. Anthropocentrism and dualism can be found in the Scriptures, but they do not dominate there. The employment of Greek categories in the theology of the ancient church and the Middle Ages aggravated both, but it was in modern philosophy that they reached their apex. This philosophy has shaped the natural and social sciences. And this extreme anthropocentrism and dualism have been deeply internalized in major forms of the liberal Protestant tradition.

We participated in the broader Western actions shaped by anthropocentrism and dualism that bear heavy responsibility for the development of the global ecological crisis. We rejoice that at ecumenical and denominational levels, Christians have widely repented. We regret that this repentance has not gone nearly far enough in effecting practical changes. It has not deeply altered century-old habits of thought and action. We still participate in a society that is deforesting the world, eroding its soils, exhausting its aquifers, poisoning the air, destroying the ocean fisheries, and in general degrading the earth. We are finally acknowledging that our activity is disastrously changing the global climate. We continue to live in ways that acquiesce in this society's unsustainable practices. But at least we no longer intentionally subscribe to the teachings that have justified it all.

We have been affected most intimately by the feminist movement and the theology it has generated. The change it has brought about in the week-by-week life of our congregations has been impressive. Such change includes the ordination of large numbers of women and new styles of leadership introduced by women at all levels of administration in our denominations. It has also resulted in renovations and innovations in liturgy, promoted especially by new, inclusive language in biblical translations and hymnals that have reduced, or even eliminated, the patriarchal bias of traditional language. We have been trying also to understand better the experience of women and to incorporate their distinctive insights into the teaching and practice of our church at all levels. Feminists showed that patriarchy's understanding of sexuality was a key source of the terrible homophobia that has characterized the church through so much of its history and for which we urgently need to repent.

We were pained to find that on this point so many of those fellow Christians who had moved with us in other changes balked. They clung to the patriarchal notion that physical expression of love of those of the same gender is a sin, and they seemed to regard it as a particularly heinous one. Accordingly, they opposed ceremonies celebrating the unions of gays and lesbians. They opposed ordaining those of homosexual orientation who would not commit themselves to celibacy. Appealing basically to the deep-seated patriarchal feelings that still hold sway among many of our contemporaries, they found a few expressions of similar feelings in the Bible and used these to justify their continued oppression of lesbians and gays. The line between progressives and other Christians became quite sharply drawn on this issue.

Are we still liberals? Since the many changes we have made express the liberal spirit, we think that, in a very important sense, we are. At this point we differentiate ourselves from others who have reacted sharply against their liberal heritage. Some call themselves "postliberals"; others, "neo-orthodox" or "radical orthodox." We differ from them in that we have approached all the new developments described above in a liberal spirit, trying to learn from them and to allow them to transform us. The tendency of those who now strongly reject the label "liberal" is to emphasize their close continuity with the older, pre-Enlightenment Christian tradition. This, of course, took shape long before many of the issues that are now so important to us arose. Those who adopt these labels do not necessarily reject all these new criticisms and demands for change. But their priority is continuity with earlier forms of Christianity.

We, on the other hand, affirm our liberal heritage as an important part of our total heritage. We do not look to any earlier epoch in the life of the church as free from distortions and limitations. We see much to criticize in traditional orthodoxy and in Reformation theology as well, and we often side with earlier liberals in these criticisms. We hope to continue to find better ways of formulating and acting out our faith, richly informed by the past, but not accepting any stage in that past as fundamentally superior to all the others.

We, too, seek continuity. But we believe that at its best the church has always been learning and growing. The more deeply the church is rooted in its own history, the freer it is to appreciate criticism and to learn from new realities and ideas. We read the Bible itself as the story of repeated transformations. As christocentric believers, we hope to respond creatively to the challenges and opportunities of our day as Christians of other times have, at their best, responded to their challenges and opportunities.

Nevertheless, we do not call ourselves "liberals." Many people today understand the term *liberal* to identify the form of liberalism criticized by Reinhold Niebuhr or by liberationists or by ecologists. We affirm all these criticisms. Also, some of those who emphasize their liberalism take an Enlightenment, even a "scientistic," worldview for granted and affirm only those Christian ideas that can pass muster in that context. This style goes back to eighteenth-century deism, but today it is likely to affirm even less. For us, the many challenges to which we have responded lead to enrichment of belief, not to its impoverishment. We do not associate ourselves with those "liberals" who are much clearer about what they do not believe than about what they affirm and live by.

The term *progressive* is by no means ideal. It could mean that we believe that a great deal of progress has occurred and that we can expect more. As will become clear, this is far from our current conviction. There was a major "progressive" movement in American history, and it had all the strengths and limitations associated with any political movement. It is not our model.

Nevertheless, the term *progressive* currently connotes views of the sort we hold. In any case, it is far more open than *liberal* to fresh definition of the sort we are offering here. As a shorthand definition, we may say that "progressive Christians" are those who stand in the liberal, social gospel tradition as it was later transformed through the influence of Niebuhrian criticism and also as by liberation theologies, especially those developed in black, Latin American, and feminist circles. We have also been deeply affected by our awareness of the ecological crisis and the contribution that traditional Western theology has made to it, as well as by our increased understanding and appreciation of other religious traditions and indigenous spirituality.

Progressive Christians long to become a community that is radically inclusive. However, most of us, as of now, are middle-class Euro-Americans. We hope that much of what we say will make sense in other communities in the United States and that in time we will not have to acknowledge this limitation. But for now, while we can learn from the poor and from other ethnic groups, we cannot speak for them. For the most part this book expresses the experience of one segment of American society and is largely addressed to other members of that segment. We are calling for repentance for crimes that this segment has inflicted on others and continues to inflict.

REFORM AND RESISTANCE

Writing theology is largely a matter of reflecting on ourselves as Christians. This has certainly been true of our writing on resistance. We realized that our normal approach to problems has been to analyze them, suggest solutions, and identify steps that can be taken to move toward those solutions. That is, we have been committed to *reform*. We have understood that the normal meaning of "reform" in American history has been to improve the situation in the direction that as Christians we affirm. We have been distressed to see how this term has been co-opted by those who want changes of a different sort, changes that favor the interests of the few against the common good. We want to recover the historic meaning of the term, and we favor such reform when it is possible. Seeking reform requires both thought about where one hopes to go and about what current steps have the best chance of moving in that direction. We continue to involve ourselves in these concerns.

However, at some times and places it seems that an unjust or destructive order is so entrenched that reform is not possible, or that we cannot settle for the moderate reforms that may be possible. In some contexts, under circumstances of this sort, the talk is of violent revolution. Some Latin American liberation theologians supported revolutionary movements of this sort in their countries. Whether as Christians we can ever participate in the destruction and killing involved in that kind of revolution is an issue of great importance in Christian ethics, but it is not directly relevant to our current practical decisions. Even though we see the current U.S. administration as having violated the law and the Constitution, none of us views the present situation in the United States as one that calls for violent revolution.

On the other hand, we see what is happening in our country and in the world as moving, overall, in the wrong direction. This is a reversal of the dominant liberal point of view in recent centuries. Under the influence of the Enlightenment our forebears have seen their context as one that has the possibility and actuality of progress in the sense that ideals they viewed as Christian were having increasing effects in the ordering of society. This came to a climax in the early stages of the social gospel. After World War II, many of us retained or renewed that positive perception of world affairs. As Christians we saw the defeat of fascism and Nazism, the political liberation of former colonies, the rebuilding of Europe and Japan, and the emergence of a new international order as embodying genuine progress. This general sense of progress was strengthened by the successes of the civil rights movement and feminism. We saw our churches repenting of their racism and patriarchalism, and also of their anti-Judaism and exclusivist theology. We saw some progress toward the reduction of poverty. We saw great improvement in relations between Protestants and Catholics as a result of the Second Vatican Council.

We were by no means content with the progress that was being made. We saw that racism and patriarchalism and anti-Judaism were still with us. We saw that much more reform was required in order to meet the basic needs of the poor. We saw that we were far from the unity of the church for which we longed. We were aware of the threat of nuclear war. We were appalled by what happened in Vietnam. We were discouraged by the slow pace of economic development in the third world and by the diversion of enormous resources into the cold war. But we could still see the needed changes as possibilities to be worked for. Far more reforms were urgent, but at a deep level, history seemed to be on our side. Our churches on the whole supported movement in the direction that would further reduce human misery and injustice.

Within the movements toward reform there were acts of resistance. Civil disobedience was a technique of the civil rights struggle and of the efforts to end the Vietnam War as well. Refusing segregated seating and tearing up draft cards were clear acts of resistance. But for the most part these acts of resistance were for the sake of genuinely possible changes, and in fact they contributed to the ending of legal segregation and the Vietnam War. We generally evaluated them according to their contribution to reform.

The change for those of us who now identify ourselves as progressives is that we no longer see the deeper historical trends as promising. Our society was once oriented toward encouraging good citizenship. Today it is oriented to producing workers for the market. A once-widespread concern for the common good is now being increasingly replaced by the aim to achieve competitive success in the market. The formal institutions of democracy remain, but the level of public participation and public discourse about issues declines. Public opinion is manipulated in increasingly sophisticated ways by the media through political advertising and by editorial control. There is reason to think that when the results still do not satisfy the plutocracy, it can directly manipulate the counting of votes. And if even that fails, it can still manipulate most of those elected to office. Indeed, few politicians can mount an effective campaign without making commitments to moneyed interests. Even if improvements are effected here and there, the broader move toward plutocracy seems unstoppable.

Plutocratic control means that national and global policies are geared toward the increase of wealth and power for the already rich and powerful. The means by which this is accomplished not only destroy human community everywhere but also devastate the natural environment. Statistically the world becomes richer, but nations are less and less able to provide a good life for their citizens. The whole system is geared in a way that makes life for most people less enjoyable and further undercuts the possibilities of a good life in the future. The new effects of global warming are an important illustration of the continuing decline, but by no means the only one.

To organize the whole world to serve ends that degrade life, human and natural, is strictly and literally insane. Yet the world's most powerful governments, and especially our own, work with corporate wealth and manipulate the Bretton Woods Institutions to achieve just these ends. There is little criticism of these global commitments, or even discussion of them, in the public media, partly because many believe that no other world is possible. From those who can envision no alternative, little opposition can come, only the effort to protect themselves and their families from the devastating results of the basic policies.

What do we do when we see the forces that are leading to a destructive end as so powerful and pervasive that we cannot imagine how any act on our part can stop them? Do we then simply acquiesce? Surely not! We are called to *resist*. But what form can or should such resistance take?

When we ask this question, we see early Christianity in a different light. No Christian in the first two or three centuries of Christianity supposed that any acts of Christians would reform the Roman Empire. Yet they saw the principles and values on which the empire was established to be fundamentally contrary to Christian teaching. For them, to live by Christian principles and values was a form of "resistance," an immensely important one. In this sense, the communities established by Paul were centers of resistance. Paul did not try to abolish the institution of slavery in the empire, but within these Christian communities slaves were treated as full human beings. Paul did not try to overturn patriarchy, but within these communities women could exercise leadership. Paul did not try to abolish poverty, but within these communities widows and orphans were cared for. His communities strove to order their lives by mutual love rather than according to principles of controlling power.

In other words, one major form of resistance is simply to live, individually and in communities, in a countercultural way. If people do this in order to have a wider effect, they will almost always be disappointed and consider their efforts to be a failure. This form of resistance is not undertaken as a means to reform. But if Christians live in a countercultural way because they are called by God to that way of life, the concern about an influence on the larger society fades, and paradoxically, in the long run, the actual influence may increase.

A clear instance of this kind of resistance in recent times is that of the Confessing Church in Nazi Germany. It had no prospect of changing the course of events of world history. Bonhoeffer himself did try to do this by participating in a plot to assassinate Hitler. But those who created the Confessing Church and participated in it had no such goal. Christians did so simply because faithfulness to Jesus Christ required that they do so. The fact that they did has been important for the self-understanding of Christians, especially in postwar Germany, and it is increasingly important for us today. But this sort of influence on the future was not the reason for establishing this confessing community.

Postliberals, such as Stanley Hauerwas, have for some years called for the church to concentrate on its own interior faithfulness, setting aside the issue of how it affects society. We can be grateful for his witness. Progressives have been slow to appreciate the need for this kind of resistance.

Still the difference between us and these postliberals is considerable. Some of the things we feel most strongly that we should resist were not objects of resistance until recently. The degradation of the earth by human activity was a problem of which few Christians were aware in previous centuries. Progressives who feel called to live counterculturally may adopt principles that are not too different from those to which Hauerwas calls Christians in the name of traditional faithfulness. But there will be a significant difference in the analysis and motivation, one that will also affect the way people act.

The most significant difference with such postliberals is that wherever progressive Christians can identify actions that have a chance of making a positive difference, we will pursue them. If the world can yet be saved from the worst effects of global warming, as individuals and denominations we will do what we can to effect the needed changes. Often the best response to the dominance of what many Christians experience as demonic power is a combination of countercultural living and public and political action. There are still open to us possibilities of influencing the course of events that were not open to Christians in the first centuries or in Nazi Germany. We should use them as we can.

A second difference is that when we continue to seek for ways to make a change, we will try to form alliances with all who can help us make that change, whatever their religious positions. Even while we resist the basic drift of our culture by living from countercultural values, we will work together with many who share our opposition to this or that expression of this drift to make what gains we can.

A third difference is that we not only deplore the dominant currents of society and opt out for ourselves, we also hold up the picture of an alternative, not just for the church but also for the world. This may seem utopian and be ridiculed or ignored. But it is important that people know that the self-destructive world in which we now live is not the only possible one. Together with those who gather in the World Social Forum, we must proclaim that "another world is possible" and then make this possibility visible.

THE BOOK

The chapters in this book were written as position papers of Progressive Christians Uniting, an independent ecumenical organization in the Los Angeles basin organized about ten years ago. PCU has a Reflection Committee charged with preparing papers for discussion by the Board of Directors and eventual approval. Most of the writing was done by the committee, but suggestions and criticism stemming from discussions by the board have also contributed.

The astute reader may have noticed that there is a tension in what has been said above between a focus on Protestantism and on Western Christianity as a whole. This is a tension we have felt for a long time. The original group that established (in 1996) what later became Progressive Christians Uniting did not include Roman Catholics. We thought that our problems as Protestants were somewhat distinctive and that we needed to maintain that identity as an alternative to the Christian Right, which is clearly a Protestant movement. Our relation to the Enlightenment and to the dominant culture of the United States has been different from that of Roman Catholics. We also thought that organizations already existed within Roman Catholicism for dealing with comparable issues whereas progressive Protestants seemed at that time surprisingly unorganized.[4] Hence we decided to recognize that our issues and efforts would be related to the Protestant churches, basically to those that we now call "old-line."

On the other hand, we have always been delighted to receive assistance from our Catholic friends. This has been significant. We have had Catholics on our board and as members of the Reflection Committee and Catholic leaders as well as participants in our conferences and other activities. One of the chapters in this book was written by a Catholic. The critical help of Catholics in other chapters should be acknowledged. Today on many issues Catholics and Protestants face similar problems in similar ways. Nevertheless, the work of PCU as a whole is shaped in terms of the Protestant situation, a situation that Catholics can help us to understand.

Most of our position papers have treated current social issues. The views of progressive Christians on many of these issues are similar to those of other liberal Christians and many conservative evangelicals, although our perspective is quite different from that of the politically slanted "religious Right," which has so shaped the public image of American Protestantism. We believe that our views should be heard and recognized as an important expression of contemporary Christian faith. Of course, *we* believe that our perspective is far *more* faithful to Jesus Christ than much of what the American public has recently been led to believe constitutes the Christian agenda for society.

We have published one volume of essays,[5] and we have adopted additional position papers of this kind since then. However, before publishing them, we want to share our deeper thinking about the perspective from which we write. This book deals more directly with the way we think about our faith and our basic situation and calling.

Our earlier book was presented as our collective work. In this book we identify primary authors, even though valuable contributions were made throughout by unidentified members of the committee.

The earlier book is primarily a call for reform. The shift of focus to resistance took place gradually. It was as much a growing recognition of a position we already held as a change of stance. But its articulation was personally and collectively important for us. We hope it will be clarifying for others as well.

Not surprisingly, perhaps, the shift took place during our protracted discussions of the position paper on the authority of the Bible. We took up this topic shortly after adopting the paper on liberation theology that comes later in the book. We came to the conclusion that the Word of God that comes to *us* through the Bible today is first and foremost a call to resist the dominant forces in our world. We have placed that chapter first.

Resistance calls for deeper levels of conviction and commitment than does working for reform. It must be sustained without perceived results even when these include widespread hostility and even persecution. Elements of such resistance have characterized the lives of great Christians in every generation. Martin Luther King Jr. represents the highest expression of such resistance in our own country. Christians such as King have strengthened their ability to resist through prayer. Our second chapter recommends that Protestants reemphasize the life of prayer and recover forms of prayer they have neglected.

Resistance is not directed to all aspects of society and culture. There is much in American life that we continue to celebrate and affirm. It is important to identify clearly what as Christians we are called by the Word of God to resist. We have selected five features of our society. Part 2 consists of accounts of these features.

Chapter 3 proposes that the dominant religion of our nation, even of many who think of themselves as Christians, is consumerism. It is astonishing how rapidly consumerism has overwhelmed religious traditions whose teachings condemn it and how little objection these traditions have offered. If we are to resist consumerism effectively, we must understand what it is and how it has won its way as well as the reality of other ways of understanding life and organizing society.

Chapter 4 deals with the growing gap between rich and poor. Although the increase in this gap has long been occurring globally both between and within nations, our focus is on American society. Much of the Bible is written from the perspective of the poor and oppressed, but it is too easy for those of us who belong to the affluent segment of society, even though we claim to recognize its authority, to be silent in the face of this trend. The forces that are reshaping society in this way are powerful, but we can still identify them and resist them.

Chapter 5 views American history and our present role in the world in light of growing recognition that from the beginning the United States has functioned imperialistically. By vigorously advocating imperial policies, the neoconservatives have enabled us to see what has been there all along, usually in ways more hidden from public awareness. We realize that simply "throwing the rascals out" will not change the basic course of American foreign policy. We see no practical way to bring American foreign policy in line with Christian teachings, but where it runs in a diametrically opposite direction, we are called to resist.

Chapter 6 turns attention to a question of worldview. Liberals have rightly appreciated the truly wonderful accomplishments of the natural sciences and of the universities that provide them with a home. Sadly, it becomes clearer and clearer that scientific formulations have bound themselves to the Cartesian understanding of nature as a machine, the implications of which are profoundly damaging. This view is so well entrenched that it is hard to imagine freeing the Western mind from its hold, but we must do what we can to liberate ourselves and deny our support.

One of the areas in which the dominant Western worldview has done great harm is with regard to the natural environment. The attitudes, policies, and actions that this worldview has encouraged threaten the future of life on the planet. There is nothing that calls more clearly for our resistance than human destruction of the environment. Chapter 7 focuses specifically on global warming.

Part 3 turns directly to theology. As we call for resistance to dominant trends in our society, we find that we are not alone. Indeed, we have arrived at our understanding of the need to resist only because of the theological work of others.

The preceding chapters are most directly influenced by Latin American liberation theology. Chapter 8 deals with that. To understand both the ways we can appropriate this theology as our own and the limitations of such appropriation, we need to learn what it is and how it came into being. To understand how to relate to it today, we need to see that it, too, is evolving.

Chapter 9 deals with feminist theology. This strikes closer to home. Many, perhaps even most, progressive Christians are women! And most of these women identify themselves, at least in part, as feminists. With respect to our daily lives, our professional activities, and our churches, it is feminist theology that is of greatest immediate relevance. Because patriarchal habits of mind are so deeply entrenched, it may be that the task of feminist theology is the most basic and the most difficult of all.

Part 4 concludes the book with reflections about ourselves and our churches. There is no unambiguous way of responding to God's call. Both as churches and as individuals, we are always caught in dangers and dilemmas. The call to resist, which now seems so central to us, heightens these ambiguities. We need to think about our actions critically without being inhibited from action.

This book primarily addresses progressive Christians as individuals and as groups. But most of us are committed to our local congregations and to the institutional church. What the church can and should do in response to God's call needs separate consideration, and we devote chapter 10 to this topic.

Chapter 11 focuses on forgiveness, which is important in two ways. First, the act of resistance easily leads to hostility toward those who carry forward the ideas, policies, and practices we resist. Those who resist often feel some pride in their righteousness and courage. Against these tendencies Jesus places forgiveness in a central place. Second, forgiveness is a test case of the extent to which specifically Christian virtues have a role in political action. We conclude by celebrating those rare occasions when it has contributed to the politics of reconciliation.

Resistance can seem purely negative. However, crucial to effective resistance is a vision of an alternative, the "other world" that is possible, or the *basileia theou* ("kingdom of God," or, as we prefer, the divine commonwealth) proclaimed by Jesus. In all our chapters we try to give at least some indication of this other possibility for which we actively hope. Living from and toward this possibility can subvert the widely held assumption that acceptance of the status quo is the only realistic way to live

It is not always clear what resistance can mean in concrete terms. We have added an afterword to discuss and amplify the practical implications of what we have written. We are still struggling to understand what God calls us to be and do in a society uninterested in the common good, a nation constructing an empire sometimes in the name of the empire-opposing Jesus, and in a world bent on a suicidal course. This book expresses our effort to understand what it means here and now to be faithful to Jesus.

The first chapter begins with a selection from the Accra Declaration of the World Alliance of Reformed Churches, and the fourth chapter ends with another. We associate ourselves with that call to resist, and we include the full statement in an appendix.

We make no pretense of being exhaustive at any point. The Bible plays many positive roles in our lives besides the one we have highlighted. There are many forms of prayer we have not discussed, and prayer contributes to the Christian life in other ways. The five chapters on what we are called to resist present important examples, but there is much more that could be said. Liberation and feminist theologies are not the only theologies of resistance. Forgiveness is not the only Christian teaching that is relevant to our concerns, nor is the political order the only one in which Christians need to apply their beliefs. Throughout the book we are saying something of importance that is especially relevant today. We are glad that others are saying other things.

Over the period of the writing of these chapters, the following persons have been members of the Reflection Committee: Ignacio Castuera, John B. Cobb Jr., Gordon Douglass, Jane Douglass, Eva Fleischner, Dean Freudenberger, Jack Jackson, Barbara James, Philip James, David Larson, Lois McAfee, Ward McAfee, Claire McDonald, Lee McDonald, George Pixley, Rod Parrott, Herman Ruether, and Rosemary Ruether. Among those whose names do not appear as author of any chapter, I note especially the contributions of Jane Douglass to many of them. Also this is an occasion for recognizing the invaluable work of Pat Patterson who, as a board member, has given a close reading to the committee's work and suggested numerous improvements. Richard Bunce, executive director of PCU until 2004, and Peter Laarman, his successor, have occasionally attended our meetings and have consistently given us the support without which our work would not have been possible.

PART I

Resistance

Why and How

1

The Bible's Call to Resist

George Pixley

The major divide among Christians today is not between those who embrace the use of secular-historical methods in the study of the Bible and those who reject them. It is between those who hear the Bible as a call to oppose the basic direction society is taking and those who do not. American Christians, even progressive ones, are not yet clear about this, but many Christians in other parts of the world are.

On August 12, 2004, a major world body of Christians brought the Bible to bear on their appraisal of what is happening in the world. Their conclusion includes these emphatic statements.

> Gathered in Accra, Ghana, for the General Council of the World Alliance of Reformed Churches, we visited the slave dungeons of Elmina and Cape Coast where millions of Africans were commodified, sold and subjected to the horrors of repression and death. The cries of "never again" are put to the lie by the ongoing realities of human trafficking and the oppression of the global economic system.
>
> Today we come to take a decision of faith commitment. . . .
>
> We have heard that creation continues to groan, in bondage, waiting for its liberation (Rom 8:22). We are challenged by the cries of people who suffer and by the woundedness of creation itself. We see a dramatic convergence between the suffering of the people and the damage done to the rest of creation. . . .
>
> As markets have become global, so have the political and legal institutions which protect them. . . . This is a global system that defends and protects the interests of the powerful. It affects and captivates us all. Further, in biblical terms such a system of wealth accumulation at the expense of the poor is seen as unfaithful to God and responsible for preventable human suffering and is called Mammon. Jesus has told us that we cannot serve both God and Mammon (Lk 16:13). . . .

Speaking from our Reformed tradition and having read the signs of the times, the General Council of the World Alliance of Reformed Churches affirms that global economic justice is essential to the integrity of our faith in God and our discipleship as Christians. We believe that the integrity of our faith is at stake if we remain silent or refuse to act in the face of the current system of neoliberal economic globalization. . . .

We believe that any economy of the household of life given to us by God's covenant to sustain life is accountable to God. We believe the economy exists to serve the dignity and wellbeing of people in community, within the bounds of the sustainability of creation. We believe that human beings are called to choose God over Mammon and that confessing our faith is an act of obedience. Therefore we reject the unregulated accumulation of wealth and limitless growth that has already cost the lives of millions and destroyed much of God's creation.[1]

INTRODUCTION

The Accra statement and similar ones by other Christian bodies pose at least two important questions: (1) Is it actually the case that current patterns of economic globalization violate the teachings of the Bible? (2) If so, because the Bible was written by people who lived centuries ago in very different circumstances, why should anyone care about what it says?

This chapter addresses both questions in a distinctive way. It does not propose that we establish the authority of the Bible for Christians and then apply what it says to the economic trends of our time. Neither does it propose that we select from the Bible those passages that appear to support conclusions we have already reached on other grounds. Rejecting both methods, the first of which is more common in conservative Christian circles and the second in liberal ones, this chapter advances a truly progressive alternative. It outlines an interactive relationship between what the Bible teaches and what we otherwise have good reasons to believe.

A century ago, some of the forebears of today's progressive American Christians read the Bible as a social gospel and felt called to challenge the injustices that industry was committing against defenseless immigrants. Some of their writings rang with a conviction about the implications of the biblical message not unlike the recent Accra declaration of the World Alliance of Reformed Churches. Nevertheless, in the struggle of liberals against the fundamentalist reading of the Bible, the commitment to economic analysis and justice fell into the background. In this generation we rarely hear from our denominations or from our pulpits a radical call to transform or to resist the basic direction society is taking, nationally or globally. We can no longer ignore the cries of the victimized to which the World Alliance of Reformed Churches has responded so powerfully. These cries call us to consider afresh the meaning of the Bible in our individual and collective lives.

This chapter addresses the questions of what the Bible is, how it functions and how it should function for progressive Christians today. What authority does it have for us? What is its basic message? If we take it seriously, can we continue to go about business as usual? Or does its demand of justice call us to truly difficult decisions? Wrestling with these questions pushes us to reflect on our heritage as progressive Christians and on the crisis we now face.

AUTHORITY IN THE CHURCH

In much of the world, the chief determinant of the distinctive religious identity of people are the Scriptures to which they turn for guidance, inspiration, or challenge. Those who turn to the Torah are Jews. Those who turn to the Buddhist sutras are Buddhists. Those who turn to the Qur'an are Muslims. And we who turn to the Christian Bible are Christians. Whether people treat the Scriptures to which they turn as inerrant or engage in extensive critical reflection about them, although important, is a secondary consideration.

With all other Christians, progressives look to the Bible. Like all other Christians, we are informed by subsequent tradition, by reason, and by experience. More than many other Christians, we emphasize the positive role played by reason and experience in informing our religious convictions and in understanding both the meaning of the Bible and its role in our lives and in our thinking.

Tradition is present everywhere, and apart from it there could be no shared life. Everyone comes into a community that has beliefs and practices shaped by its history, and all assimilate many of them before being in a position to evaluate them. Everyone engages in some process of selection among the elements in this tradition, and some incorporate elements from other traditions. This process is shaped by what makes sense and by personal and collective experience.

Reason is a critical tool that can be used to liberate us from cultural habits and ancient traditions, but it is not a purely neutral activity. It is also affected by the cultural context and by one's location in society. The premises on which those informed by biblical traditions build their arguments as well as the questions they ask are not universal human premises and questions but products of a particular history.

Similarly, our experience remains a decisive test of whether beliefs are meaningful and plausible. There is no way of approaching the Bible or anything else that is not part of that experience. We can interpret the Bible and integrate ideas derived from it into our lives, or we can reject those ideas only in terms of our experience. But what we experience and the way we experience it are culturally informed, and that means they are also informed by the Bible.

In short, those of us who have grown up in cultures deeply influenced by the Bible have no tools of inquiry or bases of judgment that are themselves fully independent of the Bible. Critical historical study of the Bible arose among us at least partly because we learned to think historically from the Bible. Moral criticism of the Bible arose among us because the Bible taught us to think morally. Criticism of biblicism arose among us because the Bible taught us to oppose every form of idolatry. Criticism of Christian otherworldliness arose among us because of the prophetic message of justice, so central to the biblical texts.

WHAT IS THE CHRISTIAN BIBLE?

Given the crucial role of the Bible in all Christian traditions, we must ask what it is. Many Christians feel that they can just point to a book on their shelves and say that is it. But this has not always been the case, and even today it obscures real questions. It took centuries for the writings deemed authoritative in the church to take this form, and even today there are differences among Christians about it. Deciding which of the writings used in the Christian churches should be canonized, that is, considered to have decisive authority, was a complex process, which can only be briefly summarized here. Compared to the Qur'an, which was delivered by one man in one language in a single lifetime, the Bible is really not a "book" at all. Rather, it is a library of literature written in different languages over many centuries, determined to be sacred by its use in the communities of faith and by religious authorities.

The largest part of the Christian Bible, known today as the Old Testament, consists of Jewish Scriptures, which over centuries were written and transmitted only in the Hebrew language. However, in the second and third centuries before the time of Christ, Jews lived throughout the Hellenistic world, and many of them spoke Greek primarily. Accordingly, Jewish scholars provided a Greek version of their Scriptures called the Septuagint, most of it translated from Hebrew manuscripts. The Septuagint included what Christians came to call the Old Testament, that is, the Hebrew Scriptures plus the Deutero-canonical books, the ones found in the Septuagint but not in the Hebrew Bible. These came to be called the Apocrypha, or Intertestamental Writings. The early Christians used the Septuagint as their primary Scripture, just as did many Hellenistic Jewish synagogues.

The apostolic writings known collectively today as the New Testament circulated during the second and third centuries in four different collections: the

Gospels, which were almost always four; the Acts of the Apostles together with the Apostolic or Catholic Epistles, that is, those thought to be written by any of the twelve apostles; the Epistles of Paul, which usually but not always included Timothy, Titus, Philemon, and Hebrews; and the Revelation of John by itself. Other writings such as the Shepherd of Hermas and the Epistle of Barnabas also had apostolic authority in some churches. However, by the late fourth century our present canon of New Testament books was widely accepted.

Having the many Scriptures as a single Bible became possible only in the fourth century with the introduction of the codex, which joined many folios by sewing them into the spine of a single volume. Since every word had to be written by hand by expert scribes, producing a complete Bible was affordable at first only by the public treasury. The first Christian Bibles were the fifty copies commissioned by the emperor Constantine. However, soon thereafter many monasteries had expert scribes who made copies of the Bible and other texts.

Around the year 400, Jerome and his colleagues translated the Bible into Latin under the direction of the bishop of Rome. This edition, known as the Vulgate, became the official Bible of all of Western Christianity for more than ten centuries. During this time, the medieval age, the Bible was known to most people only in the sermons preached from the pulpit by priests who could read Latin and had access to the holy book. Though a few translations were attempted from the Latin text, none was officially recognized.

The Council of Trent in 1546 settled for the Roman Catholic communion the continued primacy of the Latin Vulgate. This included the Apocrypha, to which Protestants have given lesser authority. When it is included in Bibles used by Protestants, it is usually put in a separate section between the Old and the New Testaments.

In light of this history, designation of the Bible as the Word of God does not, and cannot, presuppose a fixed text. We have no single manuscript of the Bible that might reasonably be imagined to have been safeguarded by God from human error. Nonetheless, by the grace of God, we have a Bible through which God's Word has been heard over many centuries, which has been the primary foundation of Christian theology and which the community of faith cherishes as life giving.

HOW HAS THE BIBLE FUNCTIONED?

For Jews the Bible is a collection of books written in Hebrew. If one wishes to study this Bible, one must master the Hebrew language in which it is written. Translations may have their uses, but they are not substitutes for the Hebrew

Bible itself. Similarly, Muslims insist on the original Arabic as the only real Qur'an.

The insistence of Jews and Muslims on reading Scripture in its original language differentiates them from Christians. From the beginning, Christians used the Greek translation of the Jewish Scriptures. Later, in the West, they used a Latin translation and then translations into many different European languages. These translations have been recognized by Christians, and especially by Protestants, as valid versions of the Bible. Although the study of the Bible in the original languages is considered to be of great importance for gaining deeper understanding of the texts, most Christians study translations. Some of these translations, such as the King James Version in English, have sometimes been treated as having almost sacred authority. This acceptance of translations made an important difference in the early days, and it continues to do so.

One deep concern of the Protestant Reformers was that the role of preaching the Word of God had declined. Although special preaching services were still held, especially during Advent and Lent, by the later Middle Ages preaching had ceased to be an essential part of the Mass. Protestants restored preaching to all public worship and defined preaching clearly as exposition of the Bible. They understood it to be not merely moral teaching intended to bring sinners to confession, but rather the occasion for the Holy Spirit's revelation of Jesus Christ in the hearts of the believers, creating faith and making the text of Scripture a living Word. Some, like Luther, reformed the lectionary to reflect better their theological concerns. Others, like Calvin, in order to broaden the people's knowledge of the Bible, preached continuously through whole books. For the Reformers, hearing the Word preached in the context of the gathered community of the faithful was essential to the being of the church.

The Reformers nevertheless objected to the dependence of lay Christians on clergy for all their knowledge of the Bible. It was important that each Christian have direct access to the Word of God. This motivated the translation of the Bible directly from the Hebrew and Greek texts into the many vernacular languages.

In the nineteenth century, especially in Protestant Germany, the historical-critical approach to the Scriptures became widespread, and major theologians largely presupposed it. This movement thoroughly pursued the free inquiry initiated in the Renaissance. As never before, scholars recognized the distance between biblical and modern times and tried to situate the scriptural books in the historical, cultural, and social contexts in which they were written. This approach to the Bible has dramatically changed and, we believe, deepened the understanding of these books.

For its part, the Roman Catholic hierarchy long resisted the Protestant emphasis on biblical authority over ecclesiastical authority, holding that church authority had created the Bible in the centuries-long process of determining exactly which Christian writings were sacred sources of revelation. A logical corollary of this position was that church authority was primary and that the Bible should be understood under the direction of that authority. It was only in 1943, with the encyclical *Divino afflante Spiritu* of Pope Pius XII, that Catholic scholars were allowed openly to engage in the historical-critical reading of the Scriptures. Even then, the Roman Catholic Church did not surrender what it regarded as its preeminent authority.

WHAT IS THE MESSAGE OF THE BIBLE?

Part of what it means to be a progressive Christian is to accept the work of scholars who study the Bible as objectively as possible. One result of this scholarship has been to emphasize the great diversity within Scripture. The books of Leviticus, Numbers, and Deuteronomy contain numerous legal prescriptions and proscriptions. The books of Judges, Samuel, and Kings are historical narratives. The prophetic books are mostly collections of oracles pronounced by Israelite prophets. The Song of Songs contains love poetry. Proverbs and the Wisdom of Ben Sira are largely made up of brief proverbs. The Gospels are narrative accounts of the deeds and teachings of Jesus of Nazareth. The Acts of the Apostles is historical narrative, this time focused on Peter and Paul. The Epistles are letters of the apostles addressed to the churches. And the Revelation of John purports to be visions revealed to an unidentified John. This diversity raises the following question: Is there any unity to the books that we collectively designate as the Bible?

Despite this emphasis on diversity, recent scholarship has also shown some overarching patterns. The Bible expresses the faith of a people who understood themselves primarily in their relation to their God. It focuses on historical events through which, they believed, God was revealed. It is not a great oversimplification to say that in the Christian Old Testament the key event was the exodus, and in the New Testament, it was the life, ministry, crucifixion, and resurrection of Jesus of Nazareth.

The exodus was the move of the people of Israel out of bondage in Egypt to the desert where their God established a covenant with them, revealing the laws by which they should live. Henceforth, the God of Israel is "the LORD your God, who brought you out of the land of Egypt, out of the house of slavery" (Exod. 20:2; Deut. 5:6). The prophetic book of Hosea says,

> Yet I have been the LORD your God
>   ever since the land of Egypt;
> you know no God but me,
>   and besides me there is no savior.
>   (Hos. 13:4)

Amos 3:1 says, "Hear this word that the LORD has spoken against you, O people of Israel, against the whole family that I brought up from the land of Egypt." Samuel said in his farewell address to his people, "'The LORD is witness, who appointed Moses and Aaron and brought your ancestors out of the land of Egypt'" (1 Sam. 12:6). Psalm 105 tells the story of the exodus at some length. The historical facts of the exodus are disputed, but its mythical power to move Israel, generation after generation, to kneel before the ultimate mystery cannot be doubted.

Associated with the exodus was the giving of the Ten Commandments to Moses. These were supplemented by far more detailed laws to govern community life, to allow Israel to model a life of purity and justice befitting God's chosen people. This law was to be cherished and celebrated, not followed out of fear.

Initially, the God who freed Israel from bondage in Egypt and established a covenant with it may have been understood as a tribal deity. But as time went by, central to Israel's faith was the conviction that this liberating and covenanting God was the one who had formed the heavens and the earth. This God brought into being all living things, culminating in humanity as a whole. There is no other deity, and all creation gives glory to this one God. In this context Israel was called to be a light to all the nations.

There are two other powerful nuclei of theology in the Hebrew Bible: first, the kingship of David; second, the conquest of Israel by the Babylonian Empire, the exile of many of its people to what is today Iraq, and the return of some to reestablish the city of Jerusalem. The experience of exile and return was the historical occasion for writing most of the books of the Old Testament. But even here it is the God of the exodus who moves and saves, as beautifully illustrated in Second Isaiah (Isa. 51:9–11),

> Awake, awake, put on strength,
>   O arm of the LORD!
> . . . .
> Was it not you who dried up the sea,
>   the waters of the great deep;
> who made the depths of the sea a way
>   for the redeemed to cross over?
> So the ransomed of the LORD shall return,
>   and come to Zion with singing.

Accordingly, despite the many themes and teachings that are found in the Old Testament, at the core is an understanding that God sided not with the rulers of the powerful empire of Egypt but with an enslaved people, freed them, and blessed them with the gift of land. It is in light of this foundational liberation that Israel is to understand its covenant with God, which specifies its responsibilities and orders its life.

Of course, there is much in the biblical writings that reflects the common human tendency to celebrate wealth and earthly power over others. The Bible can be cited, and has been cited, in support of many projects that have proved far from liberating or just. But the tendency to celebrate power and wealth has been checked and qualified by the deeper commitment to the God who sided with slaves instead of their masters. The prophets in particular, although often persecuted by the authorities, called Israel back to its covenantal commitment to the well-being of the powerless: the stranger, the poor, the widow, and the orphan.

If we turn to the New Testament, the one whom Jesus called "Abba" or "Daddy" is still the God of the exodus. This is implicit throughout the Gospels and made fully explicit by the presence of Moses and Elijah in the vision known as the Transfiguration (Matt. 17:1–8). The prominence of Moses and the exodus in Stephen's speech before the accusing mob in Acts 7 and in John's vision in Rev. 15:3 shows that Jesus' followers, also after his death and resurrection, still knew God as the God of the exodus.

But the New Testament is not about the exodus. It is the story of Jesus, his teachings, his deeds, his execution by the Roman authority, and his resurrection. Nobody can doubt that Jesus is the focus of the New Testament books. What is most certain historically about Jesus is his execution by Pilate, the Roman senatorial procurator in Palestine.[2] One can safely presume that Pilate saw Jesus as a threat to the control of the empire over Palestine.

Whether Jesus consciously intended to be politically subversive is a different question, one on which we need not take a position. He certainly gave his own devotion to God rather than to any earthly authority, and he did not see any earthly authority as sanctioned by God to control his teaching or the actions of his followers. Furthermore, he specifically taught a way of life that upset the hierarchy of established values. This is inherently subversive of the authority of those who undertake to control others.

Jesus proclaimed a *basileia*[3] that echoed God's exclusive rule in tribal Israel and contrasted with that of Rome. This *basiliea theou* (commonwealth of God) was already coming in Jesus' ministry, experienced in the early church as the gift of the Spirit, and yet anticipated in its fullness as the consummation of history. Those who followed Jesus most seriously were a problem for religious and imperial authorities both during his lifetime and for a long time thereafter.

Even after the political establishment of the church, tension continued between the authorities and those who took Jesus' message most seriously. In this chapter we are asking whether progressives today are now called to a subversive role.

The resurrection is taken by Paul and the evangelists as fundamental. This makes it part of the nucleus of the New Testament. God's raising Jesus from the dead is understood as the divine denial of the "justice" of his execution (see Acts 2:36; 4:10). It is also the affirmation of God's will for a transformed earthly life. Paul brought into being communities that undertook to be faithful to the God who raised Jesus from the dead. He taught them to practice teachings like those of Jesus, placing mutual love first, free from both the laws through which most Jews sought to fulfill the covenant and the values and the authority of the Roman Empire. Paul thus opened the door of his congregations to the Gentiles, who rapidly came to outnumber Jews. Contrary to Paul's hope that the Jewish people as a whole would accept Jesus as their messiah, his teaching led to the gradual separation of a Christian church from Judaism. The life of Jesus, culminating in the cross and resurrection, are to the New Testament what the exodus is to the Old, the nourishing force behind all else.

Of course, the Bible can be read in many ways according to the interests and concerns of the reader. From any point of view, it is about much besides the alternative vision it presents as a challenge to oppressive social structures. Nevertheless, as progressive Christians we have good grounds for affirming that this challenge is its driving force.

THE LIBERAL HERITAGE
OF PROGRESSIVE CHRISTIANITY

The segment of Protestantism that most emphatically affirmed historical criticism of the Bible and accepted the new scientific theory of evolution called itself, in the United States, modernism. This was in sharp contrast to fundamentalism, which insisted on maintaining the divine inspiration of every word of Scripture. The great ecclesiastical battles of the first decades of the twentieth century were fought between these camps.

The mainline denominations sought a way between these extremes but one closer to modernism than to fundamentalism. They retained fuller continuity with the tradition than the modernists, but they accepted historical criticism of the Bible and assimilated its results. They affirmed the freedom of science and its authority in its own sphere. In this way they continued in the broader tradition of what, looking back, we call liberal Protestantism.

The roots of liberal Protestantism are partly in the humanism of the Renaissance and the Enlightenment of the seventeenth, eighteenth, and nineteenth centuries. The thinkers of the Enlightenment typically discounted the need for ancient authorities and emphasized the capacity of the human mind to arrive at truth. They emphasized individual autonomy against repressive forces of both church and state. They participated in the process of secularization, especially in subordinating the authority of the church to that of the state. They encouraged tolerance of diversity in religious belief and practice.

While American Protestant liberalism of the nineteenth century was deeply rooted in the Enlightenment, it arose more directly from the evangelical movement of the eighteenth century. John Wesley and Jonathan Edwards both drew on the Enlightenment but were immersed in the Scriptures. Both emphasized personal religious experience. The shift of focus from doctrine to experience prepared the way for more flexibility in matters of belief and more openness to new ideas.

What we now call liberal Protestantism, therefore, affirmed much of the Enlightenment and sought to integrate that with Christian belief. Indeed, it regarded the Enlightenment as dependent on Christian culture and in large part as a healthy development of that culture. The assertion of the value and rights of individuals had clear biblical warrant and grew out of medieval and Reformation theology as well. The democratic ideal that gradually gained acceptance during the Enlightenment was also understood to be an expression of Christian convictions.[4]

Liberal Protestants encouraged the extension of rights, including the right to participate in democratic processes. In this country, they supported the anti-slavery movement. Liberal Protestants believed that faith supported both openness to the results of scientific study and adjustment of theology to what is learned. They supported religious freedom and toleration of religious diversity. In addition, they celebrated the rise of material standards of living in the United States and in Western Europe made possible by the industrial revolution.

Beginning slowly in the late nineteenth century, after centuries of extreme patriarchy, and gaining momentum in the latter part of the twentieth century, liberal Protestants responded positively to the demand of women to be given coequal status with men within the churches. The mainline denominations have ordained women as ministers and priests and have consecrated them as bishops. Women scholars now give outstanding leadership in all fields of theological study. Liberal Protestants have also supported women's suffrage, equal rights in workplaces, and gender equality in marriage.[5]

The historical criticism of Scripture was part of the historical consciousness growing especially in the nineteenth century. Indeed, this new scholarly study of the Scriptures was central to the development of the historical consciousness. This focused most importantly in the quest of the historical Jesus, which was not only an expression of dominant cultural trends but also a shaper of such cultural trends. For liberal Protestants, the historical consciousness developed in the nineteenth century was an aid in freeing Christianity from its accretions of superstition and otherworldliness. This should enable it to recover its original intentions, which are capable of addressing modern social problems. The rise of historical consciousness also paved the way for the appreciation and affirmation of other religious traditions in their distinctiveness and difference.

For liberal Protestants, the impetus behind these cultural changes was understood to be Christian, deriving from the Bible. They have usually felt themselves to be in the vanguard of a Christianizing change rather than compromising with a non-Christian culture. However, they have often found their allies among more secularized thinkers and activists, some of whom have been former Christians who have rejected the church because of its resistance to needed change.

In the United States, liberal Christianity had its finest hour in the social gospel movement. By working with other liberal forces, the social gospel was partially successful in dramatically improving the conditions of labor. Its last significant expression was the support given by the mainline churches to the civil rights struggles led by the black churches and their leaders in the 1960s and 70s.

THE CHALLENGE TO LIBERALISM
FROM WITHIN LIBERALISM

The twentieth century saw a major shift in cultural tides. Aspects of the Enlightenment that had previously seemed benign have now shown their potential for massive destructiveness. For example, by curtailing the role of church doctrine and power in society, the Enlightenment early led to improvement of the situation for Jews, but in the twentieth century the secular nationalism it supported led to genocide against them. German Protestant liberalism, which had identified closely with German culture and its "progress," generally acquiesced in the new, extreme German nationalism. The only significant opposition in Germany came from those influenced by Karl Barth, gathered as the Confessing Church. Barth criticized Christian liberalism in light of the Bible, which he saw as challenging modern culture fundamentally. The Barmen Declaration,[6] the rallying point of Christian opposition to Hitler, expressed Barth's conviction that such resistance was required as a matter of Christian faith.

The content of this declaration was mainstream theology, quite acceptable to liberal American Protestants. Its fundamental assertion was that Christians should obey Jesus Christ as the one Word of God rather than follow the example of the "German Christians," who had tailored the Christian message to preaching "ideological and political convictions." But in its German context at that time, it was a profound break with the liberal tradition. In the categories proposed by H. Richard Niebuhr, it affirmed "Christ against culture" instead of "Christ as the transformer of culture." In other words it called for resistance without calculation of consequences rather than simply for practical ways of improving the situation in church or state. It expressed a view, new to the liberal community, that there are times when Christians, in faithfulness to Christ, must simply say "No" to the dominant culture quite apart from any expectation that they could influence that culture by their actions.

Since the 1960s more and more Christians have come to see the dark side of the Enlightenment. It has centered everything in human beings, depicting and evaluating everything else from the human perspective. This view, that human beings are the measure of all things, is called "anthropocentrism." It has usually been accompanied by seeing everything else as radically different from human beings, so that we humans suppose that we are sharply separated from the natural world, controlling and exploiting it from a position above. The idea that there are two types of entities, the human and the nonhuman, is one form of "dualism." The consequences of this anthropocentrism and this dualism have been disastrous. They have led to exhaustion of some crucial resources, the pollution of the environment and of human bodies, and the extinction of many species.

Even worse, we belatedly realize, it has supported an ethos of domination that has led to contempt for peoples who live within, and not above, the natural world. These indigenous people have been displaced, subjugated, exploited, and slaughtered. Only now have Western Christians recognized that the ways of life of these people were not only more sustainable than ours but also that their sense of kinship with other creatures contributes to spiritual health and richness.

Additionally, science, with which liberal Protestants had allied themselves, increasingly encouraged a scientism that had no place for human values or ethical considerations.[7] Biblical scholarship that did so much to free liberal Protestants and clarify their appropriation of the biblical message often turned into an academic exercise largely alienated from the church, including the liberal church. Historical consciousness relativized everything in a way that threatened to end in nihilism. "Progress" no longer seemed a self-evident truth. "Modern" ceased to function well as an adjective identifying that which is "better." Given the problems and limitations of modernity, some began to call themselves "postmodern." The common meaning of this term has been little more than a critique of the modern, but in its most influential expression, under the leadership of brilliant French thinkers, postmodernism has been a radical "deconstruction" of many of the deepest assumptions of modernity.

Others were not disturbed by the drift of modern culture and readily adapted to changing cultural trends. In the name of freedom, they affirmed an extreme individualism that had no place for community and readily accepted the separation of individual rights from individual responsibilities. They celebrated their libertarianism as unleashing human potential. Prizing economic growth led them to exalt the making of wealth as the supreme end of life. Freedom of inquiry and questioning of authority led to indifference to history and especially to tradition. Exalting freedom of religion and appreciation of other religious traditions led them to loss of personal religious convictions. The weakening of traditional influence, including the influence of the Bible, opened the way for the practice of social Darwinism. This sociological theory maintains that those who survive in competition are the most "fit," thus minimizing concern for the "losers." Although few avow this doctrine today, much social and economic policy is consistent with it.

The public school, which in the nineteenth century served to prepare youth from many cultures to be citizens of the democratic United States, in the twentieth century was redefined as the place for preparing the workforce. Today, public expenditures for education are justified by the advantages to the economy of having educated workers.

The state university has succeeded the liberal arts college as the basic form of American higher education. Unlike the liberal arts college, its basic mission is not to enrich cultural appreciation and the ability to contribute to society. Instead, it is expected to support economic norms and to enable graduates to succeed in an economy that is driven by greed. Few students attend these universities to improve their ability to serve others. Most seek the training they need to get well-paying jobs.

Additionally at work in this process of secularization is the socialization of youth to dominant consumer values, especially those associated with the exploitation of sexuality. This not-so-subtle influence has served to undermine the individual achievement ethic traditionally touted in American public education. In any case, in multiple ways the American public school reflects the dominant cultural trends of our time.

Meanwhile, liberal Protestants have become increasingly aware that in much of the global south, most notably in Africa, the global free market economy has not reduced poverty. It has greatly increased the gap between rich and poor nations, and in most nations it has also increased the gap between rich and poor classes. The dominant culture, in both its earlier, friendly form and in its current, hostile form, gave support to an economy that exploited many of the world's people, giving them no voice in the decisions that most affected their lives.

Not appreciating the depth of the sociocultural shift that has occurred, liberal Christians have tended to accept even obviously negative social changes with little or no protest. Instead, they try to identify what they can regard as continuing progressive elements in the culture. Where they have recognized problems, they have proposed moderate, reformist responses.

Progressive Protestants derive from this liberal, reformist tradition. However, we have reluctantly come to recognize that the culture celebrated in our heritage was never worthy of the degree of support we gave it. We now recognize that it has abandoned many of the values it derived from its Christian heritage. We are called to reconsider our relation to culture quite radically.

THE CHALLENGE OF THE BIBLE

Recognizing that liberal Protestantism in the United States has been swept along by the culture with little resistance, much as happened to the German Protestant church in the 1930s, we are forced to ask the question of biblical authority with renewed intensity. Does the Bible authorize this "cultural Protestantism" (*Kultur Protestantismus*)? If we acknowledge that it does not, how are we to relate to its authority today?

One option is to join those conservative Christians who have all along maintained that the Bible opposes many features of modern thought and life. There is no doubt that in the twentieth century in the United States, serious resistance to the dominant culture has come much more from these conservatives than from our liberal forebears. In our relation to these biblical conservatives, we have much of which to repent. Many of them have come from less-privileged social and economic classes, and too often liberals have looked at them with condescension and even contempt. We need to learn a new respect and appreciation for them. Before we recognized the dark side of the Enlightenment, some of them stood in opposition to it on the basis of their reading of the Bible.

There are, indeed, groups that have come from the heritage of conservative Protestantism with which we now have extensive agreement. The old distinctions between conservatives and liberals fade in importance. The Sojourners as a group are in the forefront of shaping the new form of Christianity to which progressive Christians now aspire. But they are by no means alone. Koinonia Farms represents another radical response of conservative Christians who have taken Scripture with ultimate seriousness. The serious

Christian commitment of conservative Protestants such as these puts us progressives to shame.

Nevertheless, we cannot follow the lead of conservative Protestants generally. In the name of biblical authority, most of them have opposed, and continue to oppose, what progressives still regard as positive features of the Enlightenment. Today many of them refuse to accept scientific findings that progressives believe are too well established to doubt. Many cling to moral teachings that are poorly based in Scripture and are deeply hurtful to other persons. Some are committed to an apocalyptic eschatology that leads them to support unjust treatment of the Palestinians while simultaneously condemning Judaism and arousing in their followers expectations that can only end in disappointment.

Recently more and more evangelicals have regretted the extent to which they have allowed themselves to be co-opted by the religious Right. Many of them recognize that the Bible is far more concerned about justice to the poor than about abortion or homosexuality. They may agree with the Bush administration on these latter issues without subordinating the Christian faith to the interests of the Republican Party. The National Association of Evangelicals is speaking out against the use of torture and continued human actions that heat up the atmosphere. The Institute for Religion and Democracy, created by the religious Right to undermine the liberal leadership of old-line denominations, has now turned its guns also on the evangelical leadership! Progressives can rejoice that the Word of God is breaking through the political filters imposed by the religious Right. Evangelicals are now meeting with liberals and other Christians to emphasize areas on which we can all work together. Shared commitment to the Bible may be replacing division over politics as the basic relationship among Protestant bodies.

Even more promising are other groups of Protestants who, in the name of the Bible and tradition, call for "renewal." Many of them come from the liberal tradition but now see that tradition as bankrupt. They intend to renew older traditions that they believe are based on deeper faithfulness to the Bible. They often call themselves "postliberal." Some of them make use of postmodernist philosophy; others do not.

The idea of renewal generally implies that there were times in the past when the church was more faithful to the distinctive message of the Bible. This healthier period is generally located before the Enlightenment and sometimes before the acceptance of Christianity by the Roman emperors. In that earlier period, Christianity was often at odds with the dominant society, and to become a Christian was a significant and sometimes costly decision. Renewal, accordingly, typically means a recovery of traditional beliefs and patterns of action that would distinguish the church sharply from the surrounding culture of today.

The tendency of those who call for renewal has been to think that the church can be faithful to the Bible only if it sets itself apart from the wider culture, leaving that culture largely alone. Some of these postliberals assume that authentic Christianity was fundamentally lost in the Enlightenment, so they attack the Enlightenment and all its accomplishments. Theologies of this sort have not yet molded many congregations, but they are now playing an important role in formerly liberal seminaries.

How should progressive Protestants relate to this response to the recognition of the weakness of our liberal heritage and its excessive alliance with Enlightenment culture? We agree that we have not taken the distinctive message of the Bible with sufficient seriousness in its challenge to this whole culture. Nevertheless, we can neither reject the Enlightenment so completely nor affirm any earlier form of Christianity so wholeheartedly as do some of those calling for renewal. Our reading of the Bible leads us to view all historical developments and all forms of Christianity as ambiguous. Based on our faith in the God of the exodus, who is the "Abba" to whom Jesus prayed, our task is to discern what is to be discarded and what affirmed in every past form of Christianity, including the liberalism allied to the Enlightenment. We trust that the Bible will also guide us in developing new forms in the future. Of course, any position we develop will likewise be ambiguous, but we believe this is the way for us to be most faithful to the Bible. It is our calling as progressive Christians.

PROGRESSIVE THEOLOGY, THE NATURAL WORLD, AND LIBERATION THEOLOGIES

Whereas most movements of "renewal" call for recovery of old traditions, progressive Christians are deeply influenced by new developments of the past few decades. For example, the recognition of the decay of the biosphere that burst on the American consciousness in the late 1960s raised fundamental questions about Christian theology. In the discussion, many became aware that the dualistic anthropocentrism of the Enlightenment, which had kept us blind to what human beings were doing to the earth, had roots deeper than the modern period. Christian teaching in the West, drawing on both Greek and biblical thought, had prepared the soil for the extreme forms of dualism articulated in Enlightenment philosophy, natural science, political theory, and economic theory. It became important to study the Bible again to see whether it committed its followers to this damaging view.

The conclusion was that it does not. The Bible as a whole is neither so dualistic nor so anthropocentric as was the theology developed from it. Returning to its authority opens the door to new appreciation of human kinship with all living things, an appreciation supported by contemporary scientific findings if not by the ethos and methodology of most science. Although the Bible clearly authorizes human beings to make use of other creatures as needed, it does not sanction the abuse and exploitation of nature that has taken place in its name, especially in the West. This suggests that the need is not so much for renewal of any past form of Christianity as for developing a new form of Christianity through attentive listening to the Bible.

The distinctiveness of progressive Christianity can be clarified in relation to responses to black theology. Liberal Christians quickly embraced the demands of blacks insofar as these were extensions of the Enlightenment affirmation of equal rights for all people. They gave blacks and women places of leadership in the church and worked for justice in the larger society. They pressed for integration wherever that was possible. More slowly they recognized that integrating blacks into structures that express white culture is not in fact giving them full equality. As liberals more fully recognize the importance and value of difference, they tend to become relativists. They have had more difficulty dealing with racism as a deeply entrenched part of the American psyche.

Conservative evangelicals have been slower to reject explicit and avowed racism in their churches and in society, but they have done so. They may have recognized the hold of racism on the American psyche more clearly than have liberals, so that for them the repudiation of racism sometimes has a fuller meaning than for most liberals. Their work against racism remains more personal and less attentive to legal and institutional changes.

Renewalists focus on the interior life of the church. There is no justification for racism in the Christian traditions and accordingly no place for racism in the church. The presence of racism in the psyche of church members expresses the failure of the church to be truly the church. The task is to socialize the members of the church into the depths of the Christian tradition.

We progressives, as heirs of the liberal tradition, have inherited all its strengths and weaknesses. However, we are trying to free ourselves from some of the latter. We are trying to listen more attentively to the voices of blacks who so often experience in white Christians a racism of which we whites are not even aware. We share with the renewalists a desire for the church to be a place where this deep level of racial feeling can be overcome. But we put emphasis also on the use of other social institutions, such as schools, for this purpose. In the difficult task of coming closer together without trying to assimilate blacks into white culture, we look to blacks for guidance and leadership.

Perhaps the deepest change in Christian teaching in the twentieth century was brought about by the sexual revolution. Whereas through most of church history sexuality as such has been viewed as unclean, by the end of the twentieth century hardly any church intended to communicate that message. However, in other respects great differences developed. We will consider the rise of feminism as a major development within this revolution since the church's teaching about women had been closely bound up with its negative attitude toward sexuality in general. The current views of sexuality and gender can help to clarify the position of progressive Christians.

Liberal Protestants welcomed Freud and the sexual revolution as helping them to free Christianity from repressive teaching in this crucial area. They rejoiced that they could recover the healthier attitudes toward sexuality expressed in the Bible, especially in the Hebrew Scriptures. Nevertheless, the liberal denominations have been profoundly divided in the further development of teaching about sexuality and gender. Insofar as feminists called for equal rights with men, liberals have supported them, and this has led to great changes in these denominations. But the profound changes in the understanding of sexuality and gender involved in freeing ourselves from patriarchal thinking have created confusion and acute controversy. Liberal churches have thus been deeply divided, especially over the full acceptance of homosexuals. Many Christians who had taken liberal positions on other points, including race, have seen homosexuality as a form of immorality against which they must take a stand. They support equal political rights and economic opportunity for gays and lesbians but will not sanction their sexual activities by recognizing their unions or allowing them to be ordained.

Conservative evangelicals are still divided in their response to the feminist demand for equality. Some believe that the patriarchal assumptions operative in most of the Bible are normative for us today. Others are prepared to give women leadership roles in the churches. Only a few seriously consider the deeper overcoming of patriarchal habits of mind that is required for the full acceptance of same-sex sexual relations.

Renewalists are not of one mind on these issues, but their tendency to look to the past for norms works against strong affirmation of the deeper implications of feminism. These implications raise profound questions about the adequacy of any major past expression of the tradition. They point us in the direction of quite new forms of Christianity.

Progressives are those from the liberal tradition who accept this call to develop something quite new. We are not free of patriarchal assumptions and habits, but we aspire to free ourselves. We see the condemnation of homosexuality as an expression of that patriarchal mind-set of which we would free ourselves. This view does not mean that we would abandon the effort to identify disciplines and patterns of sexual behavior that are to be affirmed over against many that are not. On the contrary, we see a great deal of irresponsibility and mutual damage in current sexual practice, both heterosexual and homosexual, and widespread exploitation and distortion of sexuality. But we want to work together with persons of diverse sexual orientations in formulating a Christian sexual morality appropriate to our time.

With regard to economic and political structures, Latin American liberation theology is far more forceful and explicit in its call for change.[8] It speaks from the experience of the victims of American imperialism and American capitalism. This perspective distinguishes it from all the North American theological traditions we have considered. Within the United States, only the Native Americans have experienced American society in an analogous way. In its early expression liberation theology was insensitive to the problems of dualism, anthropocentrism, sexism, and racism, but over the years it has integrated these concerns into its message. It has provided both perceptive denunciation of the evils and injustices of society and attractive annunciation of the different world that is possible.

Earlier there had been some critique of capitalism among the social gospel writers. However, even the socialists among them rarely called for revolutionary change. There was even less basic criticism of the imperialist tendencies of United States foreign policy. In the name of progress, some of the leaders of the social gospel supported America's imperialist ventures.

The picture of American liberal Protestantism that has emerged from viewing its role in relation to American imperialism and capitalist exploitation in Latin America is profoundly unfamiliar to the American liberal church. It depicts a situation that calls not for opening the door of the economic system to those previously shut out but for revolutionary systemic change. It calls for such change on the basis of a radical affirmation of the countercultural authority of the Bible. In this respect progressive Christians now hear a message that parallels Barth's call for resistance more than the social gospel's call for reform.

For many Christians around the world, this message is now the meaning of biblical authority. They do not care much about debates between those who affirm divine inspiration and those who emphasize human authorship. North American disputes between modernists and fundamentalists, still so important to American liberals, are of less concern to many Christians elsewhere. The critical question is, instead, whether God speaks through the Bible to support the integrity of creation and the resistance of the exploited.

We progressives often fail to notice that Christians who read their Scripture critically and who embrace modern science also have sometimes used the Bible in vicious ways. They have acquiesced in genocide, as in Nazi Germany, or justified ignoring it in far-off places like Rwanda and Darfur. Jesus counseled against seeing the speck in our neighbor's eye and ignoring the log in our own. Jesus' saying (Matt. 7:3) may apply in this case!

The major divide among Christians today is not between those who make use of secular methods of historical study in their interpretation of the Bible and those who do not. It is between those who oppose the profound injustice at the core of the contemporary world and those who ignore or support it, however they read the Bible. For at the heart of the biblical message is God's love for all creatures and God's call to humans to show love, mercy, and justice to one another. Jesus, in whom we find the clearest and fullest revelation of God, stands in the tradition of the Hebrew prophets and renews this ancient teaching. Some liberals continue to focus on the opposition to fundamentalism and openness to science and historical study. Progressives take all that for granted, but they seek to stand with the deepest insights of liberationists and call for radical social change.

OUR RESISTANCE TO THE CALL TO RESIST

If progressive Christians in the United States intend to heed the radical call of the Bible, what does this mean for our actual political stand? It depends on how vividly we share the view that the basic policies of the powers that be, including especially the United States, are fundamentally in opposition to the gospel. Do they violate the teaching of the Bible that all human beings are of "one blood," that is, belong to a single family, by excluding many from participation in the shaping of society and sharing its benefits? Do they violate the commitment of Christians to "the least of these"? Do they deny the value of sparrows, just because they are of far less value than human beings? Do they treat the natural world as if it existed only for human use, when God saw that it was good quite apart from the existence of any human beings? Do they ignore the call to mercy and justice? Do they encourage the concentration of wealth in a few hands, despite the frequent biblical critique of the acquisition of goods and the exploitation of the poor? Do they systematically replace the centrality of God with the centrality of powerful human beings despite the constant biblical insistence on the difference between the Creator and creatures? Do they encourage pride and greed despite the biblical call to humility and generosity? Since progressive Christians answer "Yes" to these questions, we are called to resist!

As American consumers, concerned on a day-to-day basis with our own "well-being," we progressives are part of the problem. We can take false pride in not being among the most excessive consumers in our culture. But this falls far short of resistance. To affirm the Bible as the authority for fundamental opposition to the present global market system, with which American policy is bound up, is not a natural response for most North Americans or even for most progressive Christians in the United States. It requires radical changes in the style of life we find natural and comfortable, changes we are very reluctant to consider seriously.

Some liberals find persuasive the argument that the present global economic system with all its faults is helping the poor. True, they recognize, most of the gain is going to the wealthier segments of the population, and the gap between rich and poor is growing. But they believe that there is still some gain for the poor as well, and that no other approach is likely to help them more in the long run. For those currently benefiting from the system, this comfortable perspective is powerfully seductive.

It is not that such liberal Christians are indifferent to the suffering that accompanies economic globalization. Even those who reject the wholesale condemnation of economic globalization by ecological and liberation theologians want reforms that will protect the environment and ease the suffering of the poor both in the United States and in the "developing" world, and they can find in civil society and among sensitive economists proposals for such reforms. In the familiar liberal pattern, here, too, they discern social trends with which they can identify. They may work enthusiastically for such excellent causes as the forgiveness of the debts of the most heavily indebted of the poorest countries. But they may not be sensitive to the ways in which this forgiveness is bound up with strengthening the system that oppresses so much of the world. For progressive Christians, who respond with deep feeling to the degradation of the earth, to the destitution of billions of people, and to a system that irredeemably destroys the communities and future prospects of the poor, this casual support of reform by most liberal Christians is keenly disappointing.

Nevertheless, we progressive Christians in North America find ourselves largely continuing the liberal patterns. We note that the radical rejection of the dominant system will involve, or lead to, violence. This idea is not incorrect. Those who benefit from the status quo will defend their prerogatives and the system that undergirds their wealth and power. Even those who resist it nonviolently are likely to evoke violence on the part of the defenders. The civil rights struggle showed that a challenge to the system of segregation, however conducted, had this effect. But progressives cannot simply acquiesce. We know that we are called to oppose the assault on the earth, to reject oppression, and to seek justice even if this provokes the exploiter and the oppressor to violence against us.

Despite all of the justifications that progressive Christians offer for our still-lukewarm responses, the call to resist awakens a deep uneasiness. We believe that this uneasiness today is the voice of God speaking to us through the juxtaposition of the Bible and current events. It is leading us toward a sharper break with the dominant forces in our culture and a greater willingness to resist them.

We hear more and more often that we need "a new Barmen Declaration." At the international level, as shown in the story with which this chapter opens, some American Christians are involved in calls for resistance. We hope that soon more of us progressives in the United States will so identify with the suffering earth and its oppressed inhabitants that our affirmation of the Bible's call to inclusive love expressed in justice will inform the way we live and act.

REFORM AND RESISTANCE

We are distinguishing progressive Christianity from other forms of liberal Christianity primarily by its relation to the dominant currents of society. Liberal American Christians assume the basic health of our society and work for reforms to deal with its limitations and failures. Progressive Christians are beginning to see that the basic policies and institutions that direct our nation and our world, in very important respects, are leading in the wrong direction. Accordingly, we recognize that in addition to working for reforms where they are appropriate, we must also resist. However, the idea of "resistance" is largely strange to us as heirs of the liberal tradition. We must struggle even to understand what it has meant in the past and especially what it would mean for us today.

The clearest instances of resistance in distinction from reform occur when people are powerless to change the system. In the early church, Christians could not affect the imperial policies and teachings. They could, nevertheless, refuse to accept the imperial ideology and could organize their lives around different principles. Jesus rather than Caesar was for them "the Son of God" and Lord. Paul encouraged those who responded to his message to conform outwardly to what the empire required of them as far as they could. However, this did not include the worship of Caesar. Accordingly, resistance led many Christians to martyrdom. Similarly, in Nazi Germany those Christians who joined the Confessing Church had no expectation of reforming the government. Resistance meant refusal to conform to Nazi ideas and to the practices of the too-compliant recognized churches.

In the United States, the clearest instances of resistance occur when Christians decide to break the law without regard to whether their actions would ever lead to changing the law. Those who helped runaway slaves to escape to Canada were engaged in resistance against the system of slavery. On the other hand, nonviolent civil disobedience is a form of resistance that can also be used intentionally in the service of reform. In this case, the laws are broken publicly with the expectation of accepting punishment but also of changing public opinion and perhaps the law itself.

By far the most important example of resistance in recent American history is the struggle for justice and equal rights led by Martin Luther King Jr. When he was imprisoned in Birmingham for actions that broke the laws of Alabama, liberal white ministers who agreed with him that from the Christian perspective segregation is wrong wrote to him, urging that he use only political and legal methods to oppose it. He responded in his famous "Letter from a Birmingham Jail" that black Americans had sought reform through regular political channels long enough. This approach was far too slow. He argued that resistance to unjust laws was necessary. Blacks must put their bodies on the line, breaking immoral laws in the name of a higher law. His movement garnered support among white Christians and the wider public. In this instance numerous acts of resistance, often provoking others to violence and even heightened injustice, led to reform. The movement King led provides Americans with our best example of what resistance can be and how it can take place.

Subsequently a quite different form of resistance developed in South Africa against apartheid.[9] These forms of Christian resistance have been among the forces that ended the era of legally imposed segregation and apartheid. No church now officially accepts such practices. What we are now called to resist by the Accra statement of the World Alliance of Reformed Churches, quoted at the beginning of this chapter, is the global economy. We Americans must recognize that this global economy is closely connected to American imperialism. What form can resistance to these world-impacting forces take?

A few Christians have chosen lives of poverty that involve them minimally in the market and the financial system. They do not think of this choice as a means of reforming the system. It is simply a personal resistance to which they feel called. Far more Christians engage in nonviolent protests, which they hope will contribute to changed policies. For example, many protests have been directed against the World Trade Organization. Some of the protesters want reforms that would lead to a level playing field instead of one rigged for the advantage of industrialized countries. Others believe the nature and mission of the WTO are governed by the neoliberal ideology they fundamentally oppose. They would like to see the WTO collapse, hoping that it would be replaced by institutions geared to a far-broader understanding of the earth's needs. Here the note of resistance predominates.

Many Christians participated in protests against the unilateral invasion of Iraq. Today the climate has changed, and it is possible to work in realistic political ways for the withdrawal of American troops from Iraq. Some Americans are supporting movements of resistance in third-world countries. But thus far we Euro-American progressive Christians have not found ways to resist that are even remotely comparable to the Confessing Church in Germany, the civil rights struggle in the United States, or the Christian resistance to apartheid in South Africa.

THE BIBLE AS THE WORD OF GOD

For us as Christians, the Bible is our deepest source of comfort and hope, both for our personal lives and for the world. It is for us a fountain of faith, and it shapes and informs our liturgical lives and our theology. For many of us, it is basic to our private devotions as well. It is our source for learning of God's salvific dealing with the people of Israel, climaxing for us in the coming of Jesus. In him we have our revelation of God's nature and purposes for us and for the world. Through the Bible, read in a christocentric way, we are persuaded that God loves all creatures and especially, personally and individually, every human being, whatever her or his moral character, religious beliefs, or station in life.

Liberation theologians assert that when the Bible challenges us to resist the forces of destruction and catastrophic ruin that dominate our culture, it is rightly understood as the Word of God. Liberals, preoccupied with opposing conservative distortions of the idea that God speaks, often give up that language. But rather than abandon the idea that the Bible is the Word of God to those who misuse it, liberation theologians call on progressives to join them in reclaiming this understanding. As the Word of God, the Bible authorizes us and calls us to do justice. *If the Bible is used to oppose justice, whether by those who employ historical criticism or by those who reject it, the Word of God has not been heard; and we must denounce this use of the Bible as a false claim to God's authority.* The Bible can and should be read out of a passionate concern for the well-being of God's world.

Although the Bible is an ancient collection of books from the Middle East, in Christian communities it has often become the present Word of the Living God, and we share in this affirmation. In traditional terms, it is the Holy Spirit that transforms the words on the page into the living Word that addresses each reader in her or his real-time situation. In the name of that Word, Francis of Assisi confronted the venality and lack of compassion of the clergy in the twelfth and thirteenth centuries, and Luther, the commercialization of salvation in the sixteenth century. Of course, those Christians criticized by Francis and by Luther also read the Bible. They saw it as an authoritative word giving them the right to use Christianity to oppress the believers of their time. We judge that for them the Bible did not come alive as the Word of the Living God, who called Jesus to a solidarity with the poor, which led to his execution by those who defended the social order.

The Bible is not an objective authority that restricts our freedom to think and act. Instead, through it God can speak to us in life-giving fashion. It challenges us to act for justice, and it authorizes and empowers us to engage in that action. It illuminates the injustices in this world as well as the exploitation of the earth, and it motivates us to work to rectify these evils. In short, it authorizes action for a just and sustainable world. God, as the creator of all things, has given to human beings the responsibility to care for the earth. Increasingly we are learning that to do this demands our assuming responsibility for our behavior as inhabitants of the earth. Only as we adopt a respectful perspective that acknowledges our dependence on its well-being can we be trusted to care for it.

God created all species, saw that they were good, and worked to save them. The Bible teaches that the poor and the excluded are all children of God, who takes their side in the struggle for human living. God is revealed in the Hebrew Bible as the redeemer of Israel, who chose the Hebrew people, freed them from their servitude to the Egyptian pharaohs, and brought them to a land flowing with milk and honey. God makes an option for the poor. These themes are preserved in our Christian Old Testament. The core of the New Testament affirms that although the Roman authorities executed Jesus as a subversive danger, God raised him from the dead and thus affirmed his preaching of a just and peaceful society, of the reign of God already present.

As progressive Christians, we struggle to be faithful to biblical revelation. We not only read the Bible devotionally but also affirm the use of secular-historical methods in the study of the Bible. Using this method distances the biblical world from us. Indeed, we recognize that it is truly strange to us, but in this strangeness, God can be revealed to us independently of the culture of our time. This countercultural Word from God that we find in the Bible authorizes us to confront the sin in our world and especially our own participation in it.

CONCLUSION

One way of understanding the crisis of Christianity in its relation to the Bible is to describe our time as witnessing the end of Christian culture. Liberal Christians have long recognized and even celebrated the end of Christendom, a culture that gave special privilege to the church or to Christian ceremonies. However, liberals have supposed that Christian values have survived and shaped the moral vision of our culture. They thought that the secularity they accepted as the overarching basis of our national life was itself permeated by humanistic values with which they could identify. And to some extent, for a while, this was true.

But it is no longer true. The dominant values of our society are now oriented to economic gain for oneself. The idea that life should be lived in service to others, which once seemed to be shared with secular humanistic culture, plays a decreasing role. The most intimate aspects of our lives, including sex, are transformed by our culture's dominant consumer values into entertainment, pornography, and fashion.[10] To some extent our churches also are transformed, filling "market niches" by meeting the felt needs of lonely and confused people for community, authority, and religiosity. Few of them confront contemporary society with the strange world of the Bible, which reverses the now-dominant value system. Sadly, some of them give strong support to many features of the current economic system. Even more encourage America's imperial projects.[11]

To put the issue bluntly, our society is now organized in the service of mammon or wealth. Standing in the great tradition of the Jewish prophets, Jesus told us that we cannot serve both God and mammon. We must choose. If we choose to serve God, we are called to oppose and resist those structures and policies that are in the service of mammon. Minor reforms will not suffice. We must affirm that "another world is possible" and live from and toward that other world.

DISCUSSION QUESTIONS

1. Do you believe that the United States of America's current role in the world fundamentally fulfills God's intentions, or is our nation now primarily working against them? Is it unpatriotic to assert that our foreign policy is contrary to God's purposes as these are revealed in Jesus? Is it unchristian?

2. Conservative Christians talk of being "convicted by the Word of God." Disregarding the content of the conservative message, does the idea of being convicted by the Word of God make sense to you?

3. Would your church be willing to undertake a Bible study oriented to critiquing the dominant economic values of our culture?

4. What is your personal response to the statement of the World Alliance of Reformed Churches made at Accra, Ghana, on August 12, 2004?

FOR FURTHER READING

An authoritative account of how the Bible came to be is the now-classic work of Hans von Campenhausen, *The Formation of the Christian Bible* (Philadelphia: Fortress Press, 1972). A Jewish perspective is Daniel Jeremy Silver's *The Story of Scripture: From Oral Tradition to the Written Word* (New York: Basic Books, 1990).

A good introductory treatment of how the Bible has been interpreted is Robert M. Grant and David Tracy's *A Short History of the Interpretation of the Bible* (Philadelphia: Fortress Press, 1963 and later reprints). Grant is an Episcopalian patristics scholar, and Tracy, a Catholic theologian. Fine studies of the continuing role and power of the Bible are found in the 1968 book of the Jewish theologian Martin Buber, *On the Bible* (New York: Schocken) and James Barr's *The Bible and the Modern World* (New York: Harper, 1973).

To understand the liberal background of contemporary progressive Protestant theology, we recommend the work of Gary Dorrien. He has written a three-volume history: *The Making of American Liberal Theology: Imagining Progressive Religion, 1805–1900* (2001); *The Making of American Liberal Theology: Idealism, Realism, and Modernity, 1900–1950* (2003); *The Making of American Liberal Theology: Crisis, Irony, and Postmodernity, 1950–2005* (2006), all published by Westminster John Knox Press, Louisville, Kentucky. The liberal appropriation of the Bible is well expressed in Harry Emerson Fosdick's *A Guide to Understanding the Bible: The Development of Ideas within the Old and New Testaments* (New York: Harper, 1938).

The quite different perspective of Latin American liberation theology can be found in Jose Porfirio Miranda's *Marx and the Bible* (1973; paperback ed., 2004). More recent interpretations of the Bible by liberation theologians include Gustavo Gutiérrez's *On Job: God-Talk and the Suffering of the Innocent* (1987). This is a model of theological reflection on the basis of a biblical book, in this case Job. Jorge Pixley provides another such model in *On Exodus: A Liberation Perspective* (1987). Carlos Mesters, a Brazilian Carmelite, sets out the hermeneutics implicit in his popular Bible study *Defenseless Flower: A New Reading of the Bible* (1989). All these books have been published by Orbis Press, Maryknoll, New York.

We understand our need as progressive North American Christians to reconsider the adequacy of our liberal heritage in light of our changing context and the insights that liberation theologians have derived from the Bible. Several North American authors are challenging us to think of the meaning of our faith in new ways. Among them are Ronald J. Sider, Jim Wallis, and Walter Brueggemann. Sider is an evangelical who has written *Rich Christians in an Age of Hunger: Moving from Affluence to Generosity* (Dallas: Word Pub., 1997). Wallis, also a well-known evangelical, has written *God's Politics* (San Francisco: HarperSanFrancisco, 2005). Brueggemann, a leading biblical scholar, has written numerous books that bring the challenge of the Bible to our American Christianity. One of the best is *The Prophetic Imagination* (Minneapolis: Fortress Press, 2001). There are approaches from many other perspectives; among them is that of Cain Hope Felder (ed.), *Stony the Road We've Trod: African-American Biblical Interpretation* (Minneapolis: Fortress Press, 1991).

Recently New Testament scholars have recognized that the Gospels and Epistles were written in the context of the Roman Empire and are intentional in proclaiming an alternative to the society it dominates. A leading writer in this field is Richard Horsley, who together with Neil Asher Silberman wrote *The Message and the Kingdom: How Jesus and Paul Ignited a Revolution and Transformed the Ancient World* (Minneapolis: Fortress Press, 1997). In 2003 Horsley published *Jesus and Empire: The Kingdom of God and the New World Disorder* (Minneapolis: Fortress Press).

2

The Strength to Resist:
The Life of Prayer

Lois McAfee

See. Pray. Act.
> *Flag appearing on the home page of the Progressive*
> *Christians Uniting Web site*

To clasp our hands in prayer is the beginning of an uprising against
the disorders of the world.
> *Karl Barth*

I am increasingly convinced that we will fully grasp the meaning
of peacemaking only when we recognize not only that prayer is a
form of resistance, but also that resistance is a form of prayer.
> *Henri Nouwen*

INTRODUCTION

Throughout most of our history, we Euro-American Protestant Christians in
the liberal tradition have sought to bring about reforms to unjust laws and
practices by working within major currents in the broader society. These
efforts have been aimed at bringing about the desired paradigm shift to a just,
peaceable world. But today we are more aware than ever that that is not
enough. The Bible calls us also to *resist* many of the directions in which our
society is taking us. This is a paradigm shift, and a lot is at stake for most of
us. But, according to Dorothee Soelle, with the additional responsibilities of
vocation comes the power to live into it and the social displacement accom-
panying it:

If we are not living with resistance, we are not in possession of the powers given us. When we dread going, we can experience the miracle of what the Bible calls "the strength of the weak." The basic experience of resistance is receiving the gift of power. An exodus from imposed and self-generated impotence takes place. Life gains a new direction. . . . What I am commending here is a practical-existential step that includes confronting the life-threatening power. It is costly and it disunites and unites anew. It is an irreversible step that we can forget or undo only at the price of self-betrayal.[1]

When we join those non-Christians who are already actively resisting injustice, we may (1) focus on educating, organizing, and activating citizens and collaborating with other groups for long-term engagement in relevant nonviolent social action;[2] or (2) absent ourselves from our cultural frame of reference, geographically and/or internally, in order to "go to those places where suffering is most acute and build a home there." There we can hear from community members what justice would look like for them and join them in acts of compassion and resistance from their vantage point.[3]

Resistance necessitates risk taking on the part of progressive Christians, requiring that we engage in what Henri Nouwen terms "voluntary displacement" from our dominant societal group's frame of reference of cultural superiority. It requires motivated individuals to question the validity of and to let go of the distinctive identity we carry in this society so that we can live under its radar screen in an alternative milieu, as did God in Jesus. Nouwen reminds us that "voluntary displacement" has stood at the origins of all great religious reforms.[4] The times we live in surely call for a great religious reform. Christians can engage the world fortified not only by biblical precedent, as we have seen, but also by prayer, a practice of *inner* voluntary displacement.

This chapter responds to the many fresh calls for prayer and for spiritual renewal among progressive Christian communities who are honoring the biblical admonition to resist dominant cultural forces. It briefly discusses the recent and current societal situation in the United States, presents our beliefs about prayer, and argues for the integration of prayer with reflection and action. It then describes forms and functions of prayer available from our Christian heritage.

OUR RECENT AND CURRENT SITUATION

With the rise of modern industry in the late nineteenth century, U.S. society underwent profound changes that awakened liberal Christians. They saw how individuals, particularly the poor, were suffering severely under new social forces. They concluded that it was not enough to deal charitably with the victims of the system. Nor was it enough to continue preaching solely for the salvation of souls. Jesus' preaching of the realm of God showed them that the preeminent goal of Christian work was to bring into being a more just and peaceful society. They recognized the importance of prayer in the conversion of the world as in that of individuals. Walter Rauschenbusch (1851–1918) wrote in the introduction of his small volume of prayers for "social Christians,"

> Public prayer . . . may carry further than we know. . . . If we had more prayer in common on the sins of modern society, there would be more social repentance and less angry resistance to the demands of justice and mercy. And if the effect of our prayers goes beyond our own personality; if there is a center of the spiritual universe in whom our spirits join and have their being; and if the mysterious call of our souls somehow reaches and moves God, so that our longings come back from him in a wave of divine assent that assures their ultimate fulfillment—then it may mean more than any man knows to set Christendom praying on our social problems.[5]

However, in the wake of world wars, much of the energy of the social gospel dissipated as mainline churches offered solace for survivors by addressing personal needs and supporting families. At the same time, the individualistic evangelical tradition, stressing the importance of private prayer and Bible reading, became increasingly legalistic. Other Christians, realizing how Christians on both sides of conflicts prayed for the success of their cause, began to question whether prayer could affect the course of events at all. Still others decried prayer's being used to avoid dealing with social relationships and institutional responsibilities. In numerous congregations the groups that met for prayer and those that sought to orient the church to public issues had little apparent overlap.

Most of the heirs of the social gospel continued to worship with their communities of faith and to be inspired by the Bible, but many of them failed to take the discipline of prayer seriously. Rectifying injustices seemed self-evidently important; disciplines of prayer did not. Of course, there are notable exceptions, such as Martin Luther King Jr.

The diminution of prayer by many social activists has served to undermine its very purpose. Realizing that many of their fellow Christians are not with them, some have become discouraged. Others have burned out in their zealousness, and some of these have left the work altogether, giving in to what Thomas Merton termed "organized despair." Others have plodded on, fortified by Native American traditions or Eastern or Catholic monastic practices.

These days there is a growing awareness among progressive religious leaders of the need for activists to receive the inner nourishment, vision, and inner strength that come with a deepened prayer life. For the last twenty years, Rabbi Michael Lerner has been organizing political activists into "spiritual progressive" communities around universal spiritual principles and practices that embody love and compassion for all, including the activists themselves. Walter Wink has been arguing persuasively that

> combining prayer and social action is not just a theological necessity, dictated by the need to integrate all of life around the reality of the living God. It is a matter of sheer survival. The evils we confront are so massive, so inhuman, so impervious to appeals and dead to compassion, that those who struggle against them face the real possibility of being overcome by them.[6]

Henri Nouwen has also warned against depriving social action of prayer, and vice versa: "Prayer and action . . . can never be seen as contradictory or mutually exclusive. Prayer without action grows into powerless pietism, and action without prayer degenerates into questionable manipulation."[7]

Taking such warnings to heart, and recollecting our heritage of activists who took prayer seriously, this chapter advocates the practical and dynamic uniting of reflection, praying, and action. Active resistance to the injustices both in the world and in ourselves requires deep inward grounding in the biblical faith, a grounding that is rarely attained without the ongoing disciplines of prayer and reflection.

When we put these three activities together, we find that each is strengthened by the others. Without critical *reflection* we are apt to focus our attention—and subsequently our prayers and actions—solely on symptoms of injustice, ignoring their deeper and complex causes. Critical reflection can also reveal the many biases that flaw our perceptions of what appear to be clear-cut situations and help us think more critically about our proposed actions.

This chapter proposes that this reflection take place prayerfully with God. We who pray have faith that the mystery we call God exists, that this mystery underlies and infuses all of life, and that all people may access God's sustaining power. Praying keeps this different context and horizon in view as it "brings our moment-by-moment connectedness to God into our consciousness."[8] We believe that it is God's nature to love unceasingly and to be responsive to human need, and that in some mysterious way our prayers can affect what God can do. Praying reminds us that God is already there in each situation as we enter it and is mysteriously involved in all our reflection and action. And, over time, if we persist in our prayers, their content and our intent evolve and align more completely with the just, expansive, and peaceable realm God desires for the whole of creation. Theologian Marjorie Suchocki goes so far as to say that *prayer itself* is a unifying medium for this realm.[9]

Reflection and prayer are often deepest and most clear when they take place in the service of *action*. To acknowledge that there are hungry people needing food and to pray that the hungry be fed is most meaningful when it leads one to act so that the hungry *are* fed and to work for the eradication of hunger. As public policy continues to increase the number of hungry people, the Bible causes us to resist.

PRAYER PRACTICES FOR TODAY'S RESISTERS

Throughout our history, prayer has sustained Christians as they responded to the Word of God—including those moments when doing so meant running against dominant social forces. In this section, we examine the forms of prayer they used in light of our mandate to pray with all our being for God's purposes to be fulfilled on earth.

Historically, Protestants have trusted that each person may pray to God unmediated by another human being. Within liberal Protestant Christianity we have favored the meditative form of prayer. However, through the ecumenical movement, students and practitioners of other forms of prayer have shown that they can be adapted for use in many venues of life. Concurrently, many progressives have discovered their need for inner renewal and strengthening and have found meditative prayer only partially satisfying that need. In fall 2005, Jim Wallis told a gathering of West Coast clergy that progressive Christian leaders needed to learn to pray contemplatively for their lives and ministries, and his remark met with nods of agreement.[10] In February 2007, Marcus Borg advised a gathering of five hundred progressive Christians in southern California that "mysticism and the empowerment that comes from it are very critical for resistance to the way things are, because through mysticism—centering in God—you know that the way things are *can* be different."[11]

This chapter does not aim to be a comprehensive study of Christian prayer, which like the Bible has other important roles. Since we are writing about prayer and resistance, the following pages contain abbreviated versions of the most common prayer forms Christians use for this purpose. Readers are encouraged to seek out more-thorough source material if they find one method particularly appealing.

We encourage readers to pray in as many different ways as they find nourishing and fruitful. We invite readers to assess the appropriateness and effectiveness of types of prayer by the extent to which (1) they strengthen their will and sustain their capacities to resist features in the dominant culture that are false, unjust, and destructive; (2) they provide insights into the ways they themselves contribute to the world's injustices and discern which actions they may undertake that are most likely to be just for all concerned; and (3) they offer a glimpse—perhaps an experience—of the loving unity underlying all things and of the alternative, just, world for which we long.

MEDITATION

> If the moral demands of our higher social thought could find adequate expression in prayer, it would have a profound influence on the social movement.
>
> *Walter Rauschenbusch*[12]

This form of prayer is the one that most of us know best, and thus it is the one that we are the most comfortable using. In meditation, the prayer thoughts of our outer life and the stirrings of our inner life come together in the form of words. In the *discursive* form of meditative prayer, we use reason and concentrate on our thoughts. In the *affective* form of meditative prayer, we may also draw on our feelings: as is the case in many of the psalms, we express such feelings as love, trust, surrender, and anger.

Since a spoken word is an outward expression of our inner state, it is always wise to move into silence first to identify the current disposition of our heart, also giving a quick glance at the messages our body language is conveying. This pause lessens the likelihood of manipulating our prayer to fit our personal preferences, falling back on generalities or formulaic and predictable prayers, or as John Wesley warned, engaging in hypocrisy and deadness in praying.[13] Then, too, because language has the power to create reality, it is important to remember when offering meditative prayers on behalf of the people gathered before us that a carelessly spoken word has the potential to harm. Collections of prayers by others may help us find language for the urgings of our hearts.

In a group context, most of us offer words of thanksgiving, petition, and sometimes confession. A broader Protestant formula for meditative prayer includes adoration/awe, contrition/confession or penitence, thanksgiving or gratitude, supplication for self (petition) and for others (intercession), and a voluntary attitude of submission, surrender, consecration, and dedication. We can remember this formula by the acrostic ACTSS.[14]

As the opening phrase of the Lord's Prayer reminds us, God's very name is holy. We cannot recognize the presence of God with us without some feeling of awe and adoration. To think of God at all is to get in touch with the wonder of God's work within the vastness of creation. This moment is not one to hurry through, in order to "get down to the business" of the prayer, but a

moment to savor. It helps us reenter the universal perspective of the human-
God relationship.

Serious *confession* is not something most of us undergo willingly. It involves
our admitting not only that there is an underside to our cultural worldview but
that this exists also within our individual psyches and consequently our actions.
Sometimes it is confrontation by angry others that awakens us to our participation in this skewed and illusory, worldwide economic and military hegemony benefiting a wealthy and privileged portion of humanity while wreaking
havoc on the natural environment and on other human societies. At other
times the need for confession of our social sins may overtake us in the midst
of our daily rounds. The paradoxical good news is that Paul's admonition to
"pray without ceasing" (1 Thess. 5:17) can not only awaken us; it also takes us
through the humbling and soul-searing process of admission, decomposition
of our old ways, and gradual recomposition of our selves more in keeping with
the good for all if we stay the course. Those who follow this course of voluntary displacement from self-delusion may find they resume the pursuit of justice in humility and gratitude, willing to be held accountable by others and by
a forgiving God. Many Christian hymns, in effect meditative prayers set to
music, provide entries into confessional prayer.

Thanksgiving may also bring about contrition and confession. If we enter
into our thanks deeply, we cannot help but become aware that while we offer
thanks for the bounty that enriches our lives, others are begging God for a
meager share. In fact, no prayer of thanksgiving is complete without confession and a passionate cry for change of both self and society. We may also
gratefully celebrate those surprising instances where walls dividing nations
have come down, political prisoners have been released, impoverished downtrodden villages have succeeded in community development projects, or
where a peaceful solution was found to regional or internal national conflicts.[15]

Most of our public meditative prayers move into intercession, *supplication*
for an end of injustice. In this movement, we are encouraged to pray not only
for those who suffer but also for all parties involved in a particular injustice,
for everyone, the powerful as well as the powerless, is caught in one way or
another in the same web of injustice. Douglass Steere comments that when we
pray for others and the world, their and our own inner thresholds—our resistance to experiencing God's loving presence—is lowered. We do not even have
to know what is needed or what happens because of our prayer: with the lowering of our and their defenses, God's love becomes more visible and invit-
ing.[16] This happens when we pray for our "enemies."

Suchocki has several reasons for advocating intercessory prayers: "God
needs our prayers: God's power is exercised in the form of possibilities that the
world has the power to reject." She believes as did Rauschenbusch that "God
needs us to do the praying: they actually make a difference to what God can

do." Further, "even though we may be a distance from the scene or people we pray for, our prayers change what is possible because God is never at a distance."[17] The journals and letters of the saints attest that over time others' meditative prayers change and empower them. Mother Teresa often spoke of how the prayers of convalescing retired nuns of her religious order afforded her the *extra*human strength needed for her mission. Prisoners of conscience whom organizations such as Amnesty International have succeeded in having released have similar testimonies.

Finally, this prayer concludes with our *submission*, our voluntary giving ourselves over to the God of love and justice. In this step, we consecrate and dedicate ourselves to seeking God's direction for living out these values. We offer all that we have been given to God, for God to use as God will. This means that we accept a task God wants done, or we accept inactivity. We take on small acts of faithful, just living, or we rise to the occasion of spectacular ones if so called. We give up applying the talents we have to our Christian vocation if some other work is needed, or we use further what we have been given for the common good. Sincere, full, meditative prayer is not for the faint of heart. This prayer in its entirety is a significant act of voluntary displacement. The more we pray and reflect on what we are praying, the more we realize that indeed there is an alternative way of living in the world and that we can be released from the grip of the violent and unjust competitive world in which we are immersed. This realization activates our inner boldness. We want to live out our prayer's promise.

There are many time-tested methods to pray the ACTSS formulation. We explore here the methods of the examen, Scripture reading, singing or chanting, guided meditation, divine reading, and psalm shouting. Developed by Ignatius of Loyola (1491–1556), the examen consists of two parts. The first is an *examen of consciousness*, when the pray-er (i.e., the one who prays) moves into an attitude of openness and asks for God's help in recalling those situations where God was present to him or her during the day and they worked together. Along with significant acts with social implications, this recall includes God-attended simple acts like slowing down to let someone catch up, saying a needed word, refraining from being wasteful, or being patient and pleasant in line. These recollections can evoke thanksgiving.

The next step is to enter an *examen of conscience*, asking God to show us those places where we blocked God's work. Then we ask ourselves why we did that and what might we need to do now or next time. Working out and living out such questions is an exercise of rededicating oneself to God. We can pray the examen's two components whenever during the day a nagging sense of "missing the mark" arises. Groups can use this method for discerning the rightness of a proposed strategy or checking the justness of their work.

There are many Scripture-based forms of discursive and affective meditative prayer. These call for the ability to read, hear, or recite Scripture *formationally* (allowing the Scripture to address oneself for the purposes of change) rather than *informationally*. The classical prayer here is "Lord Jesus Christ, Son of God, have mercy on me, a sinner." When abbreviated to "Lord, have mercy" or "Lord, mercy," the one praying can match the words rhythmically with his or her breathing or walking until it is internalized. When we pray the communal prayer Jesus taught us with a reflective pause between each phrase—a prayer expressing awe, confession, and supplication with significant social implications—we increase the likelihood of its addressing each of us formatively.

Scripture may also be used for guided meditation, similar to Jesus' use of storytelling in parables. A pray-er may find that using the five human senses to imagine the scene described—for instance, blind Bartimaeus calling out to Jesus—and placing himself or herself or social group in one or more roles within that scene, supplies an opening to both new personal and social insights subversive to present realities. The five-volume Bible offered by first-nation and other scholars of the southern hemisphere, who insist that the earth has its own agency and voice and it is time we listened—provides new interpretations of Judeo-Christian scriptural texts from the perspective of Earth that are timely for guided meditation.[18]

In another form of meditation, lines of Scripture may be sung or chanted. In a practice that can puzzle those in the dominant culture, communities of exploited people joyfully celebrate God's presence with them and the rightness of their cause by singing praise psalms and Scriptures, even as their continued efforts at liberation fail. People from many religious backgrounds become instant community by singing one of the simple scriptural chants for the just reconciliation of the world, crafted by the international ecumenical Taizé Community. The Jewish tradition of chanting psalms alongside the dying, to lament and protect the transitioning soul from evil until burial—as Jesus began to do for himself on the cross and as Orthodox Jews did on shifts around the clock at the 9/11 World Trade Center site until retrieval operations ceased—is a practice progressive Christians may want to adopt in similar tragic circumstances, or when others suffer grave injustices right before our eyes, or when future world circumstances might dictate that we are the ones to suffer.

Protestants are also engaging in the early Christian practice of *Lectio Divina*, or "divine reading," with components of *lectio* (selecting and attentively reading a line or phrase of Scripture), *meditatio* (ruminating on the reading until a word emerges), *oratio* (responding to the insight with prayers of rejoicing or requests for help, etc.), *contemplatio* (resting and experiencing a moment of simply being with God), and finally *incarnatio* (returning to the scriptural insight to apply it to their life and work). One group form—*collatio* (shared meal)—follows the same pattern; additionally, a facilitator feeds back to the group a common thread he or she discerned in their sharing for the groups to confirm or deny, a common insight that might provide future direction.

Among his many prayer suggestions, George McClain, former executive director of the Methodist Federation for Social Action, offers a form of corporate prayer of shouting the psalms, substituting "we" for "I."[19] Such ancient public prayers present a strong challenge to the power of unjust authorities, provide those praying with collective energy, and if prayed regularly with openness to God, can significantly change the purposes and course of a group's action.

The Psalms can help us own our complicity with injustice, the evil that we—I, you—do, through unjust political and economic systems. For instance, we progressives might try shouting confessionally and as petition Prov. 30:7–9:

> Two things I ask of you;
>   do not deny them to me before I die:
> Remove far from me falsehood and lying;
>   give me neither poverty nor riches;
>   feed me with the food that I need,
> or I shall be full, and deny you,
>   and say, "Who is the LORD?"
> or I shall be poor, and steal,
>   and profane the name of my God.

In the broadest sense of the term, every action toward a just world is a form of prayer, a way of "praying without ceasing." Meditative-prayer acts of resistance include passing out petitions for collecting signatures, calling or writing congressional representatives on pending legislation, organizing for political action, marching to draw attention to the plight of the disenfranchised, picketing or boycotting businesses that exploit workers, training others in nonviolent resistance, offering registration opportunities on school campuses as alternatives to campus draft registrars, and conducting consciousness-raising "reverse money" tours to impoverished countries for the financially well-off. We can also act our prayer publicly by creating drama, stories, photographs, and poetry, and, as socially aware rock stars have discovered, by composing music.

OTHER FORMS OF CHRISTIAN PRAYER

Centering Prayer

If you love truth, be a lover of silence. . . . Silence will unite you to God.

Isaac of Nineveh

Centering prayer, an experiential gateway to God, moves us from discursive prayer into a prayer without words, into silence, and thus into an alternative culture. In our frantic culture of sensory overload, we rarely experience silence, and extended silence can make us uncomfortable. Yet interfaith groups have proliferated in this traditional prayer mode in the last two decades, finding silence surprisingly pregnant with God's communication. For many of us, to risk entering this silence requires that we rely heavily on the biblical knowledge that God desires our good and the good of this world.

Centering prayer removes us as the primary actor determining the content of prayer into a posture of waiting for God. It begins with focusing on a sacred word such as *Kyrie, Iesu, Abba, peace,* or *shalom* as a way of signifying intent to enter in humility into God's presence and allow God to act within. Setting a timer with no audible ticker for twenty minutes, we sit attentively with eyes closed and back straight, and gently bring the sacred word into consciousness. We focus on this word lightly—to do so heavily would reengage thinking—until the word disappears. If distractions come to mind, we gently reintroduce the sacred word. When the prayer time is up, we remain in silence for a moment before adjusting again to external senses and reentering the world with the possibility of bringing this interior atmosphere of silence into its din.

Those new to centering prayer may be disappointed when there is no subsequent sense of closure or direction following this prayer, a regular consequence of sincere meditative prayer. They may also be tempted to give it up because usually nothing noticeable to us happens during this prayer: its fruits of inner clarity and stability will appear later in our daily lives. Others may be the first to notice its effects on us.

Most of us are familiar with public forms of this prayer: we can recall the nonviolent presence of silent marchers and counter sitters in the civil rights movement of fifty years ago and the silent witness of groups gathered at governmental buildings or weaponry sites to protest the proliferation of war or nuclear testing. We also see this form of prayer among those who spontaneously gather in candlelit silence with offerings of flowers, leaving notes addressed to God and those directly affected at what become public "sacred sites" associated with a tragedy. For some observers, the colors, lines, and movements of sculpture, visual arts, and dance speak a social message to them that is louder than words.

This prayer displaces us from our culture at another significant venue: when Dorothee Soelle observed young people in shopping malls gathered to make a silent witness "where the golden calf is venerated," she commented, "They make God visible simply by standing in those places. In silence they speak of God's presence . . . [and] openly acknowledge and own their lack of power. . . . It is a silence that follows after information, analysis and knowledge. . . . In silence, God is *presenté*."[20]

Contemplative Prayer and Its Mystical Culmination

Contemplation is not a state of coma, or of religious reverie. If it is genuine prayer, we find our inward life quickened. We sense new directions, or our attention is refocused on neglected ones. We find ourselves being mobilized and our inward resources regrouped in responses to the new assignment. We find, in short, that we have been reenlisted in the redemptive order, that in these ranks, our former reservations are brushed to one side and a new level of expendability emerges.

Douglas Steere[21]

Contemplative prayer, another form of silent prayer, is another instance of inward voluntary displacement in which we open our inner selves to God and then remain attentive at each moment. In contemplative prayer, we place ourselves on the threshold between the concreteness of what we know as our portion of daily reality and divine reality, in actuality one reality. Veteran contemplatives live within a constant awareness of these two aspects of reality. In this manner Brother Lawrence (1605–1691) continually practiced God's presence, whether in chapel or in the kitchen doing chores.

More than centering prayer, contemplation requires that we temporarily restrain our powers of agency and quiet our minds. In this prayer, we are not focused on the past or future but are in the present moment, and we are letting go of our ego and agenda. Soelle proposes this inner form of resistance as a way of overcoming our culture's default egocentric and competitive consciousness, a way that reminds us that we are not God and that goodness already exists: "It is only when I can experience myself as a passive being that I know that I have not made myself, and that from its inception, life was goodness."[22]

Many teachers of contemplation stress the need to silence our ego's dominance so that we can grow in attentiveness. This is particularly important when we struggle to resist unjust institutions: the ego may try to convince us that resistance has no chance of succeeding against such power.[23] Soelle offers insights from the fourth-century-BCE mystic Lao Tzu, who understood our egos to be on loan to us by the universe, connecting us with all others in time. Soelle concludes, "An ego thus understood can leave itself behind and weave itself into larger communal webs in the cosmos. The name for this self that has come free of the ego is 'Christ in me.'"[24]

While our mind predominates in meditative prayer, the will predominates in contemplative prayer. We respond to what we later realize was a God-initiated urge, an urge that will not go away. We decide to put aside our usual ways of self-assertion and control. In simplicity of purpose and trust, we intentionally move from wanting to know *about* God to wanting to know God. In fear and trembling we seek this relationship as an immediate end in itself, all the while knowing that its effect on us will transform how we see, think, and thus act in our exterior life. We know that making ourselves available does not mean we will experience God's presence. God's timing is not ours; we may not be ready to receive God or bear some truths of a private or societal nature (John 16:12–13).

If we enter this prayer deeply, we may know God's participation in our contemplation in one of three ways: acquired contemplation, infused contemplation, and "Dark Night of the Soul." In *acquired contemplation*, the Divine briefly overcomes our heart, will, and mind. This overcoming brings a simple sense of peace we can feel but not rationally understand, and when we experience this peace and the concrete knowledge that comes with it, we have a different reference point for our subsequent thoughts and actions. We find our heart enlarged, our ability to see the realities around us heightened, our will to persevere strengthened, and our reasoning powers enhanced. As we stay in this kind of prayerfulness, we may acquire a new sense of what to do. While we may begin by practicing contemplation only in the silence of our room, we may come to pray contemplatively while actively participating in the world, a practice William Callahan calls "noisy contemplation."

Infused contemplation occurs unbidden and unexpectedly. As Paul reported (2 Cor. 12:2–4), God breaks into historical time and initiates the soul into a transforming union. In this unitive moment, the soul is completely overtaken and lifted by God. The inner self helplessly receives infinite nurture flooding the body, comes to see things beyond sight and reasoned knowledge, senses some gift for Christ's service being activated within, and, as historical time returns, fervently desires with all of one's being to respond in love and service to all people and creation itself. In the moments afterward, according to Marcus Borg, one realizes that for the entirety of one's life up until that moment, one has been asleep.[25]

A unitive contemplative experience is a particularly wonder-filled surprise. Like Paul on the Damascus Road, we are speechless. Knowing from our experience in this boundless space that we have been given a piece of God's wisdom, awakening to the realization that God similarly loves *all* others and that they have other pieces—and that all of these are needed for the just, peaceable world for which we long to be realized—we become right-sized. From then on, recipients can experience growing dissatisfaction with the distorted way that things are, and can choose—or not choose, since God does not force us— to begin to live, by degrees, counterculturally—"in the world but not of it," seeking out others to learn their wisdom and conjoining strengths for resolutely resisting its hideous distortion together in God.

The third possible outcome of praying contemplatively is "no-thing," which paradoxically is a significant event for the pray-er. The overall term from our rich tradition is "Dark Night of the Soul." John of the Cross (1542–1592) defined two phases. One of these is the dark night of the senses, when aspects of our personalities not aligned with God's character or desires may surface, demanding healing and therapeutic attention and prompting our desperate prayers for a clean heart and right spirit. In the other, the dark night of the spirit, after years of communing in God, one may bitterly experience the seeming absence of God. God is not here or anywhere.[26] While this experience is unique to each person, it is also a place of unitive being with all that is: God's purpose for the pray-er, who is both a wounded and wounding person, is the inner cultivation of a deeper faith, humility, truthfulness, and fundamental dependence on God that can see us through the persecution that our resistance may attract. Additionally, "Dark Night" reminds us that God desires that we love God radically for God's self alone and not for what God does or does not do. And it reminds us beyond a doubt that God is beyond our full comprehension.

The more we voluntarily displace ourselves into the inner practice of contemplative prayer, the more certain we become that we are to pray continually out of love for the *shalom* and unity of the whole world. This stance of nonviolent, nonpossessive, and inclusive love is reminiscent of Gandhi and Martin Luther King Jr. It is greatly to be desired for actualizing a just world, particularly for us whose desire and ability to act justly is compromised by the prevailing individualistic ethic.

Radical inclusive love characterizes what ecumenics professor John D'Arcy May terms an *ethic of care* or a *contemplative ethic*. He explains the contemplative ethic in terms of two other systems, the ethic of consumerism and the ethic of asceticism. The *consumerist ethic* may be understood as "'I want it all and I want it now.' This easily becomes the stuff of politics. That assures that conflicting interests will remain the norm." By contrast, "the *ascetic ethic* of environmentalists might be formulated as 'I want it but I don't need it'—because others need it more, or it is harmful, or there is not enough of it, so I will do without it." While commendable, holders of this ethic cannot convincingly evoke the broad consensus from others needed to effect transformative change. The *contemplative ethic*—the *ethic of caring*—is based on *being* rather than *having*. Found in the spiritualities of the world's religions, it "can be formulated as 'I don't want it because I love it' in and for itself, so that possessing it or exploiting it would seem like a betrayal of myself and my world."[27]

While this perspective may seem to be naive and romantic, and certainly unrealistic from the perspective of those immersed in the consumerist ethic of our culture, this *shalom* love nevertheless embodies the felt sense as well as the ethical sense of the just culture we are striving for. It becomes the way by which we seek to relate to all others, hoping to spread the contagion. And being severely countercultural, it requires disciplined maintenance.

This radical, just stance is expressed in another way: practitioners refrain from demonizing their activist adversaries because they know all people are part of the same whole. It is within that perspective that King claimed that the tradition of mystical unity was valid for antisegregationists and segregationists alike. To segregationists, he said,

> We shall match your capacity to inflict suffering by our capacity to endure suffering. We will meet your physical force with soul force. Do to us what you will and we will still love you. We cannot in all conscience obey your unjust laws and abide by the unjust system, because non-cooperation with evil is as much a moral obligation as is cooperation with Good, and so throw us in jail and we will still love you. Bomb our homes . . . and we will still love you.[28]

As King found out, the practice of contemplative disciplines often leads to forms of experience that can be called mystical. Protestants traditionally have thought of mysticism as disconnected from ordinary reality. This is true to the extent that our proclivity to mysticism begins when we no longer feel at home in a world of violence and competition. On the other hand, as the above examples show, mysticism also displays the oneness and wholeness of actual life, while at the same time displaying its fragmentation and moving us deeply into the suffering of those oppressed by injustice's means. Mystics are also able paradoxically to hold social wholeness and fragmentation together, as well as the opposites of peace and suffering and of love and hate, because they perceive aspects of the whole picture and see how each aspect is permeated by the other and by God's hopeful, compassionate, and suffering love.

However expansive it may be, though, mysticism is not self-sufficient. As Soelle emphasizes, "Scripture's two voices—the mystical and the prophetic—belong together, and in fact are senseless without each other. The ethical-prophetic voice speaks in the place of God and in that respect it speaks 'about' God and God's desires. But that is not enough of a witness. Prophecy is dependent on the language of mysticism, which is always a speaking 'to' or 'in' God."[29]

In recent years, liberation theologies have brought a critically conscious lens of suspicion into Christianity for interpreting social groups' actions and motives on behalf of justice. Mystics avow that a second interpretative filter, one of universal yearnings and hunger for beauty, creativity, and inclusive radical love, is called for, a pairing contained in the phrase from early twentieth-century women's labor movements: "Give me both bread and roses." The two filters work in creative tension. Soelle calls for articulation of this second interpretive lens, this lens of "hunger" on behalf of "the world where hope itself is exiled, where it has, so to speak, no work permit among us."[30] Aware of how easy it is to lose hope when we face the death-giving tendencies of institutions and systems that desire no social connection, she reminds us that "loving life, even where it has been condemned to death, even from its very beginning, is an old human ability to go beyond what is. That ability, called transcendence or faith or hope, is the most important movement that human beings can learn in their lives."[31] This ongoing contemplative prayer of nonpossessive love for all—a state of mind, heart, and soul in which one continues to care and to love after hope appears dead—is a powerful tool for persevering when our acts of resistance meet with violent confrontation, belittlement, or, worse, no response at all.

Historically mystics have functioned as subversive agents, using renunciation, disagreement, divergence, dissent, and rebellion against the world's corruption and injustices as they existed in their time. Through the ages they have attracted conflict, because their love for God has run headlong into institutions' preoccupation with regularity and order.[32] They have remained engaged in the spiritual and concrete battles for justice, even though it may be hard for us to understand their participation as social activism, for "the language of this world is articulated in terms of egoism, rationality of purposes and hierarchy and excludes authentic unity."[33]

Another oddity to many of us is the mysticism that bypasses the power of possessiveness and domination ethics. Soelle suggests a way into this extraordinary state of voluntary displacement from the culture: being amazed, resisting, and letting go. Soelle would convince us that the first-world soul *urgently* needs amazement: "the repeated liberation from customs, viewpoints and convictions which like layers of fat accumulating around us make us untouchable and insensitive."[34] In radical amazement, scientists report their findings about our universe and rescript long-held theories on its workings. In radical amazement, Dorothy Day beheld the Christ in each person she served in the Catholic Worker's outreach kitchen. Similarly, the focus of the Protestant Reformation was to activate in every layperson a new, then-radical vision of observing and serving God in daily life.

In spite of the surround-sound numbing of technological life, many of us are still stirred to awe when touched by a piece of music. A weeklong withdrawal "into desert barrenness and lying on rocks that are older than we know" reassured one activist and restored her perspective, hope, and gratitude for being alive after a gut-wrenching experience of civil disobedience.[35] Becoming aware of God's omnipresence in *this* moment, actually seeing where we are as if this is our last moment on earth, feeling a piercing and deep gratitude that we can barely stand for merely being alive, realizing as we look around that the very human community in which we are immersed is actually God's Beloved—all of these experiences can evoke awe and rid us of our culturally constructed selves. We remain with one foot in the dualistic, competitive world, with the other in the unified world, in creative tension.

This transformation takes time. The enculturated "I" that I am was built over a lifetime. We would do well to ponder Soelle's re-forming questions in our prayers of examen: "What do I perceive?" "What do I keep myself away from?" "What do I choose?"[36] To these we can add Nouwen's questions: "How am I understanding God's caring action in the world in which I find myself?" "How am I asked to let the dead bury the dead, to keep my hands on the plow and not look back?"[37] The answers can help us uncover our unique God-given vocation in this moment in history.

Corporate Prayerful Discernment

> If you, even you, had only recognized on this day the things that make for peace!
>
> *Jesus*[38]

There are acute situations of injustice that require a great commitment to resistance, but one is not clear how to proceed. What is needed is corporate discernment. Discernment (*discernere* [L.], to separate, distinguish accurately one object from another) is a historical process that allows us to see, without confusion and ambiguity, what differentiates things. For resisters, discernment involves being able to tell which action out of many possible actions for this given moment and situation (and the next, and the next) is the one God desires for us to undertake.

This process is countercultural, again calling for an intentional, voluntary displacement away from our results- and efficiency-oriented culture. The process is based on trusting the premise that God's desires may be known more fully to the gathered community simply because each person has a piece of God's wisdom.

Discernment relies heavily on trusting God. First, it requires that we give it all the time it needs. If we do not have enough time and if the exigencies of the moment are urgent and our desire to move ahead is without guile, we are encouraged to respond to these urgencies as minimally as possible to meet them. While the whole matter is still fresh, we set aside time to revisit it in discernment, in order to discover God's desires in the core of it. Second, we accept that God's timing may not coincide with ours; we need to trust that a "No" from God at this time is given out of love for all concerned. Third, as Jesus did, we seek to know God's desires in this matter above all else and commit to them before we know what they are. This distinguishes this prayer process from others in which we seek to learn what God might desire, before we make that specific a commitment. Additionally, valuing honesty highly, corporate discernment requires that we admit and temporarily suspend our own preferred outcome—that is, move into an attitude of indifference and hospitality to others—in order to hear what those with additional relevant factual information might have to add, even though we anticipate that that information will work against the fulfillment of our perceived outcome. Faithfulness to the process requires that we discern pertinent portions of the biblical tradition and that we also hear from contemporaries who have the most to gain and those with the most to lose, and from those who would be peripherally affected by our undertaking this action—including our loved ones and particularly those who would be direct recipients of the proposed action.

When we want to rush pell-mell into action because we see some direction from initial discernments, our fellow discerners may encourage us to "try on" the proposed action: first, live with it for a period as if it were in effect; then live as if its opposite were in effect; and then weigh the pros and cons of the results.

Corporate discernment may reveal that there is more than one question to be answered: for instance, "Should the initiator of the discernment process proceed in a particular way in confronting injustice?" and "How should the gathered community heed and support the prophetic word given their colleague at this time?" John Woolman (1720–1772) called a Quaker Committee of Clearness together to help him discern the genuineness of the call he sensed from God—a call to travel to all the Societies of Friends in the colonies and preach that they release their slaves. After much searching for God's enlightenment, they discerned that he had genuinely heard God's call. They also discerned that God was not yet calling them to release their slaves, and they further discerned that they were to support Woolman the month each year that he would be gone by caring for his family and his crops. For many years after returning from his travels, Woolman raised the question before a newly gathered Committee of Clearness. By 1787 "it seemed good to them and God" that they release their slaves, and they did so. Throughout this nonviolent process, members of the community remained in respectful peace with one another.

As this prayerful process proceeds, we may find that our proposed action is on the wrong track altogether. Or our insights may be confirmed, and next steps become apparent. Or there may seemingly be no answer from God, in which case we let the matter rest until an impulse arises, and the group feels it is time to try it again. Finally, when a discernment of God's desires for action seems to have emerged, it is wise to let it "rest"—at least overnight—to see if it continues to hold true before acting. When a true discernment arises from our weighing all the possibilities, there usually is a sense of rightness, a palpable corporate experience of peace, and a felt sense of inner harmony and recognition of its validity among all participants. At that time, prayers of gratitude and dedication are appropriate.

CONCLUDING REMARKS

Progressive Christians know that in many respects our world's human society is terribly askew, that the human constituents of the dominant social system may desire justice, but in practice, we fail to uphold a just order. The following chapters detail some ways in which this is so. Additionally, as indigenous groups throughout the world have been trying to tell us, the earth beckons us to undergo another radical and voluntary displacement, this time away from human society in its entirety, a displacement where it and its other constituents await our listening to them.

If there is to be a healthy human society on a healthy planet, the changes that are needed go far beyond what liberal reforms can effect. As progressive Christians, we have much to resist, in the world and in ourselves. And we can clarify and fortify our efforts of reflection and resistive work with immersion in prayer, praying before and in God who loves all, in ways that resonate with our hearts. We can share with God our passionate hope that this endangered planet can become a location of peace, with sustainable, eco-based social justice for all. We can admit that we carry this hope in the broken vessels of our socioeconomic, political, theological, and religious systems—and of ourselves, who are as much in need of transformation as are these systems. And in this spirit of humility, we can offer to help. Purposefully recombined, this triad of reflection, prayer, and action can provide a unified way for our living resistively as progressive Christians into a better world.

DISCUSSION QUESTIONS

1. Who taught you to pray? What did you learn? How much is praying a part of your personal life? Of your societal life as a Christian? What concerns you about praying?
2. Reflect on your discourse with other progressive Christians. What does it concern? Can you imagine talking about how you pray, what happens when you pray, and what way is most effective for you? Can you imagine listening to someone else who has a different experience and a different way to communicate effectively with God? Our forebears engaged each other in this way with great frequency and earnestness.

3. One challenge for U.S. progressive Christians, most of whom do not suffer very much, is to discern what it is we are to resist and what it is we are to suffer. Start jotting down a list and keep adding to it. Where will you begin? With whom? For what do you want to be held responsible? By whom? What role might prayer play in this process?
4. What single issue facing the world today engages your passion? Does praying change your way of understanding and dealing with it?

FOR FURTHER READING

Prayer and Resistance

Crosby, Michael H. *Thy Will Be Done: Praying the Lord's Prayer as a Subversive Activity.* Maryknoll, NY: Orbis Books, 1977.

Grey, Mary C. *Sacred Longings: The Ecological Spirit and Global Culture.* Minneapolis: Fortress Press, 2004.

Hanh, Thich Nhat. *Living Buddha, Living Christ.* New York: Riverhead Books, 1997.

Heschel, Susannah, ed., *Abraham Joshua Heschel, Moral Grandeur and Spiritual Audacity: Essays.* New York: Farrar, Straus & Giroux, 1997.

Ruffing, Janet K. *Mysticism and Social Transformation.* Syracuse, NY: Syracuse University Press, 2001.

Vennard, Jane E. *Embracing the World: Praying for Justice and Peace.* San Francisco: John Wiley & Sons, 2003.

Whitmire, Catherine. *Practicing Peace: A Devotional Walk through the Quaker Tradition.* Notre Dame, IN: Sorin Books, 2007.

Relevant Prayer Practices

Bourgeault, Cynthia. *Centering Prayer and Inner Awakening.* Cambridge, MA: Cowley Publications, 2004.

Callahan, William R. *Noisy Contemplation: Deep Prayer for Busy People.* Hyattsville, MD: Quixote Center, 1994.

Del Bene, Ron, et al. *The Breath of Life: A Simple Way to Pray.* Nashville: Upper Room, 1991.

Driskill, Joseph D. *Protestant Spiritual Exercises: Theology, History, and Practice.* Harrisburg, PA: Morehouse Publishing, 1999.

Keating, Thomas. *Open Mind, Open Heart: The Contemplative Dimension of the Gospel.* Boston: Amity Press, 1986.

McClain, George. *Claiming All Things for God: Prayer, Discernment, and Ritual for Social Change.* Nashville: Abingdon Press, 1998.

Morris, Danny E., and Charles M. Olsen. *Discerning God's Will Together: A Spiritual Practice for the Church.* Bethesda, MD: Alban Publications, 1997.

Mulholland, Robert. *Shaped by the Word: The Power of Scripture in Spiritual Formation.* Rev. ed. Nashville: Upper Room, 2001.

Michael, Chester P. and Marie C. Norrisey. *Prayer and Temperament: Different Prayer Forms for Different Personality Types.* Charlottesville, VA: Open Door, 1984.

Vennard, Jane E. *A Praying Congregation: The Art of Teaching Spiritual Practice.* Bethesda, MD: Alban Institute, 2005.

Wolff, Pierre. *Discernment: The Art of Choosing Well, Based on Ignatian Spirituality.* Ligouri, MO: Triumph Books, 1993.

Related Prayer Collections

Brandt, Leslie F., with Corita Kent. *Psalms/Now.* St. Louis: Concordia Publishing House, 1986.

Brueggemann, Walter. *Awed to Heaven, Rooted in Earth: Prayers of Walter Brueggemann.* Minneapolis: Augsburg Press, 2003.

Rauschenbusch, Walter. *Prayers of the Social Awakening.* Boston: Pilgrim Press, 1909; new ed., 1925.

Welle, Janice, OSF, and Ansgar Holmberg, CSJ. *Table Graces: Prayers for Meals Reflecting Earth Charter Principles.* LaGrange, IL: St. Joseph Press, 2005.

PART 2

What to Resist

3

Consumerism

Gordon Douglass and Ward McAfee

I belong to the Cult of the Next Thing. It's dangerously easy to get enlisted. It happens by default—not by choosing the cult, but by failing to resist it. The Cult of the Next Thing is consumerism cast in religious terms. It has its own litany of sacred words: more, you deserve it, new, faster, cleaner, brighter. It has its own deep-rooted liturgy: charge it, instant credit, no down-payment, deferred payment, no interest for three months. It has its own preachers, evangelists, prophets, and apostles: ad men, pitchmen, celebrity sponsors. It has, of course, its own shrines, chapels, temples, meccas: malls, superstores, club warehouses. It has its own sacraments: credit and debit cards. It has its own ecstatic experiences: the spending spree. The Cult of the Next Thing's central message proclaims, "Crave and spend, for the Kingdom of Stuff is here."

Mark Buchanan[1]

INTRODUCTION

People have always been tempted by possessions, and envy of those who possess more of them is nothing new. What *is* new is a culture that encourages an infinite expansion of wants and measures human worth by how far individuals satisfy these wants. This chapter is a call to Christians to resist consumerism. To do so thoughtfully requires an understanding of how this new religion came to gain so strong a hold on our culture in general and on so many of us as individuals.

Most Americans have escaped the elemental struggle that has plagued human societies in all previous times. Their general standard of well-being is high and no longer restricted to a powerful few. Indeed, by fifty years ago, all but the very poor succeeded in meeting their basic needs for food, shelter, clothing, and health care (though access to health care now is getting worse). Since then, the percentage of income spent on the basics has declined steadily as incomes and spending on discretionary items—larger homes, designer clothes, recreational travel—has grown, especially for the well-off. Others, whose incomes have grown sluggishly, chose to work longer hours and to go deeper into debt to maintain their consumerist habits.

The United States is not alone in this newfound condition. The countries of Western Europe, Japan, Canada, Australia, New Zealand, and even a few late developing countries are beginning to experience this broadly shared affluence. But for most of the world's people, including even the very poor of affluent societies, toiling to survive remains a common burden.

The economic system that made possible the relative affluence of modern industrial societies brings with it a challenge unknown to earlier peoples: the dilemma of plenty. "For the first time since his creation," John Maynard Keynes wrote more than seventy years ago, "man will be faced with his real, his permanent problem—how to use his freedom from pressing economic cares, how to occupy his leisure, which science and compound interest have won for him, to live wisely and agreeably and well."[2] Thus, the social challenge that confronts all prosperous societies—discovering how to live "wisely and agreeably and well" with their abundance—confronts Americans and the affluent others with an unknown future.

In the latter half of the twentieth century, American society answered this social challenge by creating a culture of hard work to earn more income in order to acquire more goods and services—in short, by consuming more rather than working less. Americans on average work longer hours than their counterparts in other leading industrial economies, as much as three or four hundred more hours per year. They also save less of their income than their counterparts, sometimes (as at present) spending virtually all discretionary income on consumer goods. They seem infused with ambition for "more"—more income, more assets, more consumer goods, seemingly without limit.

This phenomenon has come to be called a "consumer society," which is best described as one in which the possession and use of an increasing number and variety of goods and services is the principal cultural aspiration and perceived to be the surest route to personal happiness, social status, and national success. Why, we must ask, do so many Americans seem to believe that consuming more goods is the likeliest way to "the good life"? What is there about using much of our nonworking time to acquire more things that cost money—and the spending of money itself—that makes us think we're better off and happier? How does the prevailing culture of consumption affect those who cannot afford the standard of respectable membership that is set by the society? And why does our culture of consumerism tend to ignore or try to discredit the observable physical, psychological, and economic consequences of our behavior?

These questions raise religious issues concerning the meaning and purpose of life. The culture of consumerism is profoundly contrary to the Christian gospel. Indeed, in the interior life of the United States, we believe that "consumerism" is the religion that most fundamentally challenges Christianity. We are called to resist. Yet the churches deal with this spiritual problem only tangentially. Every church should make consumerism a matter of central concern. Given the firm hold of this materialistic culture, our delivery from this idolatry may require disciplined prayer.

This chapter addresses consumerism as a theological issue. To do so it begins by considering how consumerism arose and came to dominance in our society, and then proceeds to assess its effects on the individual, community, and society. To be sure, consumerism has spread to many other societies, often in response to the export of American cultural preferences. Even so, we focus on the American experience, suggesting how a progressive Christian understanding of living "wisely and agreeably and well" can provide an alternative to this culture.

THE RISE AND EFFECTS OF CONSUMERISM

The Rise of Consumerism

In order to review how consumerism came into being, we must first briefly recount how capitalism, which is its root source, developed. At its beginnings, capitalism was solely focused on capturing new markets within emerging nation-states seeking to gain economic advantages over each other. Early capitalism flourished in this environment, bringing wealth to a new class of entrepreneurs as well as income and glory to the monarchical head who allowed the system to operate. In a seminal book, *The Wealth of Nations* (1776), Adam Smith preached that wealth could grow even more rapidly if governmental policy did not play favorites, as it had in the beginning of the capitalist economic reformation. Smith advocated that capitalism should become as free as possible, unrestricted by Navigation Acts favoring one country's products over those of another. Free trade would lead to increased production and more wealth.

After a century of great economic progress, World War I wreaked great destruction on such European powers as Britain, France, Germany, Russia, Austria-Hungary, and Italy. The United States was spared, and in 1918, it emerged from "The Great War" as the economically dominant nation in the world. The perception of the United States as the land of abundance and opportunity was magnified.

During the 1920s, the automobile became a new economic force, transforming both urban and rural life and necessitating expanding industries in petroleum, steel, rubber, and glass. Advertising blossomed within the decade, as a new American urban lifestyle emerged triumphant. The new motion picture industry propagandized consumerist styles that Americans readily adopted and persons of other countries came to envy. Capitalism appeared to be entering into a new, more-glamorous stage, highlighted by innovative processes involving an efficient assembly line capable of achieving mass production, which necessarily assumed a sufficient supply of consumers to purchase all the new products that were being produced. Then, suddenly, progress itself seemed to collapse in an economic cataclysm that shut down banks and factories, leaving millions suddenly unemployed. Mortgages on homes were foreclosed and a desperate poverty plagued the land.

With the coming of World War II and the need for war materials to combat the fascist powers, full employment returned and worker salaries fattened bank accounts. But with the wartime focus on producing what was needed to win the war, a strict rationing of consumer items kept the development of consumerism in check. With the end of the war, pent-up demand exploded into a consumer frenzy, making up for years of spartan denial spanning both the Great Depression and World War II. Since then consumerism has come more and more to dominate American culture.

We have presented this victory of consumerism as simply the outgrowth of industrial development and the capitalist system. However, many other factors have contributed to this cultural phenomenon. We will note several of these.

1. *Economic Theory*. The discipline of economics contributed mightily to the rise of consumerism. The internal logic of economic theory originates in the notion of permanent scarcity of the means of production—scarcity confronted by limitless human needs and wants. Hence capitalism must strive to produce more output from less input; that is to say, efficiency demands the most effective allocation of resources and capital. This notion that scarcity is with us always is so deeply engrained in the American culture that it claims the highest priority in public affairs. The quest for economic efficiency regularly trumps other social goals that are not marketable commodities and have no readily assignable price. Typically the question is asked, How much might a given social improvement damage the production of "more"? Liberals and conservatives alike accept these efficiency premises, so their arguments over macroeconomic policies are generally over the best way to achieve the "more" rather than whether "more" truly contributes to true human well-being. The

difference is chiefly that liberals tend to have more interest in the redistribution of income for the sake of the poor than do conservatives.

2. *Advertising.* The manipulation of desires is an important part of consumerist society. Advertising as information about available goods is a natural and necessary part of any complex economy. But advertising as a form of propaganda, that is, the manipulation of beliefs and desires rather than information, is a distinct and important feature of consumerist society. Although propaganda of some sort has been a part of all societies, it was developed far more fully in the United States beginning in World War I. Over several decades, a profound cultural shift occurred as commercial appeals hammered at the unconscious mind, thereby weakening rational consideration in consumer decision making. The banalities of such appeals have become commonplace as material delights are displayed in ways to make them irresistible to many. Frequently advertisements assume everyone is capable of participation in what amounts to a continuous spending spree. But the effect on both the affluent and the poor is profound.

3. *Planned Obsolescence.* Advertising made it possible to sell new goods to replace old ones that still functioned well. Models of products quickly changed, requiring even more purchasing. But "planned obsolescence" went even further. It is defined by *The New Dictionary of Cultural Literacy* as "incorporating into a product features that will almost certainly go out of favor in a short time."[3] Planned obsolescence became a leading characteristic of the new economy. Garish tail fins on automobiles came and went as only one fad among the consumers of the 1950s. The children of the baby boom magnified youthful demands on parents to outdo their peers in "keeping up with the Joneses."

4. *Underlying Fear.* The global context also contributed. The emergence of the nuclear age and the unimaginable terror of "mutually assured destruction" brought into being by the Cold War between the United States and the Soviet Union encouraged the buying binge as if there were no tomorrow. "Drugs, sex, and rock 'n' roll" in the following decade increased the tempo, promising diversion from the troubling undercurrent of modern consciousness that Armageddon awaited. Patterns of consumption and pleasure seeking have been continuous ever since, with each generation challenged to outdo its predecessor.

5. *Easy Credit.* The evolving U.S. credit system allowed American households to borrow, often recklessly, for consumption. Many borrowed against their savings, with credit cards and lines of bank credit that steadily drew down the accumulated equity they owned in their homes. A mounting stream of credit card offers filled American mailboxes, each offering frequent-flyer miles, low introductory interest rates, and lower minimum payments. Before long, credit cards were pushed on adolescents so as to draw them into the culture of consumerist debt. Most of America's youth are hardly aware of any way

to conceive "success" other than full participation in the consumerist society. Today, fewer than a third of Americans avoid interest—even the exorbitant levels charged by most card companies—by paying off their credit card balances each month.

6. *Widespread Acceptance*. Well-meaning people, remembering the anguish of the Great Depression, accepted these developments as benefiting the entire society. Unemployment was kept low, both by consumer demand and the postwar arms race with the Soviet Union. American goods had no effective rivals in the years following World War II, for the industrial infrastructure of every potential competitor had been destroyed or severely damaged in the war. Unions were strong, and worker salaries were high. Prosperity allowed growth in the welfare state started during the New Deal. Initially, it all seemed part of some progressive plan to improve the commonwealth.

These factors all worked to make consumerism capitalism's wonder drug during peacetime, seemingly solving the problem of industrial overproduction. Returning military men filled jobs that had been occupied by women workers during the war, and the latter in turn became mothers as had no generation of American women since the nineteenth century. The baby boom created unprecedented family needs that were met by purchasing more automobiles, more children's items (both necessities and luxuries), and new houses to hold the growing families. Advertising spread the word regarding new kitchen appliances that became requirements in every modern home. Following years of hardship, the beneficiaries of this new economy termed it the "good life."

The Personal Consequences of Consumerism

The urge to buy is so sanctioned, reinforced, and exaggerated by the media and advertising industries that ignoring them is not an easy option. Their sales message projects a vision of the good life, usually including more luxurious and comfortable lifestyles. They employ sexual images to sell all kinds of goods, including automobiles, and they also sell goods that are claimed to make one personally attractive by meeting certain socially established norms.

Individuals often build in their imaginations a product-filled world informed by the images and stories they see and hear on television. When their actual consumption experiences fail to meet expectations, according to psychological research[4] people tend to adjust their daydreams and increase their consumption to achieve their newly formed idealized image, especially when the media and advertising persistently inform them that it is the right thing to do. And with credit more widely available, buying is easy, its consequences distant. Shopping malls are often the places where older children and youth "hang out." They find themselves judged by their peers according to whether they have the right things. They internalize these judgments and come to feel that their personal worth as human beings is determined by what they own. This view persists into adulthood. To avoid public shame, individuals and families must spend well beyond the requirements of food and shelter. Meanwhile, marketing experts work hard continuously to update the social definition of what "more" means.

Sociologist David Reisman was one of the first to raise concerns about the new society taking shape. He described what he saw as a new, "other-directed" personality type coming to predominate in American culture. This new American was not only a conformist but, and this was the chilling part, one who was also often unaware of conforming to the expectations of others even when doing so to a slavish extreme. "Peer groups," rather than parents or other traditional authorities, set value standards that guided the emerging generation. Celebrities from the new consumer field of pop culture set norms to define various styles of behavior to imitate.[5]

In the 1950s, an exaggerated social conformity was observable on the surface of life. Several decades of subsequent social development drove the impulse to be wedded to group expectations well below the surface, as self appeared to replace community in cultural trends. This change encouraged the social critic Christopher Lasch to describe in 1979 the alteration of the American personality by the impact of consumerism. He emphasized an addictive personality without proper limits and boundaries, with little or no sense of history and "diminishing expectations" for the future, requiring immediate gratification and living in a state of "restless, perpetually unsatisfied desire."[6] Since 1979, the themes identified by Lasch have continued and deepened.

National trends in both obesity and rising personal debt reveal behavior encouraged in a consumer culture. Self-restraint is minimized in favor of instant gratification. In 1980, U.S. household debt stood at 65 percent of disposable income. Today, household debt exceeds disposable income. As this trend continued, the rate of personal bankruptcies climbed along with it. Today, more than a million people file for personal bankruptcy each year, more than graduate from college.

"Bigger is better" is on display throughout American society. Automobile and truck models appear both as mechanical predators designed to intimidate others and as pseudomilitary vehicles enabling their owners to triumph in any survivalist showdown concerning individual primacy and relative status. Houses also are growing in size to demonstrate the preeminence of their owners. Governmental regulation, once a tool used to maintain an egalitarian ethic of the common good, has a declining role in our culture, in which excessive individual desire has become the primary standard.

The Communal and Global Effects of Consumerism

A capitalist market economy is constructed on a set of expectations that some observers call "the industrial package." Its critical components are that (1) output per worker (worker productivity) will advance through (2) technological and institutional innovations and (3) increased energy use and material inputs, accompanied by (4) higher average purchasing power supported by (5) a consumerist mentality which assures that the things produced will be purchased.[7]

Perhaps the most widely discussed critique of consumerism is the damage it does to the environment. A global consumer society based on the continuing spread of the richest countries' high-consumption lifestyles is unsustainable. Consumption is rising much faster than improvements in materials usage or reductions in the use of energy per unit of output (component #3 above), with dangerous implications for the natural world. Technological optimists counter that improvements in technology and management (component #2) will increase the productivity of energy and materials over time, perhaps even reducing the total flow through the economic system. Environmentalists doubt that this will happen. It does not seem possible, based on any known technology, for the people of China, India, or other large populations in the developing world to attain the consumption patterns of the North, which, in any case are already probably unsustainable.

A subtler version of the environmental critique focuses directly on consumerists' mentality (component #5). Alan Durning observes, "In the end, the ability of the earth to support billions of human beings depends on whether we continue to equate consumption with fulfillment."[8] And what is "fulfillment"? He thinks it is human happiness. Despite spending more than twice as much per capita than we did in 1957, Americans have shown no increase in the number of those who report being "very happy." In addition, cross-cultural studies show little difference between self-reported happiness in rich and poor countries. This leads Durning to propose a new social goal: A culture of "permanence." If "more" undermines the environment and does not make people happier, would it not make sense to seek a less-throwaway, more-sustainable society, a society that meets its needs without jeopardizing the prospects for future generations to meet their own needs? "Unless we climb down the consumption ladder a few rungs, our grandchildren will inherit a planetary home impoverished by our affluence."[9] Consumerism, in other words, abets poverty. But lowering our consumption of resource-intensive goods need not deprive us of things that really matter. Most of the things people name as their most rewarding pastimes are entirely sustainable. Religious practice, conversation, family and community gatherings, theater, music, dance, literature, poetry, artistic and creative pursuits, education, and appreciation of nature all fit readily into a culture of permanence—a way of life that can endure through countless generations.

Unfortunately, there is little sign that the American culture is moving in this direction. In 1960, the United States consumed approximately ten million barrels of oil a day. Today that figure has more than doubled. The United States has only 5 percent of the world's population, but it uses 25 percent of the world's automobiles, a major contributor to greenhouse gases. Despite this track record, our nation refuses to work with others to reduce global warming because such cooperation might hamper the American "lifestyle." Such a response to a critical problem expresses moral bankruptcy.[10]

The official American response to these problems is not to change American habits but rather to convert the rest of the world to join in the consumerist economy. Free-market economists claim that free trade can eventually eliminate global poverty—a long-run aim at best. Meanwhile, in the short run the earth is showing that it cannot absorb the natural disruptions already caused by consumerism. Rather than producing meaningful signs that global poverty is being gradually eliminated, free-market evangelists' most immediate success is the continuing consumer frenzy within the United States itself. This so-called success is accomplished irrespective of the loss of American jobs to overseas factories holding competitive advantages of incredibly low labor costs and virtually no environmental regulations.

The way that the new global economy has been working in the short term is this: Americans still enjoying good incomes have greater buying power by being able to purchase inexpensive foreign products. And those Americans earning less than before because of fewer factory jobs can temporarily make ends meet by shopping at megastores such as Wal-Mart, which specializes in marketing items made by foreign workers earning unimaginably low wages. Political pressures that might result from the exporting of jobs overseas are eased by tax cuts. For working families, this benefit is more symbolic than real. Tax cuts cannot compensate for wage cuts promoted by a weakening of collective bargaining resulting from unregulated foreign competition. Meanwhile, burgeoning national borrowing and trade deficits continue to finance consumerism's bubble. Simply from an economic point of view, these current trends are not sustainable.

CHRISTIANITY AND CONSUMERISM

Consumerism and the Religious Traditions

At the beginning of this chapter, consumerism was identified as "a cult." It functions as a religion. One particular irony of consumerism as a religion is its dissimilarity to the great religious traditions of humankind. *The religious sages of the past denounced the quest for worldly possessions,* and every world religion has warned against the spiritual destructiveness of craving them.

Buddhism identifies craving as the root source of suffering and the over-coming of craving as the way of freedom from suffering. Hinduism preaches detachment from all worldly things. Judaism and Islam strongly emphasize that the purpose of life is not to amass riches for oneself but rather to serve the needs of a suffering humanity.

Most important is Christian teaching, since a majority of the world's consumer class is, at least nominally, Christian. There can be no doubt that Christianity joins in the consensus of the great religious traditions in opposition to consumerist values. Jesus asks, "What will it profit them to gain the whole world and forfeit their life?"[11] The stories about the Rich Young Ruler, the Good Samaritan, the Sheep and the Goats, and the Goodly Pearls all lead us away from a preoccupation with self-gratification. Jesus taught that we cannot serve both God and mammon, whereas consumerism is the ordering of life in the service of mammon.

Given this religious consensus, it is deeply troubling to see the widespread triumph of consumerist values, shared by rich and poor alike. Hundreds of millions of the poor aspire to the consumption levels of the rich, aided and abetted by such television programs as *Lifestyles of the Rich and Famous*. Our question is, How has consumerism triumphed so widely? Why do so many American Christians in fact order their lives more to consumerism than to traditional Christian values? Why have the churches, conservative and liberal alike, acquiesced in this religious ideology?

Historical Reflections

It has been characteristic of liberal Christians that they have been prepared to adjust Christian teaching in changing contexts. Hence, for them the fact that new teachings and practices are different from those of the past, and even of religious traditions generally, is not sufficient reason to reject them. For example, liberals have adopted a cosmology, based on the natural sciences, that is quite different from the worldview implicit in the Bible. They have replaced the patriarchalism of most of the Bible and Christian tradition with a more nearly equal role for women. They have opposed slavery, even though the institution is taken for granted in the Bible. Progressives support this liberal view that traditional teachings must be reconsidered in light of the basic requirement of justice and love for others, especially for the weak and defenseless.

Accordingly, we progressive Christians must formulate our teaching about material well-being afresh in light of changing circumstances. Today, simply to repeat judgments and teachings formulated before the industrial revolution is not sufficient. They are not convincing in our context.

All the great religious traditions formulated their teachings in a time when needed goods were always genuinely scarce. Most populations lived near the edge of inadequacy in their food supply. Housing for most people was extremely simple and usually overcrowded. Sanitation was poor. Medical care was nonexistent or poor. Many children died in infancy, and life expectancy was short. A handful used their military and political power to extort goods from the many and lived in luxury.

Increased possession of goods by one person was based on reducing the amount of goods available to others. The orderly survival of society depended on all accepting their difficult lot. The survival of the poor often depended on their sharing what little they had with one another. In this context greedy behavior did great harm. Wealth could be obtained and held only at the expense of others. To give up wealth and share the common lot gave some relief to those who had no choice but to participate in it. Short of that, the rich could still be generous in alms giving to the poor.

It would have been meaningless in that context to call people to serve God by increasing the goods available to all. Improvement of basic economic conditions was not an option. The possibility for improving life was only in the spiritual realm. For that to take place, attachment to material things had to be overcome.

Jesus taught that when this attachment was genuinely given up, the goods would be shared with others. As the church accommodated itself to its social context, it made distinctions. All should give up attachment. For those truly called to what was seen as the highest form of the religious life, giving up attachment meant renouncing all possessions. They gave everything to monastic orders and were then provided the necessities of life. Others continued to live in the world in which property and property rights functioned. Possessing goods, even wealth, was no longer regarded as forbidden as long as one was not attached. Wealth was to be used responsibly for the sake of the larger community. This sensibility changed with the rise of capitalism and the expansion of wealth.

With the capitalist revolution well underway, John Wesley summarized the typical Protestant teaching as "Earn all you can; save all you can; give all you can." Hard work, frugality, and generosity were, thus, the virtues to be cultivated. In Wesley's own interpretation, the requirement to "give all you can" would have prevented any capital accumulation, but among his followers, as well as among Protestants generally, generosity was not interpreted so radically. It has been argued that the Protestant ethos encouraged the emerging capitalism. Nevertheless, Protestants were as clear as Catholics that greed was a great evil.

In any case, most Christians appreciated the new abundance, and it was difficult for them to oppose the methods by which it was produced. Yet these methods in many ways conflicted with traditional Christian values. The changed methods of production required entrepreneurial capital. It was important that people accumulate capital and then risk it in hopes of great profits. They must also be free to produce at the lowest possible costs. That entailed hiring workers at the lowest possible wages and spending as little as was strictly necessary on their safety and well-being.

The value system of the industrial revolution called for unleashing and celebrating the aim of increasing one's wealth. Money was to be used to make money, not to be distributed to the poor. The real improvement of the condition of the poor would come about, it was believed, precisely if the rich acted greedily. Instead of working for the relief of human suffering as it was immediately present, true virtue consisted in exploiting the poor now for the sake of improving the economic condition of society as a whole for future generations.

Some Christians looked for ways in which the gains of the industrial system could be continued while traditional Christian values were maintained. In its moderate form, this pointed toward modifications or ameliorations of the industrial system by improving the wages and conditions of labor within the factories and instituting a broader system of social support for the poor. In its more radical version, it called for public ownership of the means of production. At the practical level, the former response succeeded better than the latter, although it expressed traditional Christian values less fully.

Other Christians simply clung to preindustrial ways of thinking, ignoring their inapplicability in the emerging economic order. For them Christianity became a private matter, relevant to one's dealings in the family, with friends, in the church, and on a personal basis with others. These Christians might be interested in the personal morality of political leaders, and they might organize to support laws that undergirded public morality as they understood this, but they left economic issues to those in power.

Within both of these groups there was concern for the poor. Christians in the first group expressed this concern systematically through philanthropy, public policy, and institutions. Christians in the second group emphasized personal assistance to individuals in need. Neither of these groups affirmed the values of consumerism, yet neither actively opposed these values, which were assumed to be necessary for the growth of the economy. Within both groups, some have lived frugal and disciplined lives, shown great generosity, and given sacrificial service to others.

The Current Situation

Neither of these forms of Christian teaching provided a clear basis for strong resistance by Christians as a group to the seductions of consumerism. Neither was quick to label consumers' insatiable desires for "more" as greed or addiction. Both largely assumed that it was appropriate for most Christians to live according to those standards regarded as normal by persons of their class. Looking back, we may say that at some point these standards were reasonable, and a nonascetic Christianity could rejoice that it was now possible for most Christians to live that way without thereby harming others. But as explained above, the emerging economic system, which was basically accepted by almost all American Christians, is set up to expand continuously the quantity of average consumption. At some point, the expectations that the system instills in the population ceased to be reasonable, but the church had no standard of its own by which to evaluate the implied challenges. Accordingly, it drifted into acceptance of an excessively consumptive style as normative and allowed the values of consumerism to shape the actual lives of many of its members.

Today, that segment of conservative Protestantism that is called the religious Right is the most public and influential expression of Christian opinion. In general it seems to affirm current economic philosophy in such a way that love of neighbor and the expression of that love in service of others seem to be of secondary importance. The religious Right characterized in this way by no means represents conservative Protestantism generally. Some conservative evangelicals offer the most effective resistance to consumerism precisely by maintaining traditional teachings. These Christians focus less on public policy than on personal values and lifestyle. Since consumerism is a profoundly personal matter, all who would oppose consumerism can learn from them. Further, many conservative Protestants are now concerned about public policies that harm the poor. Accordingly, it is important that progressives committed to opposing consumerism look to such groups with appreciation and hope.

Liberal Protestants often focus on social issues at the expense of an emphasis on personal discipline. Many of them have reacted against legalistic teaching of guilt and self-denial in ways that make them less attentive to issues of individual behavior. There is little liberal preaching against excessive personal consumption. Mutual toleration of lifestyles is more characteristic than any effort to apply the Christian faith to habits of expenditure and consumption. Apart from annually renewed pressure to give generously to the church, liberal congregations rarely discuss the use of money and resources. The history of close connection with the cutting edge of American culture often leads liberals not only to become ever-greater consumers themselves, as their income allows, but also to accept much of the consumerist ideology that more is better. On the other hand, genuine liberals can be counted on to oppose those moves in a consumerist society that ignore the well-being of the poor and exploit them. Liberal Christianity remains committed to meeting the basic economic needs of all.

A Progressive Christian Response to Consumerism

We have written of liberals in the third person. However, progressive Christianity has only recently developed out of liberal Christianity, and the weaknesses of our liberal heritage are not easily overcome. Accordingly, the limitations of liberals noted previously still largely characterize us even as we recognize the need to change. Most of us belong to the middle class and share in its consumerist habits. We acquire far more than we need, and even those who seek to be more careful with our resources are reluctant to raise the question of the morality of such consumption in the circles in which we move. We continue to be part of the global problem and only aspire to be part of the solution.

If we are to become part of the solution, we must begin by recovering the authority of the Bible as we explained it in the first chapter. This gives us a perspective on our current context that enables us to evaluate it and to stand against it where resistance is needed. We see the enslavement to consumerist norms, based on the fear of lacking worth as a human being if one falls short, as profoundly dehumanizing. Material goods become a terrible idol, destructive of our spiritual lives, of human community, and of the earth. Commitment to the biblical God frees us from the supposition that life can find its end and meaning in wealth or consumption or measuring up to norms defined by consumerist society.

Unless this basic feature of the biblical heritage is reclaimed, we can have no Christian struggle with consumerism. If it is reclaimed, we will thereby be freed from our inner bondage to the dominant religion of our day. Our basic commitments will be altered so that the quest for material goods and economic security will have only a quite subordinate place in our lives. We can then ask more practical questions: How can we affirm that it is good to meet basic material needs, and even to satisfy economic desires well beyond the point of necessity, while condemning excessive consumption? How can the church define the "excess" it opposes?

The deepest reason for opposing greed is that it is spiritually destructive. The church's teaching against greed throughout many centuries reflected the fact that increasing one's possessions meant decreasing what was available to others. When that ceased to apply because of the industrial system of production, the church still warned against the spiritual danger of greed, but it ceased to oppose clearly its outward expressions. If action for the sake of increasing one's own wealth turns out to benefit others as well, the church hesitates to speak against it. The practical teaching against greedy behavior came to be either explicitly rejected or allowed to fade into the background. But as we again become aware of economic limits, the traditional teaching has become, once again, relevant.

The American middle class, and that identifies most people in what have been the mainline churches, including those of us who call ourselves progressives, is consuming at an unsustainable level. We are in the lead in making the present global system unsustainable. Perhaps the clearest indication of this is that our wastes are changing global weather patterns. But it is essential not to view this as an isolated problem. It is only one consequence of our unsustainable lifestyle.

Success in overcoming consumerism within the Christian community could be seen if "keeping up with the Joneses" came to mean competing in finding new ways to make fewer resources go farther as well as making fewer purchases of unneeded goods. It might mean moving into smaller houses and doing with fewer cars. An ethos of this sort would be a profound Christian competitor to consumerism. It would be the contemporary form of Wesley's adage to save all that you can. This behavioral change would express and encourage a deep spiritual transformation.

There would remain another principle: Give all that you can. Few today would dare to interpret this as radically as did Wesley. But the church might aim at capturing the reduced expenditures of its members for responding to the needs of the world. If the church could analyze these needs rigorously and identify the uses of money that have the best chance of responding to them, many Christians would give gladly. Again, we would have an alternative to consumerism that was genuinely Christian and could combat consumerism as an ideal.

The deepest source of consumerism is the lack of true meaning in the lives of so many. Even in the church we have failed to assess what is necessary for a faithful life, for a life that provides meaning. Progressives are competent at analyzing issues but less so in nurturing spiritual nomads into a transformed life of faith, one equipped to confront the idolatry that is consumerism.

Participating in saving God's world from disaster is a deeply meaningful and deeply Christian activity. Those who are engaged in community with others in doing this work will not need to buy surplus goods to satisfy insatiable cravings. They will discover the service of God through serving God's creatures to be a more meaningful way of life than searching for happiness through consumption.

Theologically it is important to add a further dimension. As Christians we believe that God loves the whole creation and is working for its health. Where humans allow it to happen, God heals it through natural processes. God works in our bodies and in our psyches in similar ways. Grace is everywhere. But God does not, by force, prevent us from damaging the world, our bodies, or our psyches. We are called to ask in faith, "What is God's intention for the creation, and what is our work to fulfill that intention?"

Our call is to work with God by allowing God to work through us to overcome our destructive ways. We can learn much about what that means through the witness to Jesus Christ in our Scriptures. These Scriptures call us to lives that are faithful to Jesus and take seriously his teachings, difficult as they are. This faithfulness is, at the same time, opening ourselves to God's Spirit. We believe that this will redirect our concerns from acquiring goods for ourselves to serving God's creation and especially those human beings who are most vulnerable.

For progressive Christians, the question is not just how this discipleship has been practically interpreted in the past. The question is what discipleship means today. How do we learn to be open to our own transformation, to be liberated from our captivity to our consumerist culture, and to develop a nurturing Christian life that invites others to this transformation? To emphasize the novelty of our situation is not to ignore traditions but rather to learn from them. In relation to consumerism, much of the past meaning of discipleship reasserts itself with new relevance and urgency.

WHAT CAN BE DONE ABOUT CONSUMERISM?

Alternative Models

Millions of Americans are resisting the siren call of consumerism and are trying to live sustainably. Their efforts have spawned dozens of books, magazines, TV specials, and environmental organizations to help them find more-nonmaterialistic lifestyles. Without this kind of personal commitment, no change can occur. But individual action and voluntary simplicity by themselves will not uproot consumerism. The institutions and interests that profit from profligacy are too deeply embedded in our culture. Consumerism can be modified only if the political and the personal are combined. It will require a deep, long-term political process to create an alternative type of capitalism that becomes visible enough for people and institutions to embrace—as consumers, workers, investors, and citizens.

It is possible to imagine a different kind of modern economic society that would be far more sustainable than the current U.S. model. Consider, for example, a prevailing vision of simplicity and a less-harried form of life. In contrast to the U.S. model, this alternative might assume that (1) the primary role of the economy is to satisfy our basic needs for a healthy and secure existence; beyond meeting these needs, the economy contributes to the good life by reducing work and expanding leisure; (2) the economy's performance is assessed by its success in meeting real material needs; (3) employment is a means to attaining the income required to meet our essential needs; and

(4) the standard of living is measured by success in attaining ample leisure and using it well. Such a society need not be characterized by austerity and self-denial but rather by a redefinition of what constitutes the "good life."

This imaginary society might also value lives of "creative work." Creative work assumes that (1) the economy contributes to the good life by providing us with work that brings intrinsic satisfaction and social respect; (2) economic performance is measured primarily by the extent to which most people have intrinsically rewarding, socially respected jobs; (3) employment enhances human creativity and economic development without harming others or the biosphere; and (4) the standard of living is measured by the quality of the work opportunities that the economy creates.

Technological advances and maintaining productivity are just as important to this alternative outlook as to the mass-consumption model. A simpler lifestyle demands productivity in order to expand leisure time and improve the public services that support simple living. Creative work requires productivity growth in many areas to offset the productivity declines that may result from making some jobs more craft oriented. Further, whereas productivity is usually understood in terms of the amount that is produced per hour of labor, it can be thought of as the amount of production in relation to the input of natural resources. Technological improvements oriented to increasing productivity in this sense are certainly also needed.

In 2002, Czech president Václav Havel advocated this alternative model while warning against European efforts to compete with the U.S. economy. During a visit to Italy, Mr. Havel spoke of the spread of American-style consumerism. He stated that Europe had a chance to inspire the world in other than consumerist values. He said it was "possible to lead a good life on this planet even when, instead of placing emphasis on creation of profits or growth of gross domestic product, priority is given to values such as the beauty of a country or a house [and] closeness to fellow beings."[12]

How realistic is this alternative? At present, European economies come far closer to modeling it than do Japanese, Chinese, or American models. However, without global agreement regarding steadfast governmental regulations and controls, competition eventually will drive even European economies to emulate the model that is most productive of material output. Fear of being left behind in the global race of capitalistic "progress," involving the production of unending categories of "stuff," will serve to undermine any society attempting to define success in ways that are oriented toward simplicity, leisure, and craft.

To date, the entire experience of the United States has been rapid development—growth and more growth. "Grow or die" could be the American credo. And by growth, Americans invariably mean physical growth in ways that can

easily be quantified—not psychological, artistic or spiritual growth and genuine personal satisfaction. This is the model that is driving global competition.
In such a model, increasing production is understood to be a requirement, yet
it is that very growth which is damaging us spiritually and threatening the survival of the biosphere.

Havel's simplicity-leisure-craft proposal is an economic model that encourages human beings to be authentic instead of robotized slaves to a mechanical
and electrical pace that is ever quickening. By contrast, "consumerism" is characterized by workaholism coupled with the numbing that accompanies over-
consumption. Our social disease needs to be raised to the level of conscious
self-criticism. Only then can attention effectively be directed at restricting it.

Given our dominant economic thinking and the system it undergirds, the
call to less consumption by middle-class people can be viewed as harmful. The
goal for the economy is growth. That requires ever-increasing consumption
to keep business profitable and thus able to employ workers. For many people, it seems that this is the only way to think of the economy. As progressive
Christians convinced that the consumerism this nurtures is bad in itself, and
in the global context unsustainable, we give strong support to those economists who are envisioning a different economy, one committed to meeting
human needs sustainably in a way that also recognizes that human relationships are far more important than unnecessary goods. We also support the
many experiments in local economies that operate on principles quite different from those that guide the global system.

Havel recognizes that his proposal is equivalent to a man attempting to
sweep back the tide with a broom. He sees modern consumerist civilization on
an inexorable march toward breakdown. Nevertheless, he refuses to abandon
his resistance by acquiescing in what he terms "the global automatism of technological civilization." He remains active in proposing models that at present
appear to have no realistic chance of being adopted. To do otherwise would
violate his existential view of human responsibility. He models for progressive
Christians what it means to resist when reform seems impossible. Such resistance can have significant effects. The proclamation of an alternative possibility can enable a society to recognize the absurdity of its ways, and ideas that
now appear unrealistic may actually guide the future.[13]

The task before us as progressive Christians is a religious one. "Religion"
may be defined as a way of binding all the aspects of life and society together.
Today, consumerism seems to be the dominant religion of the United
States even for many who identify themselves as Christian. We are called to
challenge this religion by challenging the beliefs that support it and by changing our own ways of life. This, in turn, presupposes that we become free of

many of the values that we have internalized from a consumerist culture. The practice of prayer described in the preceding chapter can help effect this inner transformation.

Evangelical Resistance: A New Social Gospel

If ever Christianity needed to reassert its living message, it is now. People hungry for meaning are spiritually starving amid vain illusions of wealth and privilege. At this moment in history, a progressive Christian evangelism is required. It needs to be trumpeted from the pulpit, awakening congregations that currently tolerate the steady moral degradation of all that they hold dear. The collective energy of common Christians has risen in the past to confront idolatries. Again, Christians are called to resist and to draw others into the circle of resistance. We should not be deceived that the way will be easy. The velvet slavery of consumerism is more seductive than the rival "principalities and powers" heretofore encountered by the church.

In the decades preceding the Great Depression of the 1930s, many anticipated that the new industrialization would bring as much harm as it did progress. While waiting for a future that they could not predict, reformers did their homework. They experimented with new avenues of public policy. They confronted authorities, challenged the law, and went to jail. They demanded altered systems. They were fully alive in their time and place. When the crash did ultimately come, their efforts served as the foundation for long-needed restructuring. Franklin Roosevelt's New Deal drew on their sacrifices and ideas. New Christian thinking primarily in the social gospel of the early twentieth century inspired the New Deal's later development. Today, we are called to nurture a new social gospel, one with a strong ecological consciousness.

We must confront powerful corporations that protect and promote the current stage of capital development known as consumerism. And yet, corporate symbols do not constitute our primary obstacle. Our bondage is in every fabric of our daily existence. An external tyrant does not force us to participate. We are often willing addicts in the manic rush of acquisition and fashion status. In this case, it may be truly said that we have met the enemy and we are it. An honest self-awareness is a necessary prerequisite for genuine resistance.

Consumerism is destroying us spiritually. It supports a socioeconomic paradigm that is profoundly unjust and destructive of human community. It hastens degradation of the natural environment and the coming of ecological catastrophes. It is an extreme form of idolatry. We have no choice. A follower of Jesus Christ is called to radical evangelical resistance.

DISCUSSION QUESTIONS

1. If your children were forced to choose between the best in Christian tradition and the most seductive elements of consumerism, which would they choose? Have they long ago made that choice? Have you assisted them?
2. Do you consider yourself living excessively? Does putting out your recyclable trash once a week assuage any sense of excessive living that might otherwise trouble you? Do you rationalize your habits by castigating others whose excessive practices are worse than your own? Is there any measurable difference between your needs and your desires?
3. How do you imagine "sustainability" affecting your "lifestyle" if and when it ever becomes a serious matter and not merely a rhetorical flag to be waved occasionally for public display?
4. Which of the world's great religions do you think has the greatest potential to achieve a pragmatic result in fostering a just economic order and sustainable planet? Is Christianity currently a meaningful competitor for this prize? Are you engaged to make Christianity a meaningful competitor in this regard?
5. What practical steps can you take now to move your family and your culture toward a practical ethic of sustainability? Are you and those closest to you willing to submit this matter to God in prayer?

FOR FURTHER READING

Cobb, John B., Jr. *Sustaining the Common Good: A Christian Perspective on the Global Economy*. Cleveland: Pilgrim Press, 1995.

DeGraaf, John, David Wann, and Thomas Naylor, *Affluenza: The All-Consuming Epidemic*. San Francisco: Berrett-Koehler, 2002.

Durning, Alan. *How Much Is Enough? The Consumer Society and the Future of the Earth*. Washington, DC: Worldwatch Institute, 1992.

Hawken, Paul. *The Ecology of Commerce: A Declaration of Sustainability*. New York: HarperBusiness, 1993.

Lasch, Christopher. *The Culture of Narcissism: American Life in an Age of Diminishing Expectations*. New York: W. W. Norton & Co., 1979/1991.

McDaniel, Jay. *Living from the Center: Spirituality in an Age of Consumerism*. St. Louis: Chalice Press, 2000.

Schumacher, E. F. *Small Is Beautiful: Economics as If People Mattered*. New York: Harper & Row, 1973.

4

Poisonous Inequality

Gordon Douglass

> Christianity stands or falls with its revolutionary protest against
> violence, arbitrariness and pride of power and with its apologia for
> the weak. . . . Christianity is rather doing too little in showing these
> points than doing too much. Christianity has adjusted itself much
> too easily to the worship of power. It should give much more
> offence, more shock to the world, than it is doing now. Christian-
> ity should . . . take a much more definite stand for the weak than
> to consider the potential moral right of the strong.
>
> *Dietrich Bonhoeffer*[1]

A pervasive spirit of consumerism has supported the shift of the national
economy away from concerns for the common good to a focus on private
freedom and ownership. The previous chapter called us as followers of Jesus
to resist this now-dominant "religion." In this chapter we examine the
economic system that, through its increasing concentration of wealth and
power in fewer and fewer hands, further undermines the community that
Christians value.

Throughout most of the twentieth century, incomes in America grew more
equal over time as gains for those at the top were accompanied by even stronger
gains in the middle and at the bottom. This trend was unlike that of the nineteenth century, when inequality widened, presumably because the nation was
being transformed into an industrial economy. That too was the British story:
greater inequality during the early stages of industrialization, followed in time
by lesser inequality as the industrial economy matured. Indeed, shortly after
World War II, Simon Kuznets[2] hypothesized that this pattern was characteristic of economic development more generally. Thus, newly developing countries

may at first see their incomes grow less equal, followed by the opposite as long as their average incomes continue to rise.

This notion of a "U-shaped" distribution of income over time has not worked out that way, at least in the United States. America's industrial revolution now is a distant memory, yet economic inequality has grown rapidly during the last four decades. Sometime in the mid-1970s, our economy reversed its earlier direction and began sending most of its rewards to those who already had the most. The share of aggregate income going to the highest-earning 1 percent of Americans doubled from 8 percent in 1980 to over 16 percent in 2005. Moreover, that going to the top tenth of 1 percent has more than tripled from 2 percent in 1980 to 7 percent recently. And that going to the top one-hundredth of 1 percent—the 14,000 taxpayers at the very top of the income ladder—has quadrupled. The result is a concentration of income and wealth that is not only higher than it has been since the 1920s but also higher than that of any of the world's other developed nations.[3]

The American middle class also is slowly being hollowed out. While real wages barely moved over all, they rose faster for the bottom quarter of workers than for those in the middle. By many measures, those in the middle of the skills-and-education ladder have been hit relatively harder than those at the bottom. Persons who had some college experience but no degree fared worse than high school dropouts. Some statistics suggest that the annual income of Americans with a college degree has fallen relative to that of high school graduates for the first time in decades. Yet the middle class historically has been essential to economic opportunity and democratic government—arguably the two ideals that come closest to defining our sense of national identity. A hollowed-out middle class cannot serve these purposes much longer.

To be sure, the distribution of income and wealth is widening in most developed countries, where global markets are creating an international upper class of people whose economic interests resemble each other's more than others in their national or local communities. This is leading most places to a political and social separation between wealthy national elites and the rest of society, a distance that is beginning to undermine the social contract (responsibilities of citizenship) that formerly connected people of all classes. Since the process that is detaching the rich and powerful from other classes is well advanced in America, this chapter focuses primarily on the sources and consequences of American inequality. This is not to say, however, that the chapter ignores the relation of American inequality to the politics and economics of the global economy. Indeed, it is the political forces shaping the global economy, of which rich and powerful Americans are dominant players, that help explain how the fate of most American citizens has been disconnected from those who own and control the world's physical and financial capital.

"NEOLIBERALISM" AND INEQUALITY[4]

Neoliberalism is a term widely known throughout the rest of the world, but it is rarely used in the United States to describe the ideology our "governing class" has tried to impose on other peoples and nations. In the United States, neoliberalism is often called conservatism. Neoliberalism is a vision of society in which competition for wealth is the dominant value and most social decisions are left to unregulated markets. Its basis in policy came into full relief with the election of Ronald Reagan in 1980, who successfully called for lower taxes (in part "to starve the beast" of government), fewer government controls on business, and a more central role for private markets ("to promote freedom and economic growth"). This conservative mantra also nurtured the policies of the Thatcher government in England and soon influenced the World Bank and the International Monetary Fund (IMF) to impose tighter controls on government spending by heavily indebted developing countries.

It was the so-called "Washington Consensus" that orchestrated this world-wide shift toward market-oriented policies. This widely held point of view found its leadership in the internationally oriented business community, the U.S. Department of the Treasury, the economics profession, and also the IMF, World Bank, and World Trade Organization (WTO). The Washington Consensus devised a top-down structure of global economic governance when crises threatened international economic stability, as during the debt crisis of the 1980s and more recently during hedge-fund failures and the Asian, Russian, Brazilian, and Argentine currency crises. Its top-down policies evolved into an intricate web of expected behaviors, especially by developing countries, as a condition for receiving some form of debt relief.

Neoliberalism, as promoted by the Washington Consensus, is arguably the most fundamental redesign and centralization of the world's political and economic arrangements since the industrial revolution. It has succeeded in transferring massive economic and political power away from most national governments and into the hands of global corporations and the trade and finance bureaucracies they helped create. Countries with cultures and traditions as varied as France and Bolivia are expected to adopt the same tastes, values, and public policies in order to assure the "efficient" working of world markets. In what Thomas Friedman describes as a "golden straightjacket," nations are put under constant pressure to streamline their economic institutions and upgrade their performance.[5] Nations that wear their straightjackets diligently are supposed to benefit through more trade, foreign investment, privatization, and more efficient use of resources under the pressure of global competition, while those that refuse to wear them are said to be doomed to stagnation. On the political front, golden straightjackets are designed to rob governments of freedom to choose political and economic policies vastly more appropriate for their unique social and cultural circumstances.

Neoliberalism permits the rich and powerful to cast off the ties that had connected them to other Americans after World War II. By redistributing income upward and weakening the bargaining power of labor, President Reagan succeeded in providing corporate investors the political opportunity to use the world economy to evade domestic regulations. The corporate investor class soon learned that their interests often coincided with investors, managers, and professionals in other countries. Since the corporate investor class was more mobile than most workers, it was easier for them to organize globally. Accordingly, the rights of workers were excluded from global rules and left to the protection of nation-states, whose authority stops at their borders.

Of course, global rules and policies inevitably limit the sovereignty of individual governments over their own economies and their own citizens' lives. Working out common rules and policies on, say, accounting, finance, safety, sanitation, property rights, technological interconnections, subsidies, and thousands of other areas are bound to be contentious, even among like-minded negotiators. Monetary and fiscal systems also must be harmonized.

Since there is no world government to develop and administer common rules and policies for integrated economies, less-formal arrangements that favor particular interests tend to form. By far the most significant of these is the virtual network of international investors that Jeff Faux[6] calls "the Party of Davos," named after the resort in Switzerland where the world's political and economic elite meets each year. Faux believes the "constitution" of the Party of Davos calls for its members to enhance the bargaining position of corporate capital in the global economy, typically by reaching informal agreements on the rules of trade and investment. These rules are carried out, he believes, by second- and third-tier corporate managers and bureaucrats.

Unlike the neoclassical competitive model of most economics textbooks, neoliberalism does not assume that world markets are composed of many unrelated buyers and sellers, who enter or leave markets freely and who share equally all relevant knowledge (or ignorance) about key factors determining product quality and price in each market. Nor does it assume all sellers have adequate knowledge of production techniques, have equivalent access to necessary supplies, and choose the least costly means of production. These are the conditions for "efficient" markets according to neoclassical economics. Rather, the markets of neoliberalism are riddled with complexities, uncertainties, and ambiguities of imperfect information, barriers to market entry, and product differentiation. They are dominated by huge global corporations that cooperate with each other on basic research and the sharing of knowledge about new technologies, production processes, and distribution techniques. By sharing the risks with others and gaining access to new capabilities, they are able to improve their chance of avoiding regulations at home and staying competitive in an increasingly global market. Complex networks of corporate alliances have multiplied so rapidly and pervasively that they recently have come to be called "alliance capitalism."

Having found a way to escape the social contract at home by nurturing a global economy, the advocates of neoliberalism continue to assemble complex bureaucratic networks to supervise the global market for the benefit of corporate investors. The methods are informal and hidden from view. They are far from democratic. Thus, both corporations and the bureaucrats that serve them escape the restraints of domestic policies.

So, does neoliberalism affect the distribution of income and wealth? Of course it does! The fact that corporate profits are at an all-time high and that wages are stagnant if not falling is a clear indication that the rewards of advances in productivity are not being shared fairly. So, too, is the evidence of dramatic increases in the share of income and wealth being acquired by the already well-off. All markets have rules and, therefore, have a politics that mirrors the balance of power held by market participants who set the rules. By promoting globalization and leaving behind the restraints of local regulations, the Party of Davos has successfully put in place a set of global market rules that assures favorable returns to capital at the expense of the rewards to labor.

DEGREES OF INEQUALITY

Since wages and salaries make up about 75 percent of total family incomes in the United States, they are an important measure of overall income inequality.[7] One would expect them to grow significantly when productivity, the best measure of economic advance, grows rapidly. In the years since 1995, for example, productivity grew more than 33 percent, yet real wages for the typical worker, including those with a high school or college degree, hardly budged. Indeed, real wages were stagnant or fell for the bottom 60 percent of wage earners over the period since 1979. The highest earners, on the other hand, have done much better than other workers for at least thirty years and especially so over the last ten years.

When income from capital expands for the very-highest-income families, inequality grows. For example, the top 1 percent of income earners received 38 percent of all capital income in 1979 compared to 49 percent by 2000 and 58 percent in 2003. This shift toward greater concentration is largely the result of income flowing into corporate profits, now the highest in thirty-five years.

American folklore often dwells on rags-to-riches stories of people who lift themselves up the income scale in a single generation. Yet international comparisons suggest less mobility in America than in other advanced economies. The sons of low-income fathers, for example, have less than a 60 percent chance of reaching above the twentieth percentile in adulthood, about a 20 percent chance of surpassing the median, and less than a 5 percent chance of ending up above the eightieth percentile.

The distribution of wealth in the United States is even more unequal than wages and incomes. In 2005, the top 1 percent of wealth holders possessed one-third of all wealth. The top fifth controlled 85 percent of the total, while the bottom 80 percent held only 15 percent. Many households, on the other hand, are left with mounting debts and little or nothing in the way of assets. Less than half of all households hold stock in any form. Approximately one in six households had zero or negative net wealth in 2004.

Household debt is another measure of inequality. It has consistently risen and is now 130 percent of disposable personal income. At least 25 percent of lower-income families have debt payments that exceed 40 percent of their income. Even middle-income families spend a fifth of their income on debt payments.

WHY IS INEQUALITY GROWING?

For at least thirty years, economists and others have searched for reasons why incomes and wealth in the United States are becoming less equal. Explanations include the exaggerated earnings of chief executives and entertainers, the outsourcing and offshoring of jobs, the "deindustrialization" of America, the weakening of labor unions, the fraying of social safety nets, the flood of baby boomers into the workforce, other demographic changes, the spread of computers and other kinds of information technology, the crisis in public schooling, and class warfare. In short, many explanations of growing income inequality are floating about because the topic is so provocative.

Early in the search for more rigorous explanations, economists found evidence that stiffer competition, technological changes, and other trends in corporate America were producing shifts in the demand for labor that were hurting many manufacturing workers. As downsized workers flooded into the service-producing industries—already the industries with the most unequal earnings distribution—overall inequality in earnings increased. Thus, "*deindustrialization*" became the favorite explanation. But subsequent researchers pointed out that wage and earnings inequality had been increasing within many industries of both the goods-producing and service-producing sectors.

Findings such as these suggested that greater inequality was not necessarily being induced by industrial restructuring. The cause of rising inequality was more elusive.

Research on how *technology* affects the mix of acquired skills yielded other explanations of inequality. Consider, for example, the effect of computers on the demand for labor. By and large, computers favor more-educated over less-educated workers, so that their widespread introduction in the workplace probably widens the wage gap between the two groups. But this computer-did-it theory also has lost favor recently. One reason is that inequality began to rise in the 1970s and 1980s, long before the widespread use of computers. Another is that supermarket clerks, bank cashiers, and data-entry clerks who use computers are clearly not getting rich from their jobs. Moreover, if computers caused inequality, why did they cause so much more of it in the United States than elsewhere?

Another long-term explanation is the changes taking place in the *composition of households*. The rise in divorce rates and marital separations, along with the upsurge in births out of wedlock, has boosted the proportion of single-person families among all families. The heads of these families, primarily women, often have low skills and poor education and therefore near poverty-level incomes. At the same time, a growing proportion of married-couple families have at least two earners. Many of these dual-earner families are in the upper half of the income distribution. Here, the influence on inequality is more from changes in the supply of labor rather than the demand for labor.

Surprisingly, researchers do not regard immigration as a major contributor to income differences. Most researchers hypothesize that immigrants reduce the earnings of host-country workers with similar skill sets but raise the earnings of complementary resources such as capital and some types of native-born labor. In order to test this hypothesis, most researchers compare native earnings and employment between high- and low-immigrant areas in host countries. In fact, studies for the United States show that a 10 percent increase in the fraction of immigrants in the local population reduces native wages by 1 percent at most. Researchers are still searching for adequate explanations of their findings.

Perhaps the most contentious explanation is the influence of *international trade* on income distribution. Most economists argue that the United States has a comparative disadvantage in selling goods that embody the labor of less-educated workers and it should therefore import such goods (e.g., sneakers, toys, clothing) from countries with more-abundant labor supplies. While this is likely to weaken the bargaining power of less-educated workers in America, and perhaps to make them more sensitive to wages abroad, most economists believe the gains of trade vastly exceed the harm done to the economic security of less-educated workers. Their losses will encourage them to return to school and seek other jobs.

But I see the relation of international trade to income distribution rather differently. Trade is a fact of life for the United States, and it produces both winners and losers. But the process by which the winners and losers are chosen is quite different than it is in the theory of comparative advantage. I believe that domestic power relations and the international connections of the ruling elites determine the rules under which we trade. Corporations, which are in the business of increasing their profits, have been instrumental in shaping these rules and the trade agreements that embody them. The trade agreements, moreover, contain much more than the rules for trade. Multilateral agreements such as the North American Free Trade Agreement (NAFTA), the General Agreement on Tariffs and Trade (GATT), and the General Agreement on Trade in Services (GATS) along with institutions such as the World Trade Organization are meant both to facilitate the movement of goods and services across borders and to make it easier for global corporations to locate in areas where they see the largest profit margins.

There is no doubt that outsourcing and offshoring are threatening the well-being of some American workers. At least 3.5 million manufacturing jobs have been lost since 2001, most of them to plants in developing countries where wage rates are much lower than in America. The scale and pace of this competitive threat is beyond anything that has happened before. The issue is not only the total number of jobs that will be outsourced to China, India, or Mexico. The real problem is that even a relatively small gap between the demand for and the supply of labor can create wage stagnation and decline at home, aggravating the inequality of American incomes.

Finally, we note that large corporations and the wealthy always have wielded disproportionate influence over our economy and society. *Money buys influence*. The problem today is that the growth of inequality means even greater influence by the well-off over the levers of power and the well-being of all citizens. Candidates seeking political office must court wealthy donors and PAC contributions from corporations and labor unions. Once elected, they dare not ignore the political agenda of their benefactors. As wealthy individuals and corporations grow stronger, the rules governing the U.S. economy accord more and more with their own interests, such as tax cuts for the wealthy, deregulation, unfettered trade and investment, privatization, and other measures of "freedom." Once implemented, these policies concentrate wealth and power still more, and the vicious cycle continues. Meanwhile, the Party of Davos nurtures the transnational bureaucratic networks it expects to assure corporate investor freedom throughout the world.

NEOLIBERAL POLICIES

If inequality has grown because the rules that govern our economy have been changed, benefiting corporations and the wealthy, then we must examine these rules and ask how they must change in order to restore fairness to the economy. Of course, the American and global economies are governed by literally thousands of policies and procedures that affect economic life. Only a limited few, the primary enablers of inequality, are examined below.

Global Trade and Investment Practices

Global corporations want *freedom* to trade and invest, but they have little interest in the principle of *equality*. To be sure, the theory of comparative advantage claims that specialization and trade yield gains for all parties. What the theory does not say, however, is what happens to the workers and owners who lose out in the competitive struggle. The losers are little more than "roadkill" to the winners. They must adjust to the vicissitudes of export-oriented trade by developing new skills and/or depend on public assistance. In countries with tattered safety nets, the losers have little to fall back on.

It is the global corporations and the multinational institutions they helped create that are largely responsible for the inability of most governments to respond to the needs of the losers. A central function of governments had been to assist the losers to adjust to change—usually by means of unemployment compensation and adjustment assistance. In essence, governments had used their fiscal powers to insulate domestic groups from excessive market risks, particularly those originating in international transactions. But recently, governments have been less able to help the losers because the slightest hint of raising taxes leads to capital flight in a world of heightened mobility of capital. The ideological onslaught by neoliberalism against the welfare state also has paralyzed many governments and made them unable to respond to the domestic needs of a more internationally competitive economy.

Consider, for example, the trading and investing rules under which all members of the WTO must abide. Under the WTO, the economic policies of all national governments are subject to its approval, including policies governing health, education, justice, and environmental protection. The only exception is the military. In signing on to the WTO, developing countries agree to ban all quantitative restrictions on imports and reduce tariffs on many industrial imports, and they promise not to raise tariffs on all other imports. Thus, they effectively give up the use of trade policy to pursue domestic objectives and therefore lose a primary tool to protect "infant" industries.

The WTO's rules, on the other hand, favor the interests of the U.S. government and global corporations. It is the United States that pushed for rules that open markets for its agricultural products, that favored expansion of trade-related investment measures, that established new protections for corporate intellectual property rights in rich countries, and that established global limits on government regulation of environmental, food safety, and product standards. The WTO system vests in secret tribunals the right to determine if a country's laws exceed the limits set by its rules, including automatic, permanent trade sanctions against any country refusing to comply with WTO demands. In short, the WTO has taken on the task of implementing globally many of the policies imposed on developing countries by the IMF and World Bank.

Or consider NAFTA, the trade and investment rules worked out between the United States, Canada, and Mexico. NAFTA was designed to protect the interests of corporate investors. It made them more competitive by giving them access to cheap labor and government assets in Mexico. It called for a steady lowering of Mexican tariffs against foreign corn and beans, thus putting small Mexican farmers into direct competition with heavily subsidized Canadian and American agribusinesses. This forced farmers off the land and into cities, where the Mexican government hoped to use them in industrialization financed by foreign capital.

NAFTA's side agreements on labor and the environment were paper tigers: the labor agreement set no common standards; any nation could still eliminate its minimum wage, outlaw unions, dismantle health and safety standards, or loosen restrictions on industrial pollution. The environmental side agreement simply urged member nations to enforce their own environmental laws. Neither agreement was part of NAFTA, thus failing the status of an international accord approved by each nation's legislature.

China's emergence as a trading powerhouse has injected a wholly new player into global markets. Its abundant supply of cheap labor and an authoritarian government permit it to keep labor costs low in an ever-expanding range of industries. It graduates 350,000 engineers a year. Even its research laboratories are impressive. As with NAFTA, American (and other first-world) multinationals sought opportunities to combine their financial capital and know-how with cheap Chinese labor. As a result of their direct (long-term) investments, 60 percent of China's exports today are shipped by foreign multinationals. This outsourcing of production to China, India, and elsewhere has not stopped with products using blue-collar workers. Multinational investment and trade, buoyed by the Internet, now allows firms to outsource virtually any occupation to wherever labor is cheaper.

As American Christians reflect on the unequal consequences of the existing trading system, they cannot avoid asking ethical questions: Does the system favor the poor? Does it eschew individualism and promote community solidarity? Does it call for progress toward a less-unequal society? Does it care for the gifts of creation? The answers, alas, are all negative. The neoliberal trading system obviously neglects the plight of the poor. It is governed by an institution, the WTO, which was designed and nurtured by U.S.-based global corporations and their allies in the U.S. government in order to promote their own interests over those of the poor. Nor does it favor community over individual interests. Indeed, the very essence of neoliberalism is its intent to serve the few at the expense of the many. Neoliberalism certainly calls for progress, but not the kind that reduces inequality. Its methods of trading are designed to deliver most gains to the well-off. And global corporations forcefully assert their right to trade in any market anywhere. Nothing should be off-limits, no matter how damaging their methods to the environment.

Inequality and Taxes

Still another reason for wider inequality at home is the impact of neoliberal globalization on the effectiveness of domestic policies to stabilize the local economy. Government taxation and spending policies, for example, are made less effective when international trade grows, because a portion of any government stimulus in the form of reduced taxes or increased spending is likely to raise incomes and leak out of the system through increases in imports. Monetary policy also is made less effective when neoliberal globalization grows. As foreign governments acquire a larger and larger share of outstanding U.S. government bonds, the Federal Reserve finds that it is less able to influence interest rates through open-market operations.

Neoliberal globalization also limits the effectiveness of policies governing individual markets. Nations now face the same dilemma as local governments when trying to tax companies within their jurisdictions. Multinational corporations with sales and factory sites all over the world can relocate—or threaten to relocate—to obtain tax concessions. When they buy from and sell to themselves many of the components required in finished products, they also can minimize their taxes by recording costs where taxes are high and reporting profits where taxes are low. Globalization and the rising importance of the Internet multiply the complications and costs of collecting corporate taxes as well as enforcing other forms of regulation. Since capital is more mobile than labor, globalization leads to a falling share of taxes paid by capital and a rising share by labor.

To assess the impact of U.S. federal tax policy on inequality, the Economic Policy Institute used Congressional Budget Office data to compare changes in the share of income accruing to each income class, before and after taxes. The data reveals that between 1979 and 2005, more than 6 percent of national income shifted from the bottom 80 percent to the top 20 percent, with most of the shift—about 5 percent—accruing to the top 1 percent. Further analysis showed that federal taxes became more regressive in the 1980s and since 2000— higher-income families saw their tax rates fall relative to lower-income families.

Once again, neoliberal globalization seems to have undermined the capacity of governments to counteract the inequality-producing consequences of the Davos agenda. By rendering government macroeconomic and microeconomic policies less effective, it saps the capacity of governments to enact policies for the common good. Clearly, the influence of the Davos agenda over tax policies discriminates against the bottom and middle classes in America. Its opposition to extraction taxes, pollution taxes, and taxes on speculative financial transactions is consistent with a lack of concern for the interests of community. Its eagerness to expand globalization denies other alternatives. And its opposition to regulatory or tax devices that more accurately reflect the true cost of corporate development activities marks neoliberalism as an enemy of the environment.

The Restructuring of Work

Starting in 1995, as noted above, productivity—the output of goods and services per hour worked—began to grow more quickly. Because productivity growth provides a basis for rising living standards for everyone, its acceleration is a positive development for the economy.

If this potential for widely shared prosperity is to be realized, however, a number of other factors must be present. These include a labor market with strong collective bargaining, an appropriate minimum wage, and a truly tight labor market. When these institutions are weak or absent, productivity's growth is likely to bypass the majority of working families. This is precisely what has happened in recent years. For several decades, unionization has withered to the point that only 13 percent of workers now are union members. The federal minimum wage did not budge in twelve years. And since 2000, slack in the labor market, despite rapid productivity growth, has meant diminished employment opportunities.

Neoliberalism's hand is evident in each of these labor market characteristics. Compared to some European countries, it is much harder to organize unions in the United States. Corporations hire union-busting law firms, intimidate workers who want to organize, and use the National Labor Relations Board to stall organizing drives. Workers who dare to lead organizing drives are fired. Governments also suppress union organizing to hold down wages, benefits, and labor standards such as minimum wages in order to attract foreign investors. They sometimes give special tax breaks and subsidies to foreign corporations and cut corners on environmental regulations.

Perhaps neoliberalism's most deliberate influence on the labor market is the dramatic way its global corporations have restructured the workplace. When U.S. corporations began experiencing intense competition from European and Asian firms in the 1970s, many turned to radical forms of restructuring to reduce labor costs. Corporations dropped the notion of long-term employment and substituted for it a core of salaried workers supported by a large contingent workforce that included temps, on-call workers, and independent contractors. The outsourcing of components and services, increasingly to foreign suppliers, also ballooned. These and other changes lowered wages and often eliminated health-care benefits and pensions. Job insecurity mounted, eroding the quality of life for millions of working families.

Senior executives of these corporations, on the other hand, did very, very well. Since 60 percent of most corporate boards are composed of senior executives from other corporations, boards tend to compensate their executives very well indeed. They are heavily represented in the top one-thousandth of the income distribution pyramid. Several hedge-fund managers reported incomes above $25 million in 2006, and the median compensation of CEOs in corporate America now exceeds $6 million. Private equity firms are reported to be giving even richer rewards to CEOs in the absence of public disclosure.

Meanwhile, the neoliberal agenda called for a rolling back of New Deal regulations that limit the exploitation of workers and the environment. These regulations included health and safety laws, environmental protections, and ordinances discouraging capital flight and runaway shops. Under the guise of "eliminating red tape" and "getting big government out of our lives," corporations seek cuts in the number of labor inspectors and the budget for the Occupational Health and Safety Administration.

Christians search in vain for evidence of fair outcomes in this story. The restructuring of work in modern corporations benefits the rich more than the poor. It undermines workplace community and jeopardizes geographical communities. It seems divorced from a vision of the common good. And it sets the environment at risk.

Inequality and Democracy

Democracy is based on the idea that people must participate in the major decisions affecting their lives. As inequality grows, however, so does the dangerous imbalance of political power. Global corporations use their money to lobby for rule changes at the federal, state, and even local levels. Corporate lobbyists with millions in campaign contributions at their disposal roam the halls of Congress, influencing legislation on trade; the environment; taxes; and health, safety, and consumer protections. They spend freely to create constituencies to support their policies. They hire public relations firms to run campaigns from the offices of lobbyists on K Street. William Greider calls it "democracy for hire."

The power of big money now renders irrelevant the votes of a majority of the U.S. population. Money has become the critical factor in winning congressional races, with 90 percent of House seats won by candidates with the most money. The cost of television advertising drives candidates toward rich donors. If they need to raise huge sums to survive an electoral campaign, they inevitably spend their time with the wealthy rather than the poor. Voting rates differ greatly by economic class, moreover. Households with incomes over $100,000 are twice as likely to vote than households with incomes under $40,000. The percentage of people registered to vote and actually voting climbs according to family income.

When decisions that affect the lives of common people get made in venues far removed from daily life—especially venues that dislike democratic participation, openness, accountability, and transparency—then democracy is a mere shadow of what it ought to be.

Liberal Christians always seek to reform existing institutions to make them more just and sustainable. Progressives support liberals in this endeavor. But we must now be alert to the way the word "reform" has come to be used. For the economic neoliberalism described above, "reform" is a code word meant to deceive outsiders into thinking that the new policies being proposed will improve the lives of the people generally. But for those who understand the code, its meaning is very clear: eliminate restrictions on imports and foreign ownership, lower regulations, cut business taxes, privatize state-owned industries, weaken labor unions, and unravel social safety nets in order to lower wages and costs. These are some of the prescriptions imposed on indebted countries by the IMF and World Bank—the multinational enforcers of neoliberalism—as a condition for granting them new loans. Writ large, they are the main planks of neoliberalism's global agenda.

The proponents of neoliberalism introduced its primary tools surreptitiously as a means of dealing with the debt crisis among developing countries. America's love of consumerism, both as a way of life and as a political ideology, spread to the rest of the world through the media and advertising. Yet its consequences were rarely analyzed or challenged before it had a life of its own, worldwide. Now, too late, we recognize how the combination of globalization and neoliberal politics has allowed the transnational corporate class to rip up the national social contract and create a global elite whose bottom-line decisions are indifferent to where they produce, sell, or buy.

JUSTICE IN PROGRESSIVE
CHRISTIAN PERSPECTIVE

The picture we have given is of a profoundly unjust world set on a course that can lead only to greater injustice as well as greater unsustainability. Justice is an aim of most political theory, but its most central role is found in the prophetic tradition of the Bible. Insofar as they accept this depiction of the situation, Christians of almost all persuasions agree that there is much here that is not acceptable. As progressive Christians, we need to clarify our own sense of justice that guides us in our response.[8]

One of the wisest American Christian ethicists of the twentieth century was Reinhold Niebuhr (1892–1971). He belonged to the American liberal Christian tradition, but he was its first great critic as well. Like liberals generally, he was committed to reform; but unlike many, he understood that any approximation of justice required a balance of power between the parties. Hence, if workers were to be justly treated, their power must be roughly equal to that of capital. The result would involve conflict and even violence, but realistic Christians must accept this as the price of justice. Liberals tended to prefer a simpler moral appeal to capitalists to act out of love for their workers. Niebuhr regarded this as naive and sentimental and called on Christians to recognize that in the real world, the distribution of power was the critical issue. He himself shifted from being a leading pacifist to a leader in support of military action against Hitler, recognizing the necessity of violence in international affairs. The quest for justice between nations as well as between classes in society is an expression of love, but in making this real in the world, it involves actions that do not always seem loving.

This point of view is often called *Christian realism* because, while it appeals to Christian ethical principles, it takes account of the existence of sin in political calculations. His critique was widely heard and accepted by liberals. Progressives recognize its deep truth and eschew the ethical absolutism and simplistic moralism to which some liberals have inclined. Accordingly Christian realism is part of progressive Christianity today.

Building on his earlier work to counter the power of early industrialists, Niebuhr embraced the ideal of equality as a regulative principle. He understood the principle of equality to say that departures from equality—for example, from the equal distribution of income and wealth—are ethical only when some exceptional "good" results from it, and then only in proportion to the degree of "good" that is gained.

To be sure, principles of this sort are not easily applied. What criteria should be used to decide what is an exceptional "good"? How does one choose between several meritorious "goods"? If a community is composed of many members with diverse tastes, how should choices be made? Christian realists understand these difficulties but insist that political institutions can be developed to think through the choices and make decisions that approximate justice.

Robert Stivers proposes that today Christian realists incorporate four additional ethical criteria, all based on consistent biblical themes. The first is the biblical *concern for the poor*, found throughout the Hebrew and Christian Scriptures. It expects those who seek justice to make relief from poverty an essential purpose.

The second criterion is the Christian understanding of *community*. We are who we are in relationship to others. To be human is to be a social being created for God's own *koinōnia*. The essence of Christian community is the spirit of fellowship and unity in Jesus Christ. People must be allowed to participate in decisions that affect their lives. Economic arrangements that violate community solidarity require special attention and correction.

The third criterion is to *move from where we are to where we ought to be*. The first pages of the Bible point out that people are made in the image of God, yet—starting with Adam and Eve—they fall into sin. The need to improve infuses the Bible. Economic and political systems must be made more equitable. Disproportions of power are intolerable.

The fourth criterion is *care for creation*. The popular notion of dominion as domination or license has finally dissipated under heavy criticism. The new emphasis is on care for creation, as in the way God cares for humans and nature. This norm stipulates that the long-term viability of an economic system must be whether it can meet genuine needs of people today without diminishing the ability of future generations to meet theirs and without shrinking the natural diversity of life on earth.

"REFORM" AND "RESISTANCE"

When Niebuhr was writing, reforming the economic system was a real possibility. For example, he sought greater equality of power between labor and capital, and at that time this was possible to achieve. Indeed, for a few decades a balance between capital and organized labor worked well in many industries. Workers there became part of the American middle class.

From time to time now there also are opportunities to support reforms that may check or slow the increase of economic inequality. We take them. But the situation is very different today from the time when Niebuhr was active. The inequality of power between capital and labor is now enormous. Given the globalization of the economy and the dominance of an ideology that supports only the interests of capital, there is no realistic political possibility of restoring a balance. Many of the reforms that are currently being discussed in liberal political circles are unlikely to do more than superficially reduce the suffering that results from the existing system. What minor improvements are possible should be made, but reforms of this sort, even when enacted, do not suffice. Accordingly, along with reforms designed to moderate the bad effects of the presently dominant system, we need to oppose that system fundamentally. This opposition takes the form of resistance. The commitment to resistance differentiates contemporary progressive Christianity from its Niebuhrian form.

The neoliberal ascendance seems so complete, its propaganda so effective, that it is easy to feel powerless and hopeless. But Christians dare not give up. Part of our vocation as church members is to confront oppression in all its forms and bear witness to Jesus' and the prophets' calls for a "new earth." However insignificant our choices of what and how to resist, Christians need to choose.

Resistance can occur at many levels. Consider first the most intimately personal. Resistance includes an inner dissociation from the system and from the claims of its supporters. It involves a refusal to be socialized into acceptance of the common assumptions of our society.

We are barraged with information that is slanted toward approval and support of neoliberal thinking and action. The word "protection" has been made to sound objectionable, as naming something that is self-evidently evil. Returning taxes on the rich to earlier levels is understood to be "class warfare." Affirming the responsibility of government to regulate business is described as bureaucratic meddling and an attack on freedom. Nationally and globally, those who oppose the globalization of the economy as demanded by neoliberalism are depicted as naive, ignorant, or vicious. Realism, according to the dominant voice, demands that we all get with the program, the only way ahead. Since we hear this from political leaders in both major parties and from the university in addition to the media, it is easy to be sucked into this way of thinking. Nevertheless, we are called to *resist*, even at the price of ourselves appearing to be naive, ignorant, or vicious.

It is hard to resist alone. To some degree our congregations are communities of resistance. In them we remind one another that the quest for wealth to which the world is currently devoted conflicts with acceptance of the lordship of Jesus. In our congregations people are valued for their spirit and their service rather than for their social status in the world. To this extent our congregations are countercultural communities of resistance.

Obviously they vary greatly in the extent to which the countercultural teaching of the Bible shapes their life and thinking about society. One role of personal resistance for Christians is to help our fellow Christians to reflect more deeply on the meaning of their faith and its relation to their socialization by the larger society. Congregations can become an alternative source of information, presenting it in the context of Christian values. In many congregations the women have access to this kind of information and are informed by it.

This resistance can lead to action. There is a variety of ways in which people can partially withdraw from the dominant system. They can buy fair-traded goods rather than free-traded ones. They can shift their investments from the stock market to microlending organizations. They can support local farmers through farmers markets and cooperatives. They can participate in the use of local currencies.

They also can participate in a movement of more direct resistance to the further extension of neoliberalism. In this country it expressed itself most dramatically at Seattle in 1999, in disrupting the WTO meeting there. It was badly set back by the aftermath of the attack on 9/11, however. The Patriot Act makes resistance more dangerous. Nevertheless, resistance continues.

The movement of resistance in the United States is a minor part of the global movement, but it is very important for the future that people everywhere know that resistance is also present here. Global resistance has expressed itself at a number of meetings of the Bretton Woods institutions. It has put the WTO on the defensive. Now the emphasis has shifted to a positive expression of resistance in the meetings of the World Social Forum. This forum calls for placing human values above those of economic growth and the concentration of wealth. It is composed both of groups that are defending the earth and the poor from the depredations of the now-dominant system and of groups that are developing countercultural local communities that extend the capacity of those communities to meet their own needs. With tens of thousands attending, the World Social Forum is meant to challenge the policy prescriptions of the World Economic Forum meeting in Davos about the same time of each year.

In the past few years, resistance has become politically significant in South America. For the time being the United States has been forced to abandon its goal of extending NAFTA to the whole of Latin America through the Free Trade Area of the Americas. Vigorous opponents of neoliberalism and the corporate domination it supports now lead Venezuela, Bolivia, and Ecuador. More moderate opposition is politically potent in Brazil and Argentina.

Even closer to the United States it is possible that an opponent of neoliberalism would have won the election in Mexico if votes had been honestly counted. Nicaragua has voted to become more independent of the United States. Costa Rica maintains a certain degree of independence.

Those who view the world through glasses tinted by the dominant media deplore these developments and demonize their leaders. There is little doubt that the United States is doing what it can to undermine the most outspoken of them. However, those who resist socialization into the neoliberal worldview will give and express support for this growing resistance, even if not for all of its expressions. We will also make clear our objection to underground efforts by our own government to destroy those democratically elected heads of state it regards as enemies.

IMAGINING AN ALTERNATIVE

An important part of resistance to the present order is to imagine an alternative one. We are fortunate that important work has already been done along these lines. The other world that is possible, affirmed by the World Social Forum, is usefully described by the International Forum on Globalization. The Forum is an alliance of leading activists, scholars, economists, researchers, and writers representing sixty organizations in twenty-five countries, many who are active in the World Social Forum.

Its remarkable report, *Alternatives to Economic Globalization,*[9] is a rich trove of governing principles for establishing sustainable societies, as well as detailed proposals for protecting vital goods and services from corporate exploitation, managing international trade and capital movements, adjusting tax policies, supporting unions, limiting corporate privileges and power, and rebuilding economies to make them more responsive to human needs. We recommend this report to all our readers. What follows are brief précis of a few of its findings with which we heartily agree.

Subsidiarity

Neoliberal globalization is quickly severing the ties of individuals to their local communities. An economy that is based on exports by global corporations is hostage to decisions by distant authorities over which local people have little say. They easily can destroy local livelihoods and community self-reliance. Yet decisions ought to be made as close as possible to the individuals who bear their consequences. Accordingly, "subsidiarity" favors the idea that sovereignty resides in the people. Distant authorities are subsidiary or subordinate to the authority of local people. To be sure, some things cannot be provided at the local level and must be obtained from elsewhere, sometimes from great distances. But the principle of subsidiarity calls for self-reliance as much as feasible for communities, states, and nations.

The implication of subsidiarity for the freedom of international trade and finance is profound. It would call for a fundamental restructuring of the WTO, the IMF, and the World Bank, as well as the introduction of restrictions on the free movement of trade and finance. Every community and nation should have the right to determine the terms under which they wish to enter into trade with others or invite others to invest in their economies. International trade and investment systems, moreover, should safeguard the global commons and respect and promote human rights, the rights of workers, women, indigenous peoples, and children. Neoliberal supporters of the existing trading and financial systems regard these guarantees as preposterous.

Equity

Among its significant flaws, neoliberalism favors the rich over the poor by granting those with money the right to determine what is produced but denying those without money even the most basic needs. When those who can afford meat-rich diets cause grain supplies to be diverted to the feeding of livestock, they contribute to the dynamics of hunger. When the rich buy opulent vacation homes, they drive up the price of land and housing and force the less fortunate onto the street. Greater equity both among nations and within them would reinforce democracy and sustainable communities.

Because equity is essential for sustainable societies, they must set a floor on the bottom of the income pyramid and a cap on the top, while maintaining equality of opportunity and striking a balance between equity and incentives. Setting the limits is never easy. Among the possibilities are more highly progressive personal income taxes; larger earned-income credits for individuals; higher short-term capital gains taxes; higher resource and pollution taxes; taxes on speculative financial transactions; reduced tax breaks for large-scale enterprises; reduced subsidies for large-scale energy, transport, and communications infrastructure; improved workplace health and safety regulations; retraining and relocation assistance; in general, repaired social safety nets.

The need for equity calls also for more serious controls on corporate activity by the states that charter corporations. To reinforce the need for equity, localities should have the right to require any of the following: the inclusion of labor or environmental or other stakeholders on corporate boards; restriction on the ability to acquire other businesses, especially in other localities; strict limits on capital movements by corporations; removal of corporate personhood laws that give corporations the rights of ordinary citizens without the responsibilities; abandonment of limited liability rules that protect corporate shareholders from liability for crimes; insistence on public transparency.

The Precautionary Principle

In recent decades, the United States has led the world in corporate-driven scientific and technological innovation. Among our recent developments are nuclear energy, computers, bioweaponry, space exploration, biotechnology, nanotechnology, and wireless communication. Yet few of these changes took place with much advance understanding of their impacts, and there was virtually no process for democratic evaluation. Each has brought massive social, economic, and political change, often beneficial but sometimes damaging to people and the environment. Nearly all were introduced either because of military or market considerations and without sufficient regard to their negative potentials.

Neoliberalism's introduction into the world economy is another example of flaunting the precautionary principle. This principle places the onus of proof on the proponents of new technologies or processes to prove that it is safe *before* it is generally introduced. This surely was not done in the case of neoliberal globalization.

We hope that resistance will eventually lead to profound reversals of the currents now sweeping us along. What we want is a world that is more just. But even when we cannot see the way in which our actions contribute to positive change, we are called to separate ourselves as well as we can from the dominant currents and to live by the vision of a very different world. Jesus called it the *basileia theou*—the commonwealth of God.

DISCUSSION QUESTIONS

1. Does inequality of income and wealth really matter? Can you give examples from personal experience why it matters?
2. "Mounting inequality is bound to remind even the most ideologically blinded supporters of the Davos agenda that a more just way to organize the economy is essential." How hopeful are you this will happen reasonably soon?
3. "Christians are called not only to support social reforms that work toward justice but also to *resist* those currents in society that are leading to greater and greater injustice." Explain why you agree or disagree with this statement.
4. In what ways have you personally tried to reform or resist unjust policies, programs, or systems? In doing so, how often have you felt that others regarded you as "naive, ignorant, or vicious?"
5. Are there groups or organizations in your community that are best described as part of a resistance movement? Do you participate in any of them?

FOR FURTHER READING

Cavanagh, John, and Jerry Manders, eds., *Alternatives to Economic Globalization: A Better World Is Possible*. 2nd ed. San Francisco: Berrett-Koehler, 2004.

Collins, Chuck, and Felice Yeskel. *Economic Apartheid in America: A Primer on Economic Inequality and Insecurity.* New York: New Press, 2000.

Faux, Jeff. *The Global Class War.* Hoboken, NJ: John Wiley & Sons, 2006.

Hartmann, Thom. *Screwed: The Undeclared War against the Middle Class.* San Francisco: Berrett-Koehler, 2006.

Heckman, James, and Alan B. Krueger. *Inequality in America.* Cambridge, MA: MIT Press, 2003.

Lardner, James, and Davis A. Smith. *Inequality Matters.* New York: New Press, 2005.

Mishel, Lawrence, Jared Bernstein, and Sylvia Allegretto. *The State of Working America 2006/2007.* Report of the Economic Policy Institute. Ithaca, NY: Cornell University Press, 2007.

Ryscavage, Paul. *Income Inequality in America.* Armonk, NY: M. E. Sharpe, 1999.

Stiglitz, Joseph E. *Making Globalization Work.* New York: W. W. Norton, 2006.

Stone, Ronald H., and Robert Stivers, eds. *Resistance and Theological Ethics.* New York: Rowman & Littlefield, 2004.

Thurow, Lester C. *Generating Inequality: Mechanisms of Distribution in the U.S. Economy.* New York: Basic Books, 1975.

5

American Imperialism

John B. Cobb Jr.

If I could call the proudest of Romans from his grave, I would take him by the hand and say to him, Look at this picture, and at this! The greatness of the Roman Republic consisted in its despotic rule over the world; the greatness of the American Republic consists in the secured right of man to govern himself. The dignity of the Roman citizen consisted in his exclusive privileges; the dignity of the American citizen consists in his holding the natural rights of his neighbor just as sacred as his own. The Roman Republic recognized and protected the rights of the citizen, at the same time disregarding and leaving unprotected the rights of man; Roman citizenship was founded upon monopoly, not upon the claims of human nature. What the citizen of Rome claimed for himself, he did not respect in others; his own greatness was his only object; his own liberty, as he regarded it, gave him the privilege to oppress his fellow-beings. His democracy, instead of elevating mankind to his own level, trampled the rights of man into the dust. The security of the Roman Republic, therefore, consisted in the power of the sword.

Karl Schurz, in an 1859 speech[1]

INTRODUCTION

The passage quoted above arouses some nostalgia, especially among those of us who are older. It presents a picture with which many of us would have identified in our youth and describes the Roman Empire in a way we Americans rejected. We were proud that the United States had no aspiration to empire. Its role in the world was, instead, to be a beacon of hope.

Sadly, in recent years the official statements of United States foreign policy have made clear the intention of this nation to exercise dominant power throughout the globe and to do so unilaterally when necessary. The actions of the Bush administration have been consistent with this announced policy, which in many ways is continuous with the character of American foreign policy through the centuries. Nevertheless, its blunt statement and the actions that have expressed it have shocked many citizens. The intense discussion about the merits of this program provides an occasion for radical reconsideration of America's role and goal in the world.

In earlier chapters we have affirmed that in and through the Bible we find God calling us to resist some of the dominant trends in our culture. To illustrate what we as Christians are called to resist, we took consumerism and poisonous inequality as our first examples. We noted that both of these are in the service of "mammon." Although they are primarily economic, they have important political dimensions that require separate attention. Intertwined with the religion of consumerism in the United States is the religion of nationalism. When we are told that we will not reduce our greenhouse emissions because this might adversely affect our national way of life, we understand that way of life to be identified not with democracy but with consumerism. The worship of mammon determines much of our foreign policy. Even the attack on Iraq was influenced by the desire of our oil companies to profit from the exploitation of its vast supplies of petroleum as much as by the hope of establishing a democratic government there.[2]

Still, we need to examine American foreign policy in its own terms. To whatever extent the epigraph describes our national ideals, there is little tension between them and Christian faith. But we now see that our nationalism has always in fact involved the imperialism that is rejected in this quotation, and in the administration of George W. Bush this hegemonic dimension has come to the fore. As progressive Christians we are called to resist not only consumerism and poisonous inequality but also imperialism.

The dominance of consumerism and the growing gap between rich and poor in our society are readily evident, and Christians of many traditions recognize that these are in sharp opposition to our historic teachings. With respect to foreign policy the situation is different. Many Christians, including liberal ones, still read much of American history in the way it is described by Schurz. Many still do not realize how clearly the leaders of our nation have thoroughly adopted imperialist theories and practices. Accordingly, this chapter surveys American history and then examines the theories and goals that have been articulated in the past few years.

The current advocates of global empire use the term *Pax Americana* to describe their goal. Since Christians are deeply attracted to the goal of world peace and are likely to believe that the United States should contribute to such peace, the idea of an "American peace" is not immediately offensive. After all, no other nation is in position to take the lead. Accordingly, we must take this ideal seriously. Since our conquests of Afghanistan and Iraq were in pursuit of Pax Americana, they serve as test cases of what the goal of Pax Americana requires. At this writing, a further test is the possible extension of the war to Iran and perhaps Syria.[3]

This chapter begins with a few generalizations about the history of U.S. foreign policy. It then offers a more detailed analysis of the neoconservative proposals as developed by the Project for the New American Century, surveys the actual course of recent history in relation to these themes, examines "The National Security Strategy of the United States of America" as the most official statement we have of our government's stance in the world, and, finally, considers the nature of the current opposition to these policies.

The last section of the chapter identifies progressive Christian reasons for resisting the imperialist dimensions of American policy and discusses some of the forms of resistance to which we are called.

AMERICAN FOREIGN POLICY

Themes in Past U.S. Foreign Policy

Like all nations, the United States operates on nationalist principles. However, these function in distinctive ways. Although American nationalism has often been closely connected with the English language and with Anglo-Saxon culture, it has been able to absorb people from other parts of northern Europe, from southern and eastern Europe, and now to some extent from Asia, Latin America, and Africa. The complex effects of this less ethnically determined nationalism are felt primarily in domestic politics, but they also affect American foreign policy and inform the five features of this national self-understanding we have selected for emphasis.

1. The United States at its inception decided that it did not want to be involved in the endless wars among the European powers. This initiated a strong tendency toward isolationism. Americans felt that the United States was sufficiently distant from Europe that it could concentrate on affairs in this hemisphere and be insulated from European quarrels. These views were reflected in George Washington's famous farewell address and later in the Monroe doctrine, committing the United States to "protecting" Latin America from European colonial powers.

This isolationist attitude delayed entry into both World Wars I and II. It kept the United States out of the League of Nations, and it continues to fuel opposition to the United Nations, especially to the possibility that the United States should be obliged to accept any control by the UN. This isolationist spirit has also contributed to our failure to sign international treaties and to recognize the jurisdiction of the World Court. We have been unwilling to restrict our own freedom of action in these ways. In this sense, isolationism has meant the rejection of internationalism.

In the presidential campaign of 2000, George Bush sounded isolationist themes. Our foreign policy was to be humble. We should eschew any role in nation building around the world. The isolationist patterns in American history, however, have never meant hesitation to defend ourselves. The slogan "Don't tread on me" has been inseparable from isolationist sentiment. When isolationists perceive that others are violating our rights, they have been willing to strike back. British interference with our maritime commerce provoked the War of 1812. German attacks on our ships paved the way for our entry into World War I. After Pearl Harbor, isolationist resistance to taking part in World War II evaporated. The attack on the World Trade Towers and the Pentagon evoked a desire to counterattack among those who might otherwise be disinclined to meddle in the affairs of other countries.

2. Isolation from overseas involvement has been united with the goal of hegemony or dominance in the western hemisphere. The expansion of the U.S. westward across the continent was a consistent part of United States policy until it was completed. The acquisition of Hawaii and Alaska were also part of this policy.

This expansion meant, of course, a conquest of native peoples, sometimes by sheer military force, sometimes by deceptive treaties, sometimes by contagious diseases, sometimes by destroying their economic base. At times it was genocidal.[4] At best it meant forcing the indigenous people onto land not wanted by the conquerors, land usually inadequate to support the native people in their traditional way of life. Although the term has been resisted, the policy with respect to native peoples has been imperialism.

This expansion of national boundaries has been accompanied by the policy of establishing the dominant influence of the United States throughout the western hemisphere. While Canada has usually been treated more as a junior partner, the Monroe doctrine has made the goal of hegemony clear with respect to Latin America. The primary official emphasis has been on keeping European powers out, but scores of military interventions and political subversions have been directed toward maintaining or installing governments subservient to perceived U.S. interests.[5]

It is also important to see that the general limitation of hegemony to the western hemisphere did not prevent us from an imperial venture in the Philippines. We also felt free to use our fleet to force Japan to open itself to commerce with us. The imperial spirit was never tightly contained.

3. Idealistic support of freedom, democracy, and peace has also played a role in shaping American foreign policy. It has been the strength of this idealism and its close association with American nationalism that has made it so difficult for Christians to appreciate the need to resist that nationalism. The idealism has had real effects.

This idealism was important in both world wars and came to clearest expression in presidential leadership toward international organizations in their aftermath. The treatment of Germany and Japan after the Second World War also expressed, in part, this idealism. American idealism was successfully appealed to in favor of the Marshall Plan and aid of economic development in the third world. It provided support for the World Bank as well as direct programs of assistance such as the Peace Corps.

Detailed study of policy can lead to cynicism with respect to this idealism. Few significant governmental actions have been motivated by idealism alone. However, the idealism should not be discounted. It is true that popular idealism can be, and often has been, manipulated by leaders for purposes that are different from those professed, but the idealism sometimes imposes limits on this manipulation and, in any case, must be taken into account in the formulation of policy. The neoconservatives appeal to the American idealization of democracy as a reason for imposing American dominance everywhere.

4. Interconnected with all of the above contributors to American geopolitical behavior is the deep-seated sense of American "exceptionalism." Even before the United States was formed, there was a strong sense that the colonies played a special, or "exceptional," role in divine providence. This gave the colonies both peculiar responsibilities and peculiar privileges. When the United States came into existence as a nation, this sense of American peculiarity expressed itself in the distinctive character of American nationalism.

This idea that the United States of America is different from all other nations has been involved in all the previously mentioned policies. It has justified both isolationism and imperialism. It has informed the idealism of the nation. It gave a special sense of mission to participation in both world wars. It informed the American leadership of the "free world" in its defense against the Communist bloc.

American exceptionalism has often had an explicitly Christian component. Many Americans believe that the United States is a Christian nation. Indeed, they think of it as being uniquely Christian.[6] They emphasize the role of Christian faith in the founding of the colonies by those seeking freedom to practice their beliefs. They view the founding fathers as believers in the Christian God, who sought to embody God's purposes in the Declaration of Independence and the Constitution. They justify expansionism partly as the bringing of Christian civilization to new regions. Even the enslavement of

Africans was justified as a way of Christianizing them. Many Americans saw the cold war as a struggle against godless communism. Today they are likely to think of the global struggle as, in part, against an alien religion.

To a remarkable extent the sense that this nation is different from all others was reinforced by attitudes toward America in other parts of the world. The United States has been widely viewed as the land of freedom and opportunity. Although this admiration has been severely eroded by our recent actions, to some extent it continues even today.

American exceptionalism is closely related to a remarkable American sense of virtue and innocence. Despite the near genocide of the native people of this continent, many view our westward expansion primarily in terms of the hardships and heroism of the frontiersmen and settlers. Despite the central role in our economy for centuries of the enslavement of Africans and the exploitation of their labor, we view our economic success as the accomplishment of a free people. Despite our exercise of dominant power over the Latin American nations for our own economic and geopolitical advancement, we view our relations to other countries as benevolent. Despite the actual ruthlessness with which we have treated those who stood in the way of our global policies, we suppose that our exercise of power is so benign that there is no need for us to be guided by internationally established rules of behavior. Despite our one-sided support of Israel and acceptance of its illegal settlement policies, we assume that our goals in Israel-Palestine are just and equitable.[7]

These self-congratulatory beliefs do not arise from cynical hypocrisy. Euro-Americans are often genuinely surprised that other people resent our actions. We assume that our actions have been shaped by our ideals; thus those who oppose our policies must be against our ideals. This makes Americans remarkably credulous when our leaders describe those who oppose us as morally evil. Those Americans who state that our military actions do not conform to our ideals are widely viewed as disloyal. This makes thoughtful public discussion of foreign policies difficult. The tendency to judge others by their actions and ourselves by our ideals is, of course, not limited to the United States, or to foreign policy, or even to large groups. Nevertheless, it affects American attitudes and international activities to an unusual degree.

5. Expressive of American idealism and exceptionalism is our need to see our nation as acting defensively rather than intruding aggressively into the affairs of others. Evidence of this abounds throughout U.S. history, even in situations when such a perception was totally unwarranted. For example, at the outset of the U.S. war with Mexico in 1846, President James K. Polk asked Congress to declare war on Mexico because "American blood has been shed on American soil." When Congressman Abraham Lincoln pointed out the falsity of this claim, he was attacked as being insufficiently patriotic and giving

aid and comfort to the enemy. Even in carrying out an imperialist expansion in the name of "Manifest Destiny," Americans needed to see themselves as merely responding to the unwarranted aggressiveness of others.

In this same vein, following World War II, the name of the U.S. Department of War was changed to the Department of Defense. In modern times funds have never been spent on waging wars but only on "defense." During the cold war, American foreign policy was based on a strategic plan called "containment," which suggested that an aggressive foreign enemy needed to be thwarted. Even the unprovoked attack on Iraq was justified as a response to the 9/11 attack on the World Trade Center and the Pentagon.

Much has been justified in the name of "defense"—for example, alliances with selected military dictators opposed to our principal adversaries (e.g., Chile, Guatemala, Nicaragua), and stockpiling enough nuclear weapons to destroy all civilized life. Following the cold war, "defense" has been used to justify invading nations (e.g., Panama, Grenada) that have not attacked the United States. The idea used to justify these actions is that without these preemptive strikes we might someday be attacked. This kind of doublethink might seem new in American life, but actually it has deep historic roots going back to the Indian wars during the colonial period. Many an assault on a peaceful Indian village was made in the name of defense.

Neoconservative Geopolitics

When the Soviet Empire collapsed, cold-war policies were no longer appropriate. However, there had been little discussion of post-cold-war foreign policy. Many assumed that the huge defense budgets of the cold-war period would not be needed, so there would be a "peace dividend." Some hoped for a major reduction of taxes; others, government spending to alleviate poverty and to improve infrastructure. In fact, the military budget was reduced only a little. A continuing strong military was justified by the need to be able to fight wars on two fronts simultaneously, and an extensive military presence was maintained around the world. In 2006, even apart from the new commitments of troops in and around Afghanistan and Iraq, there were 117,000 American troops in Europe; 47,000 in Japan; 38,000 in South Korea; and smaller numbers in many other places.[8]

In general, however, decisions were made in an ad hoc fashion, more as responses to changing political pressures and diplomatic practicalities than as implementing a clear vision of the role of the United States as the world's only remaining superpower. It was apparent to everyone that the United States exercised great power to advance its own interests. But it was assumed that the interests of the United States required that it maintain good relations with allies and work cooperatively with them. This style is considered to be "realist."

The realists adapted their policies gradually to the new situation of unrivaled American power. They continued the kind of global thinking endemic to the cold war and increasingly defined American interests as involving what happens everywhere. Their foreign policy was aimed to extend dominance throughout the world, but they did not articulate a new global vision to replace that of the cold war.

Only a new group calling themselves "neoconservatives" offered a reasoned and developed alternative to this kind of ad hoc pragmatic realism. Paul Wolfowitz, a member of this group, was undersecretary of defense for policy in the first Bush administration. He was distressed by the decision of the first President Bush to stop the troops of the United States and its allies at the Iraqi border. The result of the failure to remove Saddam from power was a decade of tyrannous rule and the imposition on Iraq of sanctions that generated corruption and hurt primarily its helpless citizens.

Reflecting on this failure to depose Saddam in 1992, Wolfowitz led in the preparation of a document called "Defense Planning Guidance." He proposed that "containment" should be replaced by preemptive prevention of the development of weapons of mass destruction by any potential enemy. He also argued that the United States should act alone if necessary to implement this policy. President George H. W. Bush viewed the document as too controversial, and it gained no official status. However, it has provided the basis for neoconservative thinking ever since.[9]

Neoconservatives rejected the isolationist tendency in American traditions except for its emphasis on complete independence, and they carried the imperialist tradition to its extreme limit. They emphasized the idealistic element, that is, the desire to promote peace and democracy. Whereas the United States had been the leader of the "free world" in the struggle against communism, it should now, they argued, be the leader of the whole world. Its mission is to make all countries "free and democratic." The neoconservatives emphatically asserted American exceptionalism, expecting that America, unlike other nations, would be a benevolent force throughout the world, so its dominance could be embraced by all.

During Clinton's presidency, neoconservatives advanced their thinking, especially in 1997 by establishing the Project for the New American Century. The name of the organization states its goal. This project advocated a global Pax Americana, and it spelled out what would be required in September 2000 in "Rebuilding America's Defenses: Strategy, Forces and Resources for a New Century."[10] To "rebuild" meant to reverse the Clinton cuts in military expenditures, which, the authors believed, threatened the ability of the United States to carry out its true mission. What were to be "defended" were American allies and interests throughout the world. The goal was to establish such overwhelming power in all regions of the world that no nation or group of nations would be able to challenge it. To do this, the statement argued, we must bring our military budget back to cold-war levels and then increase it. Further, the United States must be free from any restrictions on the kinds of weapons it uses, including nuclear ones. It must be free also from any international treaties that would inhibit its actions and from international courts that would presume to judge the actions of Americans.

The document also states that the United States must take complete command of outer space. It must have an impenetrable safety shield. Subsequently Donald Rumsfeld, as secretary of defense, made clear that the command of outer space will provide a basis for control of the whole world.[11] Indeed, the total military control of outer space is increasingly seen as central to the accomplishment of what is now called Full Spectrum Dominance. Other nations are not to be allowed to develop defenses against an attack from space. That China is developing such a defense is regarded as a fundamental threat.

The document goes on to call for a shift from a doctrine of deterrence to one of preemptive or preventive strikes. If a potential enemy is developing weapons of mass destruction, it is dangerous to the world to delay an attack until the enemy is ready to use these. The weapons should be destroyed before they can threaten others, and governments that are a threat to the American peace should be replaced by others that accept our leadership. We should prevent other nations from developing the ability to deter an attack by us.[12] In other words the United States should be free to impose its will anywhere.

By following these policies, it is asserted, the United States will be able to establish a unified world in which there will be no major wars. In the process it will also establish democratic regimes in countries that are now under dictators. It will maintain this situation indefinitely. This is the meaning of "Pax Americana" and the "American century."

The neoconservatives directed much of their geopolitical attention to the Middle East, which has by far the greatest oil reserves. The governments of this region are, for the most part, nondemocratic, and Islam offers the only major global worldview that opposes the corporate capitalism championed by the United States.

The United States has a special relationship with Israel, whose future remains endangered by the enmity of so many of its neighbors. The neoconservatives are closely allied with the more hawkish segments in Israeli politics. A leading neoconservative, Richard Perle, was among a handful of conservatives who wrote a white paper for Benjamin Netanyahu, then prime minister of Israel, indicating the importance of destroying Saddam Hussein.[13] In general,

the neoconservatives have encouraged Israel to ignore the international pressure to come to an agreement with the Palestinians, believing that delay and
the extension of settlements throughout Palestinian land ensured Israel's permanent control over the whole region.

This neoconservative thinking led to clear conclusions with respect to Iraq.
In 1998 Rumsfeld, Wolfowitz, and Perle, among others, signed a letter
addressed to President Clinton that included the following statement: "The
only acceptable strategy is one that eliminates the possibility that Iraq will be
able to use or threaten to use weapons of mass destruction. In the near term,
this means a willingness to undertake military action as diplomacy is clearly
failing. In the long term, it means removing Saddam Hussein and his regime
from power."[14]

The Policies of the Bush Administration

During the campaign for the presidency in 2000, George W. Bush appeared
to be isolationist. His appointment of Colin Powell as secretary of state suggested a general continuation of the realist policies of the Clinton administration with some increase of military budget. His vice president, Richard
Cheney, belongs to a group often identified as "assertive nationalists."
Although less idealistic than the neoconservatives, the assertive nationalists
agree with such policies as unilateralism and preventive strikes. In addition,
the Bush administration included a number of neoconservatives: Wolfowitz,
Perle, Douglas Feith, Lewis Libby, John Bolton, and Elliott Abrams.

Prior to September 11, 2001, the only clear shift in international policy was
a more emphatic refusal to sign international treaties. By rejecting the Kyoto
Protocol on climate change negotiated by the Clinton administration, Congress had already indicated its refusal to risk the interests of American corporations; so Bush's unqualified opposition changed little. Clinton had hesitated
to push the treaty on land mines and had shown little support for the International Criminal Court. Bush was blunt in his opposition. This could all be
understood in terms of Bush's isolationist tendencies.

The turning point was 9/11. The American people were united in their
desire to prevent future acts of terrorism against them and to punish those who
had attacked. Bush seized the moment to project himself as the leader of this
counterattack. He declared a "war on terrorism" that justified tightening control in the United States. Civil liberties took a back seat to security measures.
The hastily passed USA PATRIOT Act[15] set aside basic provisions of the Bill
of Rights of the Constitution. It allowed for searches without judicial warrant,
imprisonment without the right to counsel or the right to know the charges
against one, and even the denial of the right to trial.

The War on Terrorism became the controlling rhetoric of foreign policy. To some extent this was genuine and won the support of governments around the world. But the rhetoric has also been used to justify actions that had previously been proposed for other reasons. These actions have been widely accepted in the United States as thus justified, although people in other countries are more skeptical.

Accordingly, the United States justified the conquest of Afghanistan by the fact that the headquarters and main training camps of Al Qaeda were located there. The tyrannical nature of the Taliban government of Afghanistan, and especially its treatment of women, meant that in much of the world there was considerable support for regime change on independent grounds.[16]

Once we had attained our primary goals in Afghanistan, we turned attention to Iraq. Here, too, many Americans were persuaded that this was necessary because of Iraq's actual or potential support of terrorism. Iraq was depicted as a threat to its neighbors and especially to Israel. Hence, it was argued, its weapons of mass destruction and its capacity to make them must be destroyed, and its regime must be replaced.

Everyone agreed that Saddam was a vicious tyrant and aspired to possess the instruments of power. Economic sanctions were causing great suffering among the people of Iraq and were ineffective in changing Saddam's policies. Furthermore, his neighbors feared him. All of this gave some support to the conquest of Iraq even among those not persuaded by the argument about terrorism. Nevertheless, whereas world opinion had largely supported, or at least accepted, the invasion of Afghanistan, opposition to Bush's policy toward Iraq was massive.

One reason for the worldwide opposition was suspicion of the motives of the United States. Iraq has the fourth largest oil reserve in the world.[17] There can be little doubt that American oil companies want to profit from this resource and that the United States wants control of it. The United States had supported Saddam when he was engaged in his most vicious acts, just as it had supported Osama as long as he was fighting the Soviet Union; so the moral grounds for Saddam's removal were unconvincing. His violation of UN resolutions was less egregious than Israel's, but the United States has not permitted the UN to enforce any of its resolutions about Israel/Palestine.[18]

There were two other important reasons, however, for the size and intensity of the opposition to the attack on Iraq. One was its clear expression of the unqualified unilateralism desired by the neoconservatives. In the first Gulf war, the United States gained the support of the UN and acted, at least ostensibly, in its behalf. This time the United States made clear from an early date that it did not consider itself limited by UN votes and that it retained the freedom to attack on its own if others did not support it. If it had succeeded in gaining

UN backing, the opposition would have been greatly reduced. The peoples of most of the world, and many Americans also, find American unilateralism in foreign policy frightening.

The second of these additional reasons for strong opposition was the use of the argument favoring preemptive—or, more accurately, preventive—strikes. Previously, the general consensus of those who have hoped to introduce some semblance of order into international affairs has been that a nation is justified in taking preemptive action only if an attack is imminent. There was no imminent threat of an attack by Iraq.[19]

Furthermore, even those who wished that Saddam could be replaced were by no means confident that an American occupying force could establish a successful government. The first President Bush had been persuaded by this argument to stop UN troops at the border. He hoped Iraqis would themselves overthrow Saddam. This did not happen, but subsequent events have shown that those who could not foresee a successful outcome of occupation were correct. Though most Iraqis, at least the Shiites and the Kurds, are glad that Saddam Hussein is gone, polls have consistently shown that they want the Americans to leave.[20]

According to polls in the United States, a majority of Americans are now in agreement with the Iraqi people that continued American presence only makes matters worse. The shift to the Democrats in the 2006 elections expressed the lack of support for continuing American occupation of Iraq. However, the administration has chosen to respond to the problem in another way. It argues that a larger American presence could reduce the violence between opposing militias and bring order at least to Baghdad, where the problem was most acute. The new Democratic majority approved funding for this "surge." Its opposition to continuing the occupation of Iraq has been largely limited to unsuccessful efforts to get the administration to commit itself to troop reduction by specified times. It has not used its power over the budget to force such reductions.

The present administration has plans for an attack on Iran, primarily to destroy, or at least delay, its capacity to produce nuclear weapons, but also to weaken it politically, economically, and militarily. Although the Democratic Congress offers little or no resistance, fortunately there is opposition from the military.[21]

This does not mean that President Bush has listened *only* to the neoconservatives in his administration. They would have preferred that the United States not seek UN support for its invasion of Iraq. The failure of the Iraqi people to welcome our presence and the chaos that has resulted from it has discredited the neoconservatives with the public, and their role in the administration is reduced. Cheney's "assertive nationalism," which may also be called unqualified "imperialism," is a larger factor now.

The National Security Strategy
of the United States of America

To assess the extent to which our national policy has come to resemble the proposals of the neoconservatives, we will examine the most official statement available on American geopolitical policy: "The National Security Strategy of the United States of America."[22] This document was released in September 2002 with a letter by the President serving as a preface.

The document does not speak explicitly of a Pax Americana or an American century. It does not even speak of American hegemony. On the contrary, it emphasizes the importance of continuing on the path to a fully global market. It calls for an increase in aid for poor countries and addresses the need for a massive program to fight AIDS. It speaks of a "distinctly American internationalism" and emphasizes the strengthening of alliances rather than affirming unilateralism. In all these ways it differs from "Rebuilding America's Defenses."

The document presents U.S. policy largely as a response to the attack on the World Trade Center and the Pentagon, an attack that was not anticipated in the earlier work of the neoconservatives and has influenced their basic thinking rather little.[23] It is no doubt true that Bush's policies have been affected by this event. It is certainly true that the American people became far more willing to follow his leadership in implementing these policies because of 9/11.

Despite all these differences, what is most striking about "The National Security Strategy" document is that its major innovations follow so closely the proposals of Wolfowitz in 1992 and the recommendations in "Rebuilding America's Defenses." In short, policies that had originally been thought through independently of 9/11 were justified as a response to it. The thinking reflected in this document, like that in the earlier ones, is in response to the new global situation in which the United States is the sole superpower. Like the earlier neoconservative proposals, this one views the unique power of the United States as an opportunity to bring peace and democratic institutions to the whole world. In his introduction, President Bush wrote as follows:

> As we defend the peace, we will also take advantage of an historical opportunity to preserve the peace. Today, the international community has the best chance since the rise of the nation-state in the seventeenth century to build a world where great powers compete in peace instead of continually prepare for war.

The ambiguity of the implications of this statement is shown in the remainder of the paragraph. It implies that the possible threats to this peaceful world still come from Russia and China, and it warns them diplomatically not to challenge the United States militarily:

America will encourage the advancement of democracy and economic openness in both nations, because these are the best foundation for domestic stability and international order. We will strongly resist aggression from other great powers even as we welcome their peaceful pursuit of prosperity, trade, and cultural advancement.

Near the end of the document[24] the issue of China's policies is taken up again, with another implied warning: "In pursuing advanced military capabilities that can threaten its neighbors in the Asia-Pacific region, China is following an outdated path that, in the end, will hamper its own pursuit of national greatness." The American vision is clear. We alone or along with those nations with which we are most closely allied will have advanced military capabilities. Other countries will operate in the context of our benevolent hegemony, encouraged to participate in the global market and to develop democratic institutions. This is the vision of Pax Americana more explicitly described in the earlier neoconservative documents. The proponents of Pax Americana are confident that they can impose global hegemony throughout most of the world, but they recognize a particular problem with China.

The document discusses the issue of "preemptive strikes" at some length.[25] It points out that it is not a new doctrine. However, in the past, preemptive strikes were understood to be justified only in response to an imminent threat. Now "we must adapt the concept of imminent threat to the capabilities and objectives of today's adversaries." Their possession of weapons of mass destruction, or even their efforts to acquire such weapons, now constitutes the sort of threat that justifies a preemptive strike. It can be argued that the term "preventive strike" fits this new doctrine better.

In his introduction President Bush speaks of U.S. commitment to "lasting institutions like the United Nations, the World Trade Organization, the Organization of American States and NATO." In the body of the document the UN is listed alongside countries and nongovernmental organizations as providing "humanitarian, political, economic, and security assistance necessary to rebuild Afghanistan."[26] However, whereas there is extensive discussion of NATO and other military alliances, no significant role is assigned to the UN.

In any case, it is clear that international alliances are to be instruments of implementing our policies, not contexts in which policies will be formulated to which we will adhere: "In exercising our leadership, we will respect the values, judgment, and interests of our friends and partners. Still, we will be prepared to act apart when our interests and unique responsibilities require."[27] The United States welcomes international support in implementing policies that it formulates for the general good. It will not be inhibited from carrying out these policies by internationally established institutions or rules. This principle, that the decisions are ours to make, is implicit throughout the document. It is sometimes quite explicit. For example, we read, "We will take the actions necessary to ensure that our efforts to meet our global security commitments and protect Americans are not impaired by the potential for investigations, inquiry, or prosecution by the International Criminal Court (ICC), whose jurisdiction does not extend to Americans and which we do not accept."[28]

Finally, the document seconds the neoconservative emphasis on the need for a strong American military with bases all over the world.

> We must build and maintain our defenses beyond challenge. . . . Our military must: assure our allies and friends, dissuade future military competition, deter threats against U.S. interests, allies, and friends, and decisively defeat any adversary if deterrence fails. . . .
>
> The presence of American forces overseas is one of the most profound symbols of the U.S. commitments to allies and friends. Through our willingness to use force in our own defense and in defense of others, the United States demonstrates its resolve to maintain a balance of power that favors freedom. To contend with uncertainty and to meet the many security challenges we face, the United States will require bases and stations within and beyond Western Europe and Northeast Asia, as well as temporary access arrangements for the long-distance deployment of U.S. forces.[29]

The Opposition

Popular opposition to the invasion of Iraq was not mirrored by political leadership or the foreign policy establishment. Democrats in Congress joined Republicans in giving Bush the authority he requested. The foreign policy realists who were being displaced by the neoconservatives made no effort to oppose the invasion. Even in the 2004 presidential campaign, when John Kerry was asked whether, if he had known when he voted to support the war what everyone knew when he was running for president, he would still have voted as he did, he answered, Yes.

It is important to recognize that the discrediting of the neoconservatives is chiefly a matter of their methods, their style, their misjudgments, and their poor management. There is very little critique of their underlying purpose of establishing the American Empire. Within the existing leadership of the United States no one has denounced the goal of Pax Americana or Full Spectrum Dominance. No major leader is opposing preventive wars or American control of outer space. None are proposing a basically different direction for American foreign policy.

Unless there is a massive expansion of the war, we may expect that under either a Republican or a Democratic administration, foreign policy leadership will pass back into the hands of the "realists." Their approach will be more genteel and moderate. They will soothe the feelings of allies. They will have better judgments as to how our "liberation" of target peoples will be received, and perhaps they will avoid the astonishing levels of corporate corruption that have characterized our expenditures in Iraq.[30] But American imperialism will remain in place. Under either party's administration, we will eventually withdraw from Iraqi cities, leaving them to sectarian violence. It is unlikely, however, that we will abandon our newly built bases in Iraq and the control of Iraqi oil to which they are related. These touchstones of American imperialism will constitute our "victory" in Iraq.

A CHRISTIAN PERSPECTIVE

Christian Reflection on Recent Events

In section 1, we have tried to give a relatively objective account of American history, especially of the past few years. We have not concealed our opposition to the imperial project in general and to the neoconservatives in particular, but we have tried not to allow that to distort our account.

We turn now to describe our own point of view and what that leads us to propose. The neoconservatives have claimed the moral high ground for their project of bringing democracy to the entire world. In order to put the best possible face on their goal of global hegemony, they posit an ideal coincidence between the well-being of other peoples and perceived American self-interest. Only this would make possible the American benevolence that supporters of Pax Americana assume. In fact, however, such perfect coincidence never exists, and when there is a conflict, American leaders unhesitatingly give priority to the perceived interests of the United States.

This does not mean that the United States is likely to act simply on the principle that "might makes right." As previously noted, American idealism cuts against this, and both the neoconservatives and President Bush emphasize their commitment to freedom and democracy. Furthermore, the history of the twentieth century has generated opposition to genocide and support for basic human rights that are likely to be internalized to some degree by American leaders.

Nevertheless, the best predictor of how the United States will exercise dominant power is how it has operated in Latin America over the past century. It has intervened dozens of times in the internal affairs of Latin American countries.[31] None of these interventions have been in favor of popular movements representing peasants and workers. Most have been motivated by the desire to protect U.S. strategic interests and/or the interests of American corporations. The chief requirement of a national government has been that it support American policies and be favorable to American corporate interests.

To say this is not to question the sincerity of those neoconservatives who call for more idealistic policies. It is to question, however, the likelihood that such idealism will override economic interests and geopolitical calculations. The American record in the Middle East is not encouraging in this respect. Premier Mossadegh represented Iran's best chance to develop into a more democratic nation, but the United States arranged for his overthrow because of fear that he would not be sufficiently committed to its side of the cold war or supportive of American corporate interests.[32] American propaganda now emphasizes the viciousness of Saddam Hussein, but the United States supported him while he was engaged in his most vicious actions.

It is probable that the American government with the help of the media will be able to convince many citizens that the national actions of the United States express traditional ideals, but the rest of the world will see matters differently. The resentment that even purely benevolent control evokes will be intensified by obvious American hypocrisy. To prevent the American public from understanding what is going on will require even tighter control of information by the government and corporate media.

The above criticism of Pax Americana has been influenced by the tradition of Christian realism that opposes setting a historical goal that could be realized only among virtuous people. It does so on the grounds that this ignores the biblical understanding of the sinfulness of human beings and their societies. This understanding gives rise to the judgment that power corrupts, that is, that those who exercise power are unlikely to wield it in the impartial interest of all. Indeed, those with power typically lose the ability to understand how those over whom they exercise that power interpret what is happening.

In the establishment of the United States, statesmen influenced by their awareness of the danger of concentrating power in too few hands instituted checks and balances in the system of government. They also established constitutional guarantees of human rights, knowing how easy it is for the majority to trample on the rights of minorities through majority rule. From the Christian realist perspective it is inherently unlikely that a nation dominating the world without a rival or any other external check will be typically benevolent in its rule. That the United States has so little self-understanding of its own sinful history only makes it a more dangerous candidate for this role.

In support of his policies President Bush uses, perhaps quite honestly, religious ideas that are popularly understood to be Christian. These popular ideas tend to divide the world dualistically into the good and the evil. They identify the good with "us" and the evil with "them." "They" are easily identified by their opposition to "us." Accordingly, it is believed, "we" have a mission to bring good to the world, often at the expense of destroying our enemies. This Christian version of "jihad" is "crusade."

Precisely because the language in which the goal of Pax Americana is put forward rings so true to Americans shaped by some popular forms of Christianity, the responsibility of progressive Christians to criticize is heightened. In more-biblical Christian teaching, the line between good and evil runs through all of us as individuals and as nations. The line does not lie between virtuous and vicious nations or between Christians and persons of other faiths. The people of ancient Israel often thought God would protect them because they were God's chosen people. The great prophets typically denounced them for this false assurance. Especially with regard to national actions, purity of motive is hardly possible. God called for justice and righteousness rather than reliance on a special relationship.

This complexity does not prevent progressive Christians from judging that some governments are better than others or that real improvements are possible. It does not exclude that, in extreme cases, the United States may have the moral responsibility to bring about regime change in another country. But it warns us against self-righteousness in the process. It also reminds us how rarely the gains effected by military action counterbalance the destruction and suffering that are involved.

Most thoughtful Christian leaders of the old-line churches opposed the war from the outset for reasons such as these. If the UN had taken responsibility for conquering Iraq, deposing Saddam, and reconstructing the country, the prospects for a positive outcome would have been improved, although certainly not assured. Progressive Christians would probably have been more divided on the wisdom and righteousness of such an international intervention.

What is clearest to progressive Christians is that hierarchical domination is inferior to voluntary partnership. Being the only superpower places the United States in a position of unique opportunity. Instead of using this opportunity to impose its rule on the whole world, it could use this power to bring into being a world in which all peoples participate in making decisions that shape the global future. Progressive Christians share with neoconservatives an avowed aspiration for world peace, but we believe that genuine peace is based on justice and freedom and widespread participation in political processes, not on imperial control by one nation.

What Should Be the Christian Response?

In this book we distinguish "reform" and "resistance." When there are practical possibilities of improving the situation, progressive Christians will work with others for the needed reforms. In relation to the events recounted above, this means that at the time of this writing, progressive Christians can seek to persuade the Democratic leadership in Congress to take a stronger stance against the continuing presence of any American troops in Iraq, including those at the new bases, and to renounce all claims to Iraqi oil. We can encourage our government to seek the involvement of many Arab and Muslim states in reducing sectarian strife in Iraq and bringing order to daily life there. And we can urge the administration to use some of the funds now expended for military purposes to help rebuild the Iraqi infrastructure. That we can be broadly successful in these efforts is highly doubtful, but this does not excuse us from the effort.

However, we emphasize that much of what is wrong with our society is not accessible to change through normal political processes. Some assumptions and basic directions are so deeply entrenched in our society that they are not discussed in the political arena. This chapter has shown that American imperialism is a phenomenon of this sort. It has operated throughout American history in a variety of guises, and it has been possible, politically, to criticize some of its expressions. But the basic movement of conquest across the country and even its extension across the seas has rarely been seriously criticized. The hegemony over Latin America and most of the actions taken to express it have hardly been politically controversial within the United States. Today the political debates are about how best to pursue the program of maintaining and extending American power rather than whether that power should be extended or even maintained.

For progressive Christians, the latter question is decisive, and we can only answer that the long-continued extension of American hegemony should end. Indeed, it should be reversed, although there are no ways in which we can currently work directly to end this deep current of American life. At most we can work realistically to bring an end to its expression in the conquest of Iraq. But although we cannot organize to overcome this deep-seated drive for power, we can, indeed, as progressive Christians we must, resist it.

We can resist it by reminding ourselves and one another of who we are as disciples of Jesus Christ. Jesus lived in a great empire, but his message did not support that empire. Indeed, the empire saw him as a threat and killed him. Jesus taught us to pray that *God's* purposes be realized on earth as they are in heaven. The world for which we pray cannot be one of imperial rule of any one people over others. It must be one of partnership among peoples. Those who followed Jesus formed countercultural communities that operated by counterimperial values. We are called to think and live similarly in countercultural ways. We will summarize some of the consequences.

First, we can note that a remarkable feature of the Bible is that so much of it is written from the perspective of the oppressed rather than the oppressors. Taking our cue from the Bible, we can learn to understand ourselves as Americans more realistically by studying American history from the perspective of those who have been its victims: Native Americans, African Americans, Mexican Americans, later immigrants from Asia, and those people around the world who now suffer from the economic policies we have imposed on them. It is a painful process, for it destroys the sense of innocence that so many Americans enjoy.[33] As individuals we need the encouragement and support of the church in the process of understanding from a broader perspective who we have been and who we continue to be.

In a context in which all the major media are owned by large corporations that are part of the military-industrial-governmental complex, resistance means finding alternate sources of information and refusing to be deceived by what we are repeatedly told. Progressive Christians need one another to support the bottom-up vision of the world.

Whereas the media treat the lives of Americans as vastly more important than others, being informed by the Bible means caring just as much about the suffering of those whom the United States has declared to be its enemies as about other Americans. It means recognizing that some of those who are demonized as terrorists are struggling sacrificially for the survival or the freedom of their people. It means seeing that changes that may be costly to us as middle-class North Americans may represent a gain on the part of many of the world's peoples.

Second, even though our nation, and indeed the world, seems bent on a self-destructive course, we must refuse to become hopeless. The Christian "hopes all things" (1 Cor. 13:7) and seeks always to find the good hidden in the bad. Even when we cannot identify any plausible scenario that would lead from where we are to where we want to go, we will not despair. We will discern God at work in unexpected ways and places. Accordingly, we will not adjust ourselves to living in terms of an imperialist culture. We will nourish our hope from the Bible and find elements of promise even in the darkest days.

In Isaiah, the voice of God speaks to the forsaken Zion:

> I will appoint Peace as your overseer
>   and Righteousness as your taskmaster.
> Violence shall no more be heard in your land.
>   (Isa. 60:17–18)

It may be that in the long run various lessons concerning the limits of military power, the need for international cooperation, the need for respecting cultural differences—indeed, the fundamental error of the "National Security Strategy"—will be learned.

Third, we will resist the temptation to divide the world into those who stand with us in opposition to the imperial culture and those who participate in it. We will recognize that all of us are caught up in the imperial culture and that all also have some longing for a just peace.

To refuse self-righteousness is not to abandon judgment. We may often be highly critical of national policies and actions even if we are careful not to reject those who advocate them as evil. For example, we will be highly critical of the division of the world into good and evil nations or good and evil persons while we try to avoid demonizing those who make such distinctions and act on them. We will be especially critical of any appeal to loyalty to Jesus Christ as a justification for trampling on those regarded as his enemies.

Christian Reflection about Fundamental Alternatives

This chapter has emphasized that the explicit advocacy of Pax Americana by the neoconservatives brings to public awareness policies that have in one way or another dominated American history from the coming of the first Europeans to our shores. We have always used superior military and economic power to conquer and control others.

It would be a mistake, therefore, for progressive Christians to suppose that returning to the policies of previous administrations would be a great gain. Indeed, it might lead concerned Americans to relax into acceptance of the global hegemony that is the natural outgrowth of our historic foreign policy in a time when the United States is the only superpower. Instead we should use this occasion, when many have been made aware of this goal of American policy, to reflect much more fundamentally on the role we want the United States to play in the world. If the goal is not global hegemony, then what?

An alternative to American imperial domination is strengthening existing international organizations such as the UN, the World Court, and the new International Criminal Court. In this alternative, all nations, including the United States, would observe internationally established rules and procedures.

Some believe that an adequate international order could be attained by such strengthening of existing institutions. It would require that the UN have its own permanent military force so as to enforce its rulings. The UN would need an independent source of revenue, such as a tax on the flow of money across national boundaries or on activities in international waters.

Others argue that the structure of the UN is fundamentally flawed. In this case a major focus would be on its transformation or replacement by another international body. This might be some kind of global institution such as that long advocated by World Federalists.[34]

Still others would emphasize the need for regional bodies like the European Union to develop around the world and handle many of the matters that are now dealt with at the global level. These regions could develop interregional institutions. If the UN were retained, the Security Council might be composed of representatives of these great regions, while the Assembly continued to represent individual nations.

Adoption of any of these patterns would require a drastic shift in American self-understanding and foreign policy. Progressive Christians should bring our distinctive perspective to bear on the discussion of both goals and policies that would lead toward them. To stimulate discussion of alternatives to empire may be one of the most effective means of resistance.

DISCUSSION QUESTIONS

1. It has been said that "nature abhors a vacuum." What moral, political, and/or economic vacuum did neoconservatives move into? Under what conditions did the neoconservative initiative arise?
2. If the United States were to emphasize multilateralism in its approach to foreign policy, what would need to be dropped, reinstated, and/or added for our present challenges?
3. As Christians, what should we envision for the role of the United States in the world today? What shifts in policy would be needed to support this? How can concerned Christians most effectively help these policies to be adopted and implemented? Is a pivotal event such as 9/11 necessary in our democracy to bring about significant changes?
4. Do you agree with the author that the United States has "little self-understanding of its own sinful history"? What do you think he means by this?
5. If American Christians need to give up our innocence about who we have been and who we continue to be, are we willing to articulate in our own words the policies we have often unthinkingly accepted?

FOR FURTHER READING

Griffin, David Ray, John B. Cobb Jr., Richard A. Falk, and Catherine Keller, *The American Empire and the Commonwealth of God*. Louisville, KY: Westminster John Knox Press, 2006.

Hoffman, Stanley. *Chaos and Violence: What Globalization, Failed States, and Terrorism Mean for U.S. Foreign Policy*. Lanham, MD: National Book Network, 2006.

Johnson, Chalmers. *The Sorrows of Empire: Militarism, Secrecy, and the End of the Republic*. New York: Metropolitan Books, 2004.

Murphy, Gretchen. *Hemispheric Imaginings: The Monroe Doctrine and Narratives of U.S. Empire*. Durham, NC: Duke University Press, 2005.

Rieger, Joerg. *Christ and Empire*. Minneapolis: Fortress Press, 2007.

Ruether, Rosemary Radford. *America, Amerikka: Elect Nation and Imperial Violence*. London: Equinox Publishing Company; Oakville, CT: DBBC, 2007.

Smith, Gaddis. *The Last Years of the Monroe Doctrine*. New York: Hill & Wang, 1994.

Zinn, Howard. *A People's History of the United States, 1492–Present*. San Francisco: HarperCollins, 2003.

6

Scientism

John B. Cobb Jr.

In October 1997 the National Association of Biology Teachers adopted the following statement: "The diversity of life on earth is the outcome of evolution: an unsupervised, impersonal, unpredictable and natural process of temporal descent with genetic modification that is affected by natural selection, chance, historical contingencies and changing environments."[1] They were led to do so by their opposition to Christian conservatives who argued that evolutionism was just one theory about the development of life alongside others and who wanted to introduce the teaching of "creationism" into the public schools as having equal plausibility. Some religious leaders not associated with creationism urged the association to drop the words "unsupervised" and "impersonal" because they implied a negative judgment about theism.

At first the association refused, but three days later, on October 11, it agreed. The board of directors recognized that just as creationism invaded their territory from the theological side, these terms could be construed as a commitment to atheism, which would be an invasion of the legitimate territory of theology. The biologists asserted that their intention had been only to say that "there is no evidence the process of evolution is directed from some source." As long as theologians do not claim that such evidence exists, they are free to say what they wish about God's relation to the world based on "faith."

INTRODUCTION

How people think about themselves is profoundly affected by what they believe about the world. In ancient times the determinative beliefs were mythological, and myth continues to play a large role. But around 2,500 years ago a process of rationalization began. In Greece it was primarily philosophical and scientific. In Israel the focus was ethical and theological. In India the greatest achievements were philosophical and religious. In China the most distinctive contributions were social and political. Of course, in no case was the rationalization limited to these emphases.

When Christianity became dominant in the West, theology became the encompassing intellectual context. It included much that had been learned through philosophy and ancient science and encouraged continuing work along these lines. Christians assumed that all truth was God's truth.

Today, however, theology, philosophy, and science have gone their separate ways. The dominant ethos of the modern Western university supports philosophy in a limited role and favors science as supreme in determining how we are to think of our world. Theology is largely excluded from the conversation.

Alongside the university are the religious communities, including those in the monotheistic traditions. These continue to mediate theological traditions. Young people grow up in these communities and absorb attitudes and values from them. But they are also immersed in an educational system that gives little credence to the beliefs about the world that support these attitudes and values. Increasingly, and especially as they become more highly educated, they are likely to think of the world as they learn about it from the sciences.

The tension between the understanding of the world in the sciences and in the religious traditions often focuses on the question of God. As we saw in the story with which this chapter begins, scientists in general insist that God cannot be considered an explanatory factor in the world they study. This is just as true of history, sociology, and psychology as of biology, and it is now true also in the study of religion. To whatever extent our understanding of our world is shaped by the dominant forms of science, God is excluded from relevance. If God is to be spoken of at all, it must be in the separate compartment of "faith." From the point of view of the dominant scientific culture, "faith" means believing that for which there is no evidence. This situation has developed in the past two centuries, and liberal Christians have allowed this change to take place with little protest because of their great appreciation for science. Even today scientists can count on liberal Christians to support their freedom in the public schools. Only very conservative Christians have resisted. However, the results are highly unfavorable for a healthy Christianity.

If we judged that the empirical facts learned by the sciences were themselves the cause of this unfavorable climate, we would have no choice, as progressive Christians, but to continue to support the freedom of scientists to teach as they wish. But we judge that it is time to question whether this is the case. Are the views of the teachers of biology required by the evidence, or are they the result of the philosophical ideas with which most of Western science has long been aligned? If, as it appears to us, the latter is the case, the time has come for progressive Christians to join in resistance. Accordingly, we propose that the Bible calls us to resist not only consumerism, poisonous inequality, and American imperialism, but also the scientism that now dominates the scholarly-intellectual-cultural world.

The currently standard evolutionary theory expresses the scientism that we are called to resist. Many of its proponents draw the conclusion not only of atheism but also of ethical nihilism. The recent writings of Richard Dawkins have successfully popularized this militant atheism.[2] It is time to resist the theoretical formulations that give rise to these conclusions.

Unfortunately, Christian opposition to the current teaching of evolution has taken forms that we cannot support. What is called "creationism" in particular can be affirmed only by ignoring or denying a great deal of well-established scientific knowledge. Arguments for "intelligent design" accept the basic form of standard science but then argue that there are gaps that require a different explanation. Acceptance of these theories would undermine the whole scientific enterprise. Progressive Christians are committed to the support of that enterprise.

It is our hope that a Christianity that fully adapts to the knowledge that the sciences have undoubtedly contributed and fully supports the continuing work of science may be able to challenge the sciences to reformulate themselves in a way that is open to the contribution of wisdom from the religious traditions, including Christianity. The period in which the advance of science has meant the retreat of faith may be ending.

Any hope for change of this kind assumes that the dominant understanding of science and faith in the modern university is mistaken. In this understanding, faith is opposed to knowledge, so that the advance of science is inherently destructive of faith. The conventional picture is that believers cling to particular views of the world that derive from myth and have no foundation in evidence. These cannot withstand the onslaughts of science, which is based on an objective investigation of the facts. The church's condemnation of Galileo, based on the refusal to examine the empirical evidence, is taken as typifying the relation of the church to science. This relation is seen as having come to a head in the controversies over evolution. It is then supposed that although science has won in the educational system, some churches keep the opposition alive in the general culture.

FOUR POSITIONS

In debates about the relation of faith and science, there are currently three main positions. First, there are those who understand themselves to represent victorious science. As previously indicated, this view is dominant in our universities. It allows no positive role for religious traditions. These, at least so far as their distinctive beliefs are concerned, are depicted as superstitious and outdated. All reliable truth is to be learned from science. We call this "scientism." It was the position of those who initially formulated the statement of the National Association of Biology Teachers.

Second, there are Christians who insist that the Bible, as the Word of God, is authoritative in all fields, so that scientific findings contradicting it must be invalid. They insist that a theory consonant with their reading of the Bible be given an equal place in the teaching of biology in the public schools. We may call this position "biblicism." It is the position of creationists, and it was the reaction of the biology teachers against the political resurgence of this biblicism that led them to their strong statement.

After conservative Christians realized that creationism would not make headway in the public schools, they began to promote the theory of intelligent design. Part of the negative reaction to this doctrine came from the fact that its teaching was supported by many of the same groups who had backed creationism. From the point of view of progressive Christians who are critical of scientism, however, this theory is not as easily dismissed.

Proponents of intelligent design point to evolutionary developments that are, indeed, difficult to understand in the purely mechanistic terms of the dominant theory. They argue that these phenomena are more easily understood as results of intelligent design. Accordingly the theory of evolution should be taught with that possibility clearly expressed.

Intelligent design is more open to empirical evidence than creationism, and less offensive to science. In a broad and loose interpretation, most theists subscribe to it. We believe that intelligent purpose has played a role in bringing our world into being.

Nevertheless, the theory that has been presented under the rubric of intelligent design is highly problematic. In its usual formulation, it seems to suppose that most events in the biological sphere occur through purely mechanical causes and that only occasionally does a distinct type of causation come into play. This violates the basic scientific principle of uniformity. Thus far advocates of intelligent design have not come up with examples of evolutionary developments that *cannot* be explained by standard biological theories. Hence, they are making little headway among scientists who are not committed on religious grounds to a role for God. This theory is also theologically offensive in that it presents the divine role in the world as episodic.

Third, there are various forms of dualism. These hold that theology and science have separate spheres within which they do their proper work. For some Christians, the dualism is ontological, that is, between the sphere of mind and that of matter. For some it is methodological, with science appealing to empirical evidence and theology to revelation. For some, it is formulated as the difference between the natural and the supernatural. For some it leads to the belief that each side should leave the other alone, whereas others emphasize points of contact and hope to expand these.

A particularly influential form of dualism among liberal Protestant theologians expresses the influence of Immanuel Kant. It distinguishes between the world of facts and the world of values and meanings. Faith deals only with these latter questions. For this reason, many insist, there can be no conflict between a science that stays in its proper bounds and a theology that understands its limits. Our account of the limitations of dualism will have these theologians chiefly in view.

There are problems with all these positions. Scientism assumes that all questions of truth are to be answered by science. But scientific knowledge cannot deal with the whole range of human experience and need. Also, the science that is absolutized by scientism is couched in a mechanistic and reductionistic worldview, whose implications are humanly devastating. They even undermine the ideas and ideals of science itself.

Christians who argue against widely held scientific accounts are often rightly sensitive to their spiritually destructive implications. But biblicists attribute a kind of authority to the Bible that it cannot have. They bring disrepute to the faith when they use ancient prescientific teachings to contradict carefully developed scientific theories. At a deeper level, the Bible itself calls for openness to truth wherever it may be learned. And despite a very mixed record, the church has tended to follow this principle.

The dualists try to solve the problem by a sharp division between the realms of religious and scientific thought. But they exaggerate the separability of what we believe as Christians from what science teaches us about the world, even if we reduce the former to expressions about the meaning of life. For example, if we accept the idea that everything is determined by mechanical causes, we cannot understand ourselves as responsible beings. Beliefs about fact and value cannot be kept in airtight compartments.

A normal education today gives the impression that the realistic picture of the actual world is gained from the natural sciences. This picture is mechanistic, materialist, and, therefore, reductionist. There is a strong tendency to accept the implications of this understanding of reality for understanding also ourselves. The message that there is another realm or approach in which values and meanings are taken seriously does little to counter the belief that any such approach, being nonscientific, is less reliable. Hence the meanings that actually dominate the lives of open-minded people are increasingly informed by the worldview associated with the sciences. The sphere left for Christian reflection becomes more and more limited.

In addition to the three positions that are most prominent today, there is another that has played a large role in the past and, we believe, should be renewed: it is the idea that theology and science belong together in a single, coherent worldview. The effort to develop such a worldview has been largely abandoned since Kant. Liberals have rightly adjusted their teaching to what we have learned from science, but success required that typical scientific formulations also be modified. Liberal theologians draw back from making such a demand. Nevertheless, the current situation at the cutting edges of science encourages us, as progressive Christians, to believe that a new integration is possible.

A DIFFERENT HISTORY

We can move toward a different way of thinking about faith and science by telling a more accurate story about their historical connections. The story begins by noting that modern science was developed by Christians on the basis of beliefs derived from the synthesis of Greek and Hebraic thought and modified by the influence of Islamic scientists and philosophers. The conviction that motivated much scientific research was that behind the seeming disorder of things was a deeper order. And the reason for the confidence that this deeper order existed lay in the belief that a rational God created the world. By learning more about the creation, the early scientists believed, they gained greater knowledge of God.

Scientists were not all equally orthodox in their theology. Giordano Bruno was a pantheist, and for this heresy he was executed. He was virtually the only scientist to have been killed for his beliefs during centuries in which science transformed the human understanding of the world. This absence of severe persecution was not due, Christians must regretfully acknowledge, to any hesitation of the church to kill its enemies. During the period in which science arose, tens of thousands of heretics were slaughtered. The witchcraft trials resulted in mass killings. Scientists were largely left alone because the church basically supported their enterprise.

Then what about the silencing of Galileo? He was opposed by the Aristotelians, who dominated the science of his time. They rightly saw that Galileo sharply undercut their whole cosmology. The church had accepted that cosmology as the best available science of the time, and, therefore, it backed the dominant community of scientists against Galileo. This was, of course, a serious mistake, but it did not express a hostile attitude toward science in general. Instead, it illustrates two points: scientists committed to a dominant paradigm resist radical change; and it is difficult for nonscientists to know how to take sides in scientific debates. It is especially difficult to know when the church should oppose the scientific establishment and give its support to minority scientific voices, as we are proposing here. It would not be difficult to show that modern scientists themselves have means of silencing those who threaten their paradigms.

The rise of modern science is often presented as the overthrow of Aristotelianism by mechanism. Actually, in the sixteenth and seventeenth centuries there was a ferment of thought, much of which differed markedly from both of these options. No one label applies well to the diverse thinkers in this third group, although the recovery of Neoplatonic philosophy played a role in much of their work.

On the one side, the roots of this movement in Pythagoras and Plato led to an emphasis on mathematics that had been muted by Aristotelianism. On the other side, attention focused more on the unique powers of different things than on the motions imposed on them from without. Many of these Neoplatonic thinkers affirmed that all the entities in nature, like organisms, had an interior being and were in some measure self-moving or self-determining. Many believed that they affected one another and took account of one another, not only on contact but also at a distance, as appeared to be the case in magnetism and gravity. Frances Bacon, a member of this group, wrote, "It is certain that all bodies, whatsoever, though they have no sense, yet they have perception; for when one body is applied to another, there is a kind of election to embrace that which is agreeable, and to exclude or expel that which is ingrate. . . . And this perception is sometimes at a distance, as well as upon touch."[3]

The other opponent of Aristotelianism was mechanism. Here the model was the clock rather than the organism. The clock appears to function purposefully, but in fact every movement in the clock can be explained fully by efficient causes. These causes operate by direct contact, so there is no action at a distance. Also, there is no agency or intentionality in the elements that make up the machine. The final causes, so important in Aristotelian science, are to be excluded from science altogether.

Following this model, science views the objects of its study as purely material or passive, that is, as having no interiority or principle of action. Even living things were to be understood as explicable in terms of matter in motion, with the exception of human beings, who were understood to have a supernatural soul. Some scientists have attempted to understand gravity in these mechanical terms, but for Newton the impossibility of doing so testified to the direct agency of God. In any case, the mechanical model required that the laws of nature be imposed on the passive objects making up nature from without. Thus, in its origins, the mechanistic model was united with supernaturalism.

Scientists of all three schools made significant contributions to the advance of science. The mechanistic worldview won out not so much because it provided a superior context for research or a more comprehensive explanation of what was observed, but for theological and political reasons. René Descartes chose the mechanistic model in large part because it gave greater support to the church. His reasoning is interesting.

Important for the church's authority over its people was belief in life after death. Descartes saw that the mechanistic model gave the strongest support to that doctrine precisely by separating the soul from the body. If the soul is intimately related to the body and continuous with it, as some Neoplatonists supposed, then it may well share its mortality. If, on the other hand, the human body is simply a part of the world machine, then the soul is of a radically different order. The physical reasons for the mortality of the body have no application to the wholly different type of entity that is the soul. Whereas everything physical is ephemeral, the soul can be understood to be eternal.

Another reason for favoring the mechanistic view was the role of miracles, for which it allowed. The theoretical authority of the church was justified in large part by the occurrence of miracles. Jesus' miracles, especially the resurrection, were understood to prove his divinity. The miracles performed in the early church showed the authority of its teachings. Protestants tended to argue that once the New Testament was canonized, miracles ceased. The Catholic Church insisted that miracles continued within it and thereby demonstrated the supernatural character of the church. Most of these miracles were nonmedical healings. If these could be explained naturalistically, as the Neoplatonists tended to teach, then they provided far less support to the church's claims.

If, on the other hand, within the sphere of nature physical events are caused entirely by other physical events on contact, as the mechanistic model required, then the healing of one person by another, without medical means, is clearly outside of natural possibility. It is supernatural. The connection of such miracles with the church provided support for its claims.

The authority of the church was not of interest only on theological grounds. It was regarded as the bastion of social order. Political authorities were concerned that any weakening of its authority would endanger them as well. The support of popular uprisings by some of the members of the group we are calling Neoplatonic, such as Paracelsus, confirmed this suspicion. The view that order is imposed from above, rather than arising from the partly free movements of the beings that are ruled, suited political conservatives much better.

Initially the victory of the mechanistic worldview gave support to the church as Descartes had expected. However, the growth and spread of the mechanistic worldview led to increasing skepticism about whether *any* event had *ever* violated natural law—as miracles were supposed to do. The great debate in the eighteenth century was between deists and supernaturalists. The deists taught that God's creation was so perfect that it needed and received no interventions from its creator. The supernaturalists argued that the fulfillment of God's purposes in creation required occasional miracles. The proponents of intelligent design are reviving a similar argument.

This debate was not between believers and scientists. Both sides supported science, and both sides held to theological beliefs. The debate was between two types of theologians. Both groups assumed that the world had been created in much its present form and that this required an omnipotent and omniscient Creator, who laid down the laws of nature. The issue was only whether this same Creator sometimes overruled these laws.

Already in the eighteenth century, some doubted Christian teaching more radically. The most influential of these skeptics was David Hume, whose most radical conclusion was about causality. Hume was a thoroughgoing empiricist who argued that what is empirically given is nothing but the data of our senses, such as sounds and patches of color. If we carefully observe these data, we see that they change through time. We can discern repeated patterns of change, so when we see one billiard ball contact another, we expect the movement of the other billiard ball in a certain direction. This discernment gives rise to our judgment of causality, which typically contains an element of necessitation. We suppose that the movement of the first ball compelled the other to move, but given Hume's limitation of empirical evidence to that provided by the sense organs, there was no basis for this conclusion. By causality we are then justified in meaning only regularly observed succession.

Of course, most scientists continued their pursuit of causal relations, paying little attention to Hume's challenge, but Kant appreciated the force of Hume's analysis and understood its devastating implications for the science of his day. He was convinced that we cannot avoid understanding physical relations in terms of necessary causes, which must be contributed by the mind. Thus Kant was led to focus on the creative contribution of the mind to the ordering and interpretation of all experience.

Kant thereby "saved" the science of his day from the implications of Hume's sensory empiricism. But Hume's analysis was even more devastating for theology. God's existence as the cause of the world had seemed self-evident. But if cause is nothing but the regular succession of sense data, then God cannot be a cause. We have no sensory perception of God creating the world. A fortiori there can be no repeated patterns of succession of God's act and the emergence of the created order. Kant's response, likewise, provides no basis for thinking of God as cause of the world or of any event whatever.

Although both Hume and Kant were influential among the intellectual
elite, their exclusion of the possibility of God's creative work in the world did
not gain a popular following until the second half of the nineteenth century.
As long as people supposed that the world came into being in much the form
in which we find it, there seemed to most of them no alternative but to affirm
a supernatural Creator. Evolutionary theory changed this. What was originally
brought into being was far simpler than what now exists. Furthermore, according to Darwin's theory of evolution, the development of complex organisms
came about through natural processes. Although Darwin himself affirmed a
deistic worldview, according to which God created the first molecules with a
propensity to evolve, the perceived need for a Creator rapidly declined.

The doctrine of evolution threatened Christian faith in other ways as well.
Prior to its development, there was almost universal agreement that the human
mind or soul is not part of the world machine. But the Darwinian theory of
evolution implied that it is. Soul and body evolved together. In due course, the
soul or mind came to be identified with the brain.

There were moral implications as well that were unacceptable from a Christian point of view. Darwinian evolutionists affirmed "survival of the fittest" as
the means by which the genetic pool is improved. The implication was drawn
by some Social Dorwinists that this principle applies in the human sphere
as well. The effort to keep those who are "unfit" alive and to give them the
opportunity to propagate goes against the grain of natural advance. Instead of
preserving those who are physical and social failures, society should allow
them to die.

As a result of this new set of teachings emerging from science, for the first
time warfare between science and Christian faith did emerge on a large scale
in the late nineteenth century. The battles were complex and indecisive. The
warfare left wounds that have not healed, including the false impression that
faith is antithetical to science. Liberal theologians who were unwilling to
engage in this warfare developed three alternatives. One was to affirm Darwinian evolution but to interpret it as the way God creates. This interpretation was possible because Darwin himself did not provide a full explanation of
the emergence of the changes in the organisms among which nature selected.
However, when biologists integrated Darwin with Mendelian genetics, they
argued that random mutation of genes accounted for these changes, and it was
more difficult for theologians to connect God to this random mutation.

The second alternative was to follow the Kantian tradition. Kant excluded
any causal connection between God and the events studied by the sciences, but
he affirmed that there is another sphere in which God is rightly posited. This
is the sphere of "practical reason" or ethics. The modes of reasoning applica-

ble here, he taught, are entirely different from those suitable to the study of the natural world. This is where theology should make its home.

The details of Kant's analysis of practical reason have not been widely followed, but most theologians turned to distinctively human experience as the only place where talk of God can be grounded. Schleiermacher, often called the "father of liberal theology," built his theology on religious experience. Albrecht Ritschl based his neo-Kantian theology on the distinction of ethical experience from factual information. He argued that theology is not concerned with facts but only with their evaluation.

Neo-orthodox theologians challenged many features of liberal theology, but for the most part they accepted a Kantian separation of theology from the natural sciences. They carefully formulated their theologies in ways that left the topics dealt with by natural sciences alone. For most of them, God's revelation tells us nothing about the world that scientists study. The dualistic response of the dominant community of theologians, once established in the nineteenth century, was little questioned in the twentieth. Indeed, it has become almost an article of faith that scientific developments are irrelevant to theology.

The third alternative is to introduce a new paradigm into scientific thinking, perhaps more like that of the seventeenth-century Neoplatonists. This would make possible more positive relations between science and theology. Fortunately for this project, changes in physics in the twentieth century are calling for some such change.

A distinct community of persons interested in establishing a positive relation between science and religion has emerged. It includes both theologians and scientists, and their writings have often attracted wide public interest. One thinks of Teilhard de Chardin's *The Phenomenon of Man.*[4] Nevertheless, through most of the century the interests of this community were marginalized and ignored in both theology and science.

Toward the end of the century this community began to gain more visibility and more status. For example, the Vatican held a series of international conferences to advance the discussion about science and theology, and new centers and institutes developed, such as the Center for Theology and the Natural Sciences in Berkeley. John Templeton devoted much of his wealth to the promotion of these interests, and most of the Templeton prizes for the advancement of religion have gone to scientists with an interest in the religious implications of their work.[5] Much remains to be done before these concerns become mainstream in either theology or science, but the changes that have already occurred may point the way for the twenty-first century. We believe that this third response to scientism is the most promising for progressive Christians to adopt.

OPENING FOR NEW REFLECTIONS

Currently, three of the main foci of theoretical interest in the relation of science and religion, in addition to evolution, are quantum theory, ecology, and the big bang.

Quantum Theory

In the early twentieth century, scientists discovered within science the limits of the mechanistic worldview with which they had largely identified science itself. Recognition of these limits became inescapable in the study of quanta. This field is often still called quantum "mechanics," but the quanta cannot be treated as tiny bits of matter pushed and pulled by contiguous forces. They are better understood as bursts of energy, interconnected in a vast field of such events. These events appear to influence one another at a distance. Whereas the goal of science had been to demonstrate how mechanical principles explained all physical behavior, this goal has been abandoned here. The principle of indeterminacy prevailed.

Although many scientists have wanted to pursue their research in other areas as if the mechanistic worldview were intact, others have recognized that the implications of quantum theory should be thought through. Since everything is composed of quanta, the challenge to the mechanistic worldview associated with science is serious. Psychologically, abandoning the mechanistic model has proved to be extremely difficult, but a few have developed models more like those of the early Neoplatonists. They see the entities of which the world is composed as being self-determining agents rather than passive lumps of matter. They are more like inwardly interconnected organisms than like machines. The possibility of an alternative model, capable of accounting for the evidence, shows that the hold of mechanistic thinking over the minds of scientists is a historically contingent matter of social conditioning rather than the sort of necessity that Kant supposed.

One major line of reflection on the part of those interested in science and religion has been from indeterminacy in the realm of quanta to freedom on the part of human beings. The denial of this possibility implied by the dominant science of the past has been one main reason for the adoption of the dualistic approach by theology. The debate continues.

Ecology

A second area of public interest developing out of science has been ecology. As a subbranch of biology, ecology emerged in the nineteenth century. It encouraged attention to biological systems and their relation to geological ones. But it remained an obscure specialty until in the 1960s some of its practitioners sounded the alarm about how human actions are undermining and degrading the biosphere.

Ecology does not challenge orthodox science as radically as does quantum theory. Much of the work of ecologists is done within the mechanistic paradigm. Yet ecologists call attention to the interconnection of things in a way that is in tension with deeply entrenched habits stemming from the mechanistic paradigm. Most scientists seek the explanation of large-scale phenomena in the functioning of their parts. Ecologists emphasize that one cannot understand what is happening in any one part of the system without attending to what is happening throughout. This emphasis has encouraged systems thinking in the sciences.

To have this publicly important part of science reinforcing ideas required by the data of quantum research has helped to change the public image of the implications of science. Many now draw from science the lesson of interconnectedness instead of the lesson of reductionism. The greater congeniality to Christian theology is evident.

Ecology has also established in the public mind the practical importance of science for social policy. The dualistic view of natural science on the one side and the social sphere on the other is now recognized as problematic. Dualism has led to economic thinking that ignores the effects of human activity on the environment. It has led humanists in general to view the natural world more as a stage on which the human drama is enacted than itself an actor in that drama. Most historians long ignored the great importance of natural phenomena in shaping human behavior, resulting, for example, in the downfall of civilizations or massive migrations of people. We know now that a government concerned about the well-being of its people must listen to the natural scientists. The resistance of the administration of the younger President Bush to taking account of scientific information about the world illustrates the harm that is done by failing to listen.

We recognize that the continuing power of dualism leads to fragmentation of thought. Progressive Christians do not want to develop their theology without full consideration of what the many sciences can teach us. For theology to maintain a distance from this knowledge becomes more damaging and more difficult. Whereas liberal theology in the past dealt only with relations among human beings, now, in principle, progressive Christians want to take account of what is happening in the natural world and to relate ethically with other forms of life.

One reason for opposing scientism today is that it has eventuated in the fragmentation of knowledge, which has led the great majority of academic disciplines to ignore the great threats to the human and biospheric future. For example, most economic projections and the policies based on them continue to ignore global warming. So do most discussion of new developments in medicine and health care or even agriculture and city planning. Yet the now-inescapable changes in planetary weather are of great importance in all these areas. The lack of holistic and integrated thinking has contributed immeasurably to our failure to take account of the scientific awareness of global warming in all our thinking about the future. In the next chapter we will describe this crisis and how progressive Christians respond.

The Big Bang

The third development that has challenged the dualistic separation of theology from science has been the rise of the new cosmogony. In the nineteenth and early twentieth centuries the implication of science seemed to be that the cosmos we know had been around forever. In that context, theologians reformulated the doctrine of creation to refer to the existential dependence of creatures on God.

In the latter part of the twentieth century, a new cosmogony arose. It is popularly called the big bang. It has achieved dominance in the scientific community, although alternative interpretations of the data are still being advanced. In any case, most now agree that our universe had a beginning and moves toward an end. Of course, the time scale is vastly different from the one that theologians once derived from the Bible, but the parallels with Christian tradition remain striking. Of particular importance is the discovery of the very specific contingent principles that had to be in place from the beginning of this universe in order that life could emerge.

Although most theologians, schooled in dualism, continue to ignore the implications, the idea of an intelligent creator with great foresight and power arises quite naturally in response to the contemporary picture of the big bang. A number of scientists find this important. It is, of course, possible to assert that the adaptation of the cosmos to the support of life is pure chance, but most scientists are reluctant to appeal to chance when the probabilities, as in this case, are extremely low. At the same time, most of them oppose any opening to the use of God as explanatory of what happens in the cosmos.

We saw this opposition in the biology teachers who want to exclude any form of purpose from the explanation of evolution. We can find it among physiological psychologists, who are loath to allow conscious experience to play any role in the explanation of what happens in the brain. We can see it in the a priori denial of parapsychological phenomena despite the empirical evidence in their favor. To include mental acts as causal elements in an account of the physical world is felt by scientists in general to be nonscientific.

This view of what is scientific is the consequence of the commitment to materialism rather than of openness to empirical evidence. But even those who would not rigidly exclude evidence for the influence of mental states on physical events are likely to balk at including God as a part of the explanation of physical events. They associate God with the supernatural, and much of the history of modern science has been the quest for natural causes to supersede supernatural explanations.

Accordingly, the dominant response of scientists today is to develop amazing theories for which, at best, there is only very indirect support. For example, some propose that this universe is one of many that may be thought of as successive or as all existing concurrently. In the latter case it is theorized that these concurrent universes can have no influence on one another, so no direct evidence against (or for) this hypothesis is conceivable.

Few progressive Christians are in a position to judge whether the view that ours is but one of many universes is correct and, if so, which of the theories about this multiverse is most plausible. However, we can see that a major reason for the development of these theories has been to reduce the grounds for positing a role for intelligent purpose in the creation of this universe. We note also that in the past supporters of scientism often used against speculative philosophy and theology the argument that their theories were not in principle provable or disprovable by empirical data. The application of this criterion would exclude from science most of the work that is now being done by leading scientists on multiverses. In short, scientists are willing to redefine science itself in order to weaken apparent evidence for the role of God in the coming to be of this world. Recognizing this fact can lead us to be less uncritical in our acceptance of the authority of "science."

A DIFFERENT RESPONSE

Given the fluidity of the current discussion and a more accurate reading of history, we can approach the issue of faith and the natural sciences in a quite different way. We see that faith supported science and adapted quickly to its findings at every point except with respect to evolutionary thought. If faith is to be faulted, it is for its acquiescence and even support for the reductionist, materialist worldview that came to be associated with science. It was commitment to this worldview that generated the crisis associated with evolutionary theory. That mechanistic worldview is now in trouble within science itself, and we thus need to rethink its acceptance.

There have been changes in theology that make it more open to what can be known of the physical world. In the early modern period, it was possible to think of a purely spiritual soul inhabiting a purely mechanical body. But during the twentieth century this understanding of the relation of the psyche and the soma came under multifold attack within theology. Most theological traditions now emphasize embodiment, and biblical scholars have recovered the unity of body and soul in the Bible. This suggests that Christians should join others in proposing new models for scientific thinking, models that integrate the mental and the physical, display the connectedness of all things, and reject reductionism. The empirical evidence provided by the sciences can be formulated in terms of such a model as well as, indeed, better than, in the mechanistic way.

Since it was evolutionary theory that brought the opposition of the mechanistic model and Christian faith to a head, let us consider how that might be reframed. Instead of assuming that the evidence for evolution proves that we are nothing but complex patterns of atoms in motion, we may start with what we know best: ourselves. We know that we are living beings who feel and think and make decisions. If we are products of the evolutionary process, participants in it, and therefore closely related to its other products and participants, then it makes sense to suppose that they, at least our closer relatives, are also living beings who feel and think and make decisions. In short, instead of viewing the evolutionary process only from the bottom up, extending the materialistic ideas that are so easily associated with the simplest entities to the more complex ones, we can take seriously what we know of more complex beings and then hypothesize that, in simpler forms, similar characteristics may be present even in elementary entities.

Such a shift has practical consequences. For one thing, it changes our valuation of other forms of animal life. Just as we recognize unique value in ourselves, we are led to acknowledge unique value in them as well. We should not treat other animals as mechanisms that have their value simply as means to human ends.

At the theoretical level, the top-down view leads to a fundamental challenge to the account that is still dominant in scientific communities. We see that it is a mistake to exclude purposiveness from a role in the evolutionary process. Clearly, purposive human action today is having an enormous effect on the evolutionary future of the planet. Among human beings, it influences who lives, who reproduces, and who dies. With respect to other animals, the fate of whole species is in our hands.

Most biologists acknowledge that current human purposive action has importance for the evolutionary future, but they are less likely to affirm the extensive evidence that the purposive behavior of other animals has also influenced evolutionary developments. Consider a simple example. Some birds use sticks to spear worms inside of holes in trees. One may, of course, say that this is now instinctive. But one can trace such a species back to ancestors that did not do this. One can also find that the genetic pool has been affected by this new means of getting food.

The dominant theory assumes that this behavior was acquired by chance. That is, of course, possible. That is, the first bird to spear a worm in this way may have been engaged in exploratory behavior, without any purpose of getting food. However, if purpose played no role in bird behavior, this would have been simply a random event with no consequences. That the bird in question repeated the act and that others imitated it was surely purposeful. The birds wanted food, and they learned that this was a way of obtaining it. Those best adapted to getting food in this way improved their likelihood of reproducing. Their genes played an increasing role in the gene pool.

The neglect of this evidence by mainstream biologists indicates the power of the mechanistic model in shaping what counts as evidence. Once the inadequacy of that model for physics is fully appreciated, there seems to be no reason to insist on its completeness for the purposes of biology. Surely biology can develop better with an organic model!

To invite biologists to change their model from machine to organism is not an attack on science. Many scientists criticize the Aristotelian astronomers for refusing to look through Galileo's telescope for fear of having to abandon their basic paradigm. But all too many of them are equally resistant today to considering the evidence that their basic paradigm is inadequate. Those who are truly committed to science rather than to a now-outdated paradigm are opening themselves to the possibility of adopting a new paradigm. It is legitimate for theologians to encourage such shifts that will benefit science and also bring forth scientific formulations with which Christian teaching can be in harmony.

A major reason for excluding purpose of all types from evolutionary theory is the fear that once its reality is acknowledged, religious believers may find an opening for a role for God. The fear is justified. In particular it is justified when we have an understanding of causality that does not depend on successions of sense data. But in the foreseeable future, theologians need not ask biologists to speak of what God is doing in the evolutionary process. The process can be described and studied in a richer way with organic categories without raising the question of God.

Nevertheless, the theory formulated in this way no longer excludes a role for God. Believers think that in our own lives God calls and we respond. God does not control our responses, but even when we resist God's call, it affects us. If we are products of the evolutionary process, there is no reason to limit God's persuasive work to human beings.

This does not mean that God has a single specific goal in mind for the evolutionary process, one that will, therefore, inevitably be achieved. This is the idea that evolutionists have most strongly opposed—and with good reason. The evidence does not support this role for God. There is no evidence that God aimed at just the specific results that have been realized, that the process was preprogrammed from the beginning. On the contrary, chance and myriads of individual purposes have played a role along with necessity.

We may claim that the evidence not only allows for belief that God also plays a role but actually encourages it. There are many mysteries in the evolutionary account. The origin of life is so astonishing that some scientists find it easier to believe that it came from some other part of the universe than that it emerged here. Frances Crick commented, "An honest man, armed with all the knowledge available to us now, could only state that in some sense, the origin of life appears at the moment to be almost a miracle, so many are the conditions which would have to have been satisfied to get it going."[6]

There are many other extremely complex and somewhat improbable processes that took place rather rapidly, requiring multiple coordinated developments. Indeed, even quite ordinary events seem "miraculous" when fully considered. The repeated protests against standard evolutionary theory by those who find that it requires excessive credulity should not be dismissed lightly. There is no doubt that chance and necessity, which are the only explanatory principles recognized by the dominant theory, played a large role in this whole process. But it would all be easier to understand, and some events much easier, if we supposed that a persuasive divine influence was operative as well.

WHAT DOES THE BIBLE SAY?

What we find the Bible saying to us on the relation of faith to science depends on our way of reading the Bible. For many centuries leading Christians studied the Bible for hints about the answers to scientific questions. For example, some believed that the references to the four corners of the earth implied that the earth is flat and rectangular. Some believed they could determine the age of the earth from careful study of biblical history. Such extremes have almost disappeared, although some fundamentalists still tend in that direction, especially on questions about the beginning and ending of the world. Most Christians, on the other hand, suppose that biblical writers reflected the beliefs about the natural world that were prevalent in their day. We look for the religious meaning that shaped their interpretation of these prescientific beliefs.

If we accept a mechanistic worldview that denies any role to purpose in the forming of our world, then the values taught by biblical authors who believed that the world was created by a God who continues to act within it are undercut. If we reformulate the vast data provided by the sciences in terms of an organic worldview, much of the basic biblical vision can be reformulated and reaffirmed.

Does the Bible support this project? In one respect, there is no question but that it does. The Bible knows nothing of the separation of bodies of knowledge into airtight compartments. For the Bible all truth is God's truth. No alternative even occurs to its writers. Furthermore, Israelite faith was repeatedly modified and enriched as it incorporated elements from other cultures and traditions. For biblical writers generally, faithfulness to God and the tradition consisted in responding freshly to new situations. This process of creative transformation of tradition continued in the New Testament. New Testament authors certainly did not feel bound simply to repeat what earlier authors had written.

The Sermon on the Mount is explicit about Jesus' freedom to go beyond standard inherited teaching. Jesus is represented as saying repeatedly, "'You have heard that it was said. . . . But I say to you'" (Matt. 5:21–48). Paul repeatedly critiques the role that law played in the dominant Jewish thought of his day. Furthermore, there is no claim in the biblical writings themselves that the last word has been spoken. In John, Jesus' promises that "'when the Spirit of Truth comes, he will guide you into all the truth'" (John 16:13). Paul declares, "[Now] we know only in part, and we prophesy only in part; but when the complete comes, the partial will come to an end" (1 Cor. 13:9–10).

Of course, what is in view in these passages is not modern science; it is basic religious belief. But if we are to look forward to learning more about basic religious truth, then surely we are to be open to change and development in other areas of our thinking as well! In ways not foreseen by biblical authors, these also throw light on the meaning of our existence before God. Although biblical writers were open to change and call us to be open as well, they certainly do not encourage every form of change. Paul passionately opposed the change that he heard was taking place in the Galatian church. The nature of his response is important for our consideration today.

Many suppose that the way to prevent harmful changes is to summarize the doctrines or moral teachings that constitute the essence of true Christianity and to hold them fast regardless of historical change. Paul did not do this. He did not try to establish either an orthodoxy or an orthopraxis. He appealed instead to the fundamental nature of Christian existence: "Having started with the Spirit, are you now ending with the flesh?" (Gal. 3:3). For Paul the question was whether what is new is the work of the Spirit or a succumbing to the flesh. He provides powerful indications of the difference between what is of the Spirit and what is of the flesh (see, e.g., Rom. 8:1–17). But to apply this vision to our response to changing contexts, such as the changing context wrought in the modern world by the hegemony of scientific thinking, requires imagination and creativity.

Our judgment is that clinging to either a prescientific or a scientific cosmology in the face of negative empirical evidence is an expression of the power of the flesh, not that of the Spirit. Certainly any effort to block the pursuit of truth is an action against the Spirit of truth. To appeal to the Bible in support of the repression of science would indeed be a travesty. But equally, the acceptance of a worldview that denies the reality of the Spirit and crushes the human spirit is yielding to the flesh.

REFORM AND RESISTANCE

In these chapters we are recognizing the possibilities for reform but emphasizing the need for resistance. We have spoken of reform where there are possibilities of desirable change and means of working for it. We have spoken of resistance where the established currents are so strong that there are no apparent ways of effecting change.

The previous discussion suggests that some change is possible, so our task is to reform the way the sciences now interpret their data. Outside of academia these changes are readily discussed. For this reason the situation with respect to scientism is different from that of consumerism, poisonous inequality, and American imperialism. However, within academia and within the separate scientific disciplines, commitment to the inherited assumptions and patterns is so deep that the idea of reform is hardly relevant. Graduate education in almost any science is so bound up with socialization into the acceptance of the mechanistic worldview that few scientists are really able to contemplate the possibility of transposing their science in a new key. At every educational level the teaching of science and the inculcation of a mechanistic worldview go hand in hand with no acknowledgment of their difference.

On the Christian side, the assumption that science should be left to the scientists is so deeply entrenched among liberals and those influenced by neo-orthodoxy that they offer no real resistance to the destructive teaching of scientism throughout the educational system. The fact that conservative Christians have opposed this reductionist materialist teaching only strengthens the commitment of liberals and the neo-orthodox not to do so. They are rightly committed to the freedom of scientists to investigate anything and everything. They are rightly committed to adjust to responsible scientific findings. They rightly object to Christian interventions in science that are not scientifically responsible.

Precisely because so many of our fellow Christians with whom we are generally allied are committed to the support of scientists against criticism by Christians, I have devoted most of this chapter to arguing that developments within science call for changes that most scientists are not yet making. To encourage them to make these changes is not opposing science. It is opposing the seventeenth-century worldview with which science has been bound up. It is not antiscientific for Christians to oppose metaphysics that is both philosophically weak and profoundly damaging spiritually.

Mechanistic modes of understanding are so deeply entrenched and their implications are so widely accepted that, for the most part, Christians who reject the dualistic solution are placed in the stance of resistance. We resist by continuing within the church to insist on the reality of human freedom and responsibility. We continue to emphasize how we are members one of another and indeed of the wider community of living things. We deny that we are self-contained beings and affirm that we are largely constituted by our relations with one another and with God. To teach this interrelatedness is a crucial form of resistance because none of it makes any sense in terms of the mechanistic view that dominates so much of the culture and especially what is taught in universities.

But in this chapter we are arguing that we can go beyond this stance. There is a great deal of evidence that does not fit the mechanistic worldview. Many of the mainstream efforts to deal with this evidence remind us of the efforts to save the classical view that all heavenly bodies move in perfect circles by introducing epicycles. As more and more epicycles are required to save the mechanistic model, the likelihood increases that more scientists will be open to adopting another one. As progressive Christians we have every reason to encourage that move.

That our quarrel with current scientific formulations is about metaphysics is made clear by one of the most philosophically sophisticated defenders of scientistic metaphysics, Richard Lewontin. In a review of a book by Carl Sagan, Lewontin stated that he and Sagan and many other scientists, because of "their commitment to materialism," allow only materialistic explanations in science "in spite of [their] patent absurdity." He asserts "that materialism is absolute for we cannot allow a Divine Foot in the door." Lewontin goes on to explain that the reason God must be excluded even at the cost of patent absurdity is that the alternative would be "to allow that at any moment the regularities of nature may be ruptured, that miracles may happen."[7] Perhaps progressive Christians can show that it is possible to avoid the patent absurdities of materialism without endangering belief in the regularities of nature.

To allow for an organismic model in the teaching of biology would be a drastic reform of that academic discipline. However, in the current political and cultural context, realistic efforts to move the teaching of biology in public schools in this direction are possible. Christian resistance to the dominant mechanistic scientism might generate reform.

DISCUSSION QUESTIONS

1. Do you see any conflicts between science and Christian faith? If so, what are they, and how do you deal with them?
2. Do you think that creaturely purposes have any role in biological evolution? What about divine purpose?
3. How do you understand miracles in the Bible? Do miracles occur today?
4. Do you think that we could understand other animals better if we attributed to them some characteristics we find in ourselves? Emotions? Purposes? Memory? Intelligence?
5. Is it a good idea to connect our belief in God as Creator to the current scientific theory of the big bang?

FOR FURTHER READING

Barbour, Ian. *Religion in an Age of Science*. San Francisco: Harper & Row, 1990.

Cobb, John B. Jr., ed. *Back to Darwin: A Richer Account of Evolution*. Grand Rapids: Wm. B. Eerdmans Publishing Co., 2008.

Corey, M. A. *God and the New Cosmology: The Anthropic Design Argument*. Lanham, MD: Rowman & Littlefield, 1993.

Crick, Francis. *Life Itself: Its Origin and Nature*. New York: Simon & Schuster, 1981.

Dawkins, Richard. *The Selfish Gene*. Oxford: Oxford University Press, 1989.

Davies, Paul. *The Mind of God*. New York: Simon & Schuster, 1992.

Griffin, David Ray. *Two Great Truths: A New Synthesis of Scientific Naturalism and Christian Faith*. Louisville, KY: Westminster John Knox Press, 2004.

Henry, Granville C. *Christianity and the Images of Science*. Macon, GA: Smith & Helwys, 1998.

Polkinghorne, John. *Science and Creation*. Boston: New Science Library, 1988.

Rolston, Holmes. *Science and Religion*. Philadelphia: Temple University Press, 1987.

Van Till, Howard J. *The Fourth Day*. Grand Rapids: Wm. B. Eerdmans Publishing Co., 1986.

7

Global Warming

Lee C. McDonald

If humans pursue a business-as-usual course for the first half of this century, I believe the collapse of civilization due to climate change becomes inevitable.

Tim Flannery (2006)

Now is much too late; the damage has already been done. To expect sustainable development . . . is like expecting a lung cancer victim to be cured by stopping smoking.

James Lovelock (2006)

We need to contemplate terrible military battles in pursuit of basic natural resources between hordes of desperate people.

Peter Schwartz and Douglas Randall (2003)

We are gradually destroying the sustaining community of life on which all living things on Earth depend.

Joint statement of scientists and the National Association of Evangelicals, meeting at the Center for Health and the Global Environment, Harvard Medical School, 2007

INTRODUCTION

The previous chapters have shown that there is much for progressive Christians to resist in the policies and practices that are leading toward disaster. Still we have said little about the damage that humanity as a whole, with Americans often in the lead, are doing to our natural habitat. In this context, the activities that are changing the planet's climate seem to be the most critical of all. It is of the greatest urgency that the policies and practices that now govern most of our collective behavior be fundamentally changed. The changes needed are so basic and the practical proposals for reform now before the public for consideration so comparatively superficial that, once again, we are called to *resist*.

This call intensifies the reasons to resist consumerism, the economic policies that increase inequality, imperialism, and scientism. It shows that they are all interrelated and part of a pattern of thought and action from which we as Christians must distance ourselves radically. It also shows that however 'impractical" the alternatives may seem, they constitute the only true "realism." Since the cultural attitudes and customs that lead us to disaster are deeply internalized by all of us, many of us will require the sort of spiritual disciplines described in chapter 2 to liberate ourselves from them.

To many climate scientists, the threat we look at in this chapter is not merely growing but is of such a magnitude that humanity is approaching a precipice. Even schoolchildren now have some idea of the envelope of greenhouse gases that encircles the earth and is trapping heat. But how dangerous is it?

THE WORST-CASE SCENARIO

James Lovelock, a British chemist who in the 1970s offered to the world the "Gaia hypothesis,"[1] conceived of the earth as a living organism in which humans, animals, plants, soil, chemicals in the atmosphere, geological formations, and all sorts of visible and invisible creatures and forces work together as one organism. Since then scientific work has supported many aspects of the Gaia claim.

Lovelock's new book *The Revenge of Gaia*[2] shocks the reader by opening with the statement quoted at the beginning of this chapter. Since carbon dioxide remains in the atmosphere for a hundred years or more and the big upsurge of the greenhouse effect began shortly after World War II, quick fixes are not likely to work. The earth presently feeds 6.4 billion people, and the addition of several billion more is predicted for this century. Lovelock believes that unless the industrial system is radically changed or the earth's population is cut back to one-half to one billion, billions will die of starvation and other catastrophes before the century ends. Uncontrollable immigration will descend on the few and narrowing fertile areas.[3]

Lovelock is not the first to sound like Cassandra. The Department of Defense commissioned a study of global warming through its Office of Net Assessment, headed by the legendary military planner Andrew Mitchell. The authors were Peter Schwartz and Douglas Randall, and their report, titled *An*

Abrupt Climate Change Scenario and Its Implications for United States National Security, came out in October 2003. It argued that most views of global warming are too gradualist and do not take adequate account of such threats as a "thermohaline circulation collapse," whereby severe and sudden temperature drops in the North Atlantic region could be accompanied by increased heat and drought in many other regions of the world.

Two points in the Pentagon report were especially alarming. First, it may be too late to reverse the warming trend, leading to the possibility or even probability of ecological disaster. Second, the United States should be prepared for "violence and disruption" arising from abrupt climate changes—"a different type of threat to national security. . . . Military confrontation may be triggered by a desperate need for natural resources such as energy, food and water, rather than by conflicts over ideology, religion, or national honor."[4]

Despite his world-weary pessimism, Lovelock does not act as if a fatal end were predestined. In the course of *The Revenge of Gaia* his language shifts from "will happen" to "might happen," and he discusses possible remedies. The central part of the book is a long digression on the benefits of nuclear power, which generates no atmospheric carbon dioxide, the leading greenhouse gas culprit.

SCIENTIFIC CONSENSUS

Greenhouse gases form an envelope around the earth and trap heat from the sun. They have for centuries, and this effect can be beneficial insofar as it stabilizes weather patterns; however, the present concern arises from the fact that an accelerating increase in heat can destabilize weather patterns, leading to extreme climate change. The change is not necessarily uniform; both heat waves and uncharacteristic cold waves can be generated. Since 1900 there has been a 1.1 degree Fahrenheit increase in temperature near the surface of the earth, and half of this increase has been since 1960. The ten warmest years since 1860 have all occurred since 1990. In January 2007 the National Climatic Data Center reported that 2006 was the warmest year on record for the forty-eight contiguous states (2006 was also a record wildfire season). The average annual temperature for 2006 was 2.2 degrees Fahrenheit higher than the mean temperature for the twentieth century. Since 1970 the rise in temperature each decade was greater than in the preceding decade, and eight of the last ten years were the warmest on record worldwide.

The most authoritative reports are those of the Intergovernmental Panel on Climate Change (IPCC). This panel of several hundred climate scientists was formed in 1988 at the instigation of the World Meteorological Organization and the United Nations Environmental Programme. Its first report was in 1990; its second, in 1995; and its third, in 2001. The *Fourth Assessment Report*, issued by the Working Group on Science of IPCC meeting in Paris in January and February 2007, involved 450 authors and 2,500 expert reviewers, representing 130 nations. Whereas the 2001 report had asserted that the probability that human activities are causing global warming was 66 percent, there is now virtual certainty. The official figure was held down to 90 percent only because of pressure from China.

Using 1990 as a baseline year, the report estimates that 2101 will be from 1.8 to 4.0 degrees centigrade hotter. The sea level will rise from 18 to 59 centimeters. The report also revealed great variability in past temperature fluctuations but reaffirmed that the second half of the twentieth century was the hottest in 500 years, and probably in the last 1,300 years. Even if all greenhouse gas emissions were stopped immediately—an impossibility—the mean average temperature would continue to rise by 0.1 degree centigrade a decade, or 1.2 degrees by 2100. Moreover, the resulting shrinkage of forests, which absorb carbon dioxide, would add a comparable amount of heat.

Of particular concern is the worldwide melting of glaciers and of the Arctic ice pack, which has lost over 40 percent of its thickness since 1960. This melting accelerates global warming by reducing the surface area that reflects sunlight away from the earth. Noted climatologist James Hansen of NASA and Columbia University states,

> As with the extinction of species, the disintegration of ice sheets is irreversible for practical purposes. . . . The Earth's history reveals cases in which sea level, once ice sheets began to collapse, rose one meter (1.1 yards) every twenty years for centuries. . . . The last time that the Earth was five degrees warmer was three million years ago, when sea level was about eighty feet higher. . . . Fifty million people in the U.S. live below that sea level.[5]

Low-lying Pacific island nations like Tuvalu and the Seychelles Islands are particularly worried about the rising sea level, as is Bangladesh.

The common greenhouse gases are carbon dioxide, methane, nitrous oxide, ozone, chlorofluorocarbons, and other trace gases. Water vapor also plays an indeterminate part. Carbon dioxide is only 25 percent of the package, but it has been increasing faster than the others—an average 1.8 percent gain a year—and, as noted, remains in the atmosphere longer, a hundred years or more. Methane is more potent in trapping heat, but it dissipates in nine to twelve years. The early melting of permafrost in Siberia is adding methane to the 760 billion tons of greenhouse gases already in the atmosphere.

Ice-core probes in Greenland reveal that the concentration of carbon dioxide in the atmosphere is the highest it has been in 650,000 years, and quite possibly the highest in 50 million years. The National Oceanic and Atmospheric Administration discovered in 2004 that the shells of sea animals had been weakened by excessive concentrations of carbon dioxide in the ocean, making coral formation more difficult, thus affecting fragile marine ecosystems. Even deep-sea creatures are affected. At the bottom of the deepest Arctic seas, ice crystals trap molecules of methane under high pressure in tiny cages called clathrates. Small worms feed on the methane in clathrates.

The preindustrial level of carbon dioxide was 280 parts per million (ppm). By 2006 it had risen to 381 ppm. There is considerable scientific consensus that 450 ppm would be a dangerous level, and at present rates of change, that point would be reached by year 2030. To prevent this, carbon dioxide emissions would need to be reduced to 7 percent below 1990 levels by 2010.

A TECHNOLOGICAL CURE?

If the earth is running a fever, a symptom of a serious disease, we need strong medicine and a strict regimen to save the planet's life. Progressive Christians do not oppose reform, even reform that takes modest steps, but we resist the complacent mentality that too easily assumes modest reform can solve the ecological crisis. Reform implies a desirable series of adjustments that can improve a more or less satisfactory system. For example, rapid development of new technology is a reformist approach, and we welcome it. But the system that produced the crisis is not satisfactory and needs far more radical changes.

Many technological efforts involve the development of forms of energy that do not contribute to global warming. We noted that Lovelock advocates the nuclear option, but others deserve serious consideration.

Wind. According to Lester R. Brown[6] wind-generated electricity is growing at 29 percent a year. Germany and Spain are well ahead of the United States in total megawatts, and Denmark gets 20 percent of its electricity from wind. When California started wind generation in the 1980s, the cost was 38 cents per kilowatt-hours. It has now dropped to 4 cents at the best sites.

Solar Power. The use of photovoltaic cells to generate electricity directly from sunlight was discovered in 1952, and in 2004 the world solar-cell capacity was 4,300 megawatts, about equal to the output of thirteen coal-fired power plants. In 1994 Japan launched a "70,000 roofs" program to subsidize roof installations, and in 1998 Germany began a "100,000 roofs" program that gave consumers a ten-year loan at reduced interest. Germany reached its goal of 100,000 solar-equipped roots in 2003.

China is now the world leader in solar technology, with 52 million square meters of collectors, which it plans to quadruple by 2015. In the developing world one million village homes get electricity from solar cells, but this number constitutes less than 1 percent of the 1.7 billion people in the world who have no electricity at all.[7]

Geothermal. The use of geothermal energy from hot springs and geysers has the attraction of an almost inexhaustible supply and negligible greenhouse gas emissions. It has, of course, geographical limitations. The greatest potential for geothermal power generation is in Indonesia, Japan, the Philippines, and New Zealand. Japan, for example, has estimated that geothermal-based electricity could reach 69,000 megawatts, which would satisfy one-third of its energy needs. The U.S. capacity is 20,000 megawatts; California, for instance, gets 5 percent of its electricity from geothermal power plants.

Biomass. Biomass energy produces 2 percent of Europe's energy, but the European Commission predicts that this figure will increase to 15 percent in fifteen years. Biomass generation accounts for about 3 percent of energy in the United States. Most U.S. biomass plants are tied into the pulp-and-paper industry and burn agricultural residues and forest byproducts. Sweden, however, has pioneered more-efficient biomass plants, and a huge biomass plant just outside Tokyo provides much of the city's electricity by burning seaweed, livestock and chicken manure, household waste, and food residue with minimal air pollution.[8]

Hydroelectric power. Hydroelectric power has been with us for a long time; some operating plants are a hundred years old. Connected to multiuse dams (irrigation, flood control, recreation, and power), the investment costs seem easy to justify, and the storage of water that can be released at off-peak times for electrical use is almost the only practical way that electricity can be stored. Quebec has the world's largest hydroelectric generating system, with eight stations and 16,021 megawatt capacity. The Grand Coulee dam on the Columbia River, America's largest plant, produces 6,809 megawatts. China's famous, or infamous, Three Gorges dam system on the Yangtze now produces 9,800 megawatts but is projected to produce 24,400 megawatts by 2009.

Hydroelectric power, however, is not problem free. Dams can disrupt vast ecosystems resulting, for example, in the well-known decline of salmon populations in North America. Riverbanks downstream are affected, such as the erosion that has increased in the Grand Canyon since the Glen Canyon dam was built. Decaying plant material in newly flooded areas creates methane, and as in the Three Gorges project in China, large populations are sometimes dislocated. The World Court has also reported that hydro power has been consistently overestimated due to inattention to droughts. In Chile sixty-three dams taken together have produced 55 percent less power than projected.[9]

Biofuels. Oil shortages in the 1970s led to the creation of new plant fuels, especially ethanol from sugar cane in Brazil and from corn in the United

States. In 2003 the United States began subsidizing ethanol and biodiesel fuel at $1 per gallon. The next year the United States was producing 3.4 billion gallons of ethanol, which amounted to 2 percent of the fuel used by American autos. The same year Brazil allocated half of its vast sugarcane crop to ethanol and was talking to Japan and China about ethanol exports to those countries. By 2005 twelve billion gallons were being produced and four million U.S. vehicles were using some blend of petroleum and ethanol. India has ten ethanol plants. In 2006 a study at the University of California, Berkeley, showed that if ethanol wholly replaced gasoline, a 13 to 15 percent reduction of greenhouse gases would result. Ford Motor Company claimed it could produce cars capable of using 85 percent ethanol at a retail cost of only $150 per vehicle above the cost of a standard car.

Not fully anticipated was that at present in world commodity markets food producers and biofuel producers find themselves competing for the same corn or sugar, thus driving up the price. In 2006 the price of a bushel of corn jumped from $2.50 to $3.50. *The Ethanol Market Weekly Report* in January 2007 commented on Archer-Daniels-Midland's sudden 15-cent-per-gallon increase in the price of ethanol and predicted other companies would soon follow (ADM produces 70 percent of American ethanol), and the price of corn would continue upward. H. Sterling Burnett of the National Center for Policy Analysis has argued that it takes more energy to produce a gallon of ethanol than the energy it puts out and that the cost to produce a gallon of ethanol is 51 cents more than the cost of producing a gallon of gasoline. He cites a Department of Agriculture study that shows the dollar-a-gallon subsidy to ethanol translates into a four-dollar-a-gallon cost to taxpayer and consumer. Ethanol evaporates more quickly than petroleum and causes more localized smog. Because it absorbs water, ethanol cannot be shipped through existing petroleum pipelines. Devoting vast acreages to new corn growing further depletes the soil and affects the whole economy. The diversion of food stocks that might go to hungry people and the increased cost of food must also be recognized. According to Martinelli and Filoso, the high cost in soil erosion has been shown by "abundant scientific evidence."[10]

Hydrogen fuel. The Bush administration celebrated the potential of hydrogen fuel as an answer to carbon emissions because burning hydrogen produces no carbon dioxide. Chicago ran buses on hydrogen in 1995, and a few other cities followed. Technology prophet Jeremy Rifkin wrote an optimistic book titled *The Hydrogen Economy*, in which he states, "The Hydrogen economy is within sight. How fast we get there will depend on how committed we are to weaning ourselves off oil and other fossil fuels."[11]

Liquid hydrogen is an efficient way to store energy, but the expense and technical problems of extraction and safe storage are enormous. The cheapest way to produce hydrogen is from natural gas, a process that only generates more carbon dioxide. To avoid that problem, a process called electrolysis can be used, but it is three to four times more expensive and is highly explosive, requiring much stronger tanks than does gasoline. General Motors made a model hydrogen car (Arnold Schwarzenegger was photographed in the driver's seat, though he didn't drive it) at a cost of one million dollars, but GM hopes to have a counterpart ready to sell by 2015. Some projections suggest that the cost of the engine would have to be one hundred times what an internal combustion engine costs. Perhaps most discouraging is the estimate that it would take twenty-one tank trucks of hydrogen to haul the energy equivalent of one of today's tank trucks full of gasoline.

Substituting electricity. General Motors built an all-electric, rechargeable car in the 1970s that, according to the documentary film *Who Killed the Electric Car?* was very popular, but because it was leased and not sold, the leases were canceled and the cars were literally ground up by the automaker. There is talk of a return of the electric car, though building charging stations is costly, and at least for the present the result would be to shift the production of greenhouse gases from the car to power plants.

A more moderate use of electricity appears to work better. Honda, Toyota, and Ford are selling hybrid cars, and their popularity is growing; as of this writing, however, only 1 to 2 percent of the cars driven by Americans are hybrids. They are augmented gasoline cars, with increased mileage per tankful of gas because a battery-driven, computer-controlled electric motor replaces gasoline combustion during start-up, idling, and coasting times. A reverse flow of energy during braking recharges the large battery. Hybrids are small, and the mileage is good, so their emission of greenhouse gases is reduced.

High-Concept technology. The perceived danger to the earth and its human population has generated some proposals that aim at direct reduction either of greenhouse gases in the atmosphere or of the solar radiation that warms the earth.

Carbon sequestration involves pumping carbon dioxide deep into the ground or into sandstone deep under the ocean to get it out of the atmosphere and out of the way. Minor efforts to sequester carbon have been attempted in Norway, North Dakota, and Canada. These efforts have affected a few million tons of carbon, but the world generates 25 billion tons a year. The technological problems of carbon sequestration on a sufficiently large scale to make a significant difference are enormous.[12]

Lowell Ward and Kenneth Caldiera of the Lawrence Livermore Laboratory have proposed a sunshade, a sunlight-deflecting disc some seven miles in diameter that could be placed by rocket at the point where the gravitational pull of the sun and the earth are equal and opposite. The disc would deflect a small amount of incoming sunlight, not enough to be noticeable to most people but enough to make a difference, the authors think, in the overall heat of the earth. They have also suggested that small stratospheric balloons might do the same thing. John Latham of the National Center for Atmospheric Research has proposed the creation of devices that can stimulate the creation of clouds from ocean water to accomplish the same end. Another "solution" suggested by some scientists is adding sulfur to aviation fuel for high-flying airliners, enough for the exhaust to create sulfuric acid droplets that would block some sunlight.[13]

NO QUICK FIX

No one questions that technology can help, but there is no quick fix. Further, if economic development and population growth increase total energy use, technological improvements by themselves do little more than stop the increase in production of greenhouse gases. Catastrophe still looms.

The problem of population growth is immense and complex, and we cannot do it justice here. Suffice it to say that it is bound up with issues of poverty, immigration, family-planning services, the global economy, and the education of women. Lester Brown[14] takes heart from the fact that forty-two countries have stable or declining populations, and he thinks China and the United States are heading toward population stability. A third group of nations in Africa and Asia are growing rapidly, and some think a world population of nine billion will be reached by 2050. Brown nevertheless hopes for a peaking at 7.8 billion in 2041 followed by a decline.[15] Around the world, where education for women goes up, for example, the birthrate goes down. There is thus some hope that by the end of the twenty-first century gains in moving toward an energy-efficient, noncarbon economy will not have been swamped by population growth.

Another problem, however, with the technological solutions proposed above along with the effect of continuing in the present direction is sharply illustrated by the case of China. Growing at almost 10 percent a year, China adds an urban development comparable to Houston, Texas, every month as it streaks toward an American standard of life. As Bill McKibben points out, if the Chinese should match the United States in automobile use, "they would produce more carbon dioxide annually than the whole of the rest of the world's transportation systems."[16]

Another range of problems also exist. If the change in weather were the only environmental problem faced by human beings, *perhaps* a technological solution would be possible, but students of the earth's processes had reasons for acute concern even before this problem surfaced. The loss of forest cover, the expansion of deserts, the erosion of the soil, the pollution of the seas, the increasing transmission of diseases from animals to human beings, and the evolution of bacteria and pests immune to our poisons are only a few of the problems we confront.

Consider what continuing present patterns of growth would mean simply in terms of fishing. Thus far technological "improvements" are directed toward increasing the catch by methods of fishing that are rapidly depleting the supply and reducing the ocean's capacity to support life. If the average Chinese consumed as much seafood as the Japanese now do, China's demand by itself would exceed the current, already unsustainable, world catch.

Perhaps the most critical problem currently is the scarcity of fresh water. Even apart from global warming, the aquifers that have made irrigation possible in many parts of the world are being exhausted. Rivers are running dry before they reach the ocean; pollution has rendered many lakes and rivers unusable; and global warming adds acutely to this crisis. Lack of fresh water will make feeding the world far more difficult, and attempting to solve energy problems by using agricultural products would only worsen this fundamental problem.

If the technological responses to global warming enabled the world to continue to grow economically, all of these other environmental problems *would still be exacerbated*. The mind-set that separates each problem and seeks a technological fix for it while ignoring its wider consequences can at most stave off disaster temporarily. When the collapse comes, it will be all the more comprehensive.

The alternative to scrambling from one crisis to another is not to be found in technology. Although technology has a contribution to make, the task is to work toward a quite different world from the one created by cheap fossil fuels. It will be a world in which the needs of human beings are met with far less use of energy in ways that are consistent and in harmony with restoring the biosphere to health.

MORE RADICAL CHANGES

We need new technologies, the end of population growth, and more frugal lifestyles for the affluent, but the latter need not entail hardship and sacrifice. Our focus should be on envisioning a different way of meeting needs than the destructive ones we now employ.

One general problem with the direction we have been going is that the economic theory on which we have depended has been directed to increasing total production by enlarging markets. The goal has been a single global market within which capital and goods move freely. In the past few decades we have come a long way in that direction, and in chapter 4 we noted that one result is greater and greater inequality. Here we add that another result is more and more environmental degradation and dependence on energy.

The world needs to reverse directions. A sustainable world will be based on local economies rather than on a global one. This move toward decentralization would restore political power to local governments and make it possible for such governments to meet the basic needs of their people in a way that can not occur in a global economy. It will end the race to the bottom in wages, working conditions, and care for the environment and also greatly reduce the amount of energy needed for transportation.

This general move toward economic decentralization will help, and the new discipline of ecological economics can contribute to thinking through what will be involved. But the world needs other forms of radical reenvisioning. We will consider two topics that are central to this reenvisioning: food production and habitat.

Today there is still sufficient food, and hunger results primarily from poverty. However, our present ways of producing food are unsustainable. They depend heavily on oil; they lose top soil; and the runoff pollutes water with silt and agrichemicals. Livestock grazing in particular enlarges deserts, and this desertification intensifies dust storms. Aquifers are being exhausted, and dependence on irrigation has become problematic, especially that from rivers fed by melt from rapidly disappearing glaciers. Increases in production are now achieved chiefly by increasing use of petroleum as fertilizer, herbicide, and insecticide. These applications are damaging the quality of the soil and reducing the biodiversity that provides a healthy basis for agriculture. With demand for agricultural products increasing and the natural basis of production declining, a crisis looms.

One of the currently proposed technological fixes is the development of transgenically modified organisms. These constitute a frightening gamble with the future health of the biosphere. The temporary beneficiaries are huge transnational corporations, and the most immediate losers will be peasant farmers the world over. In the longer run, all will lose.[17]

However, another world is possible. Instead of responding to problems in ways that make them worse, that is, in ways that further damage the natural system, increase the demand for petroleum, incur unforeseeable risks, and speed up global warming, we could shift to a fundamentally different system of production. Although the great majority of research in agricultural production now moves in the wrong direction, some research shows the possibility of producing food in ways that can regenerate the soil, reduce dependence on irrigation, and reverse desertification.[18] If humanity would throw its energies into developing local systems of agriculture sustainably appropriate to each region, the earth could begin to heal from the vast damage that we humans have wreaked upon it over thousands of years, and especially in the last century.

The change will be in the direction of using solar energy, producing food for local markets, rotating crops, planting perennials and polycultures, and responding to pests biologically instead of chemically. It will also involve integrating livestock with cropping systems. The result in many places will be more nutritious food. However, eating habits will become more seasonal, and foods that cannot be locally grown, even in greenhouses, will become scarce. Meat consumption will not be ended, since grazing animals on grasslands is an important source of human food. But because feeding grains to animals is an inefficient way of providing needed protein and calories to humans, in much of the affluent world meat will be much less plentiful.

Human habitat is another acute problem, primarily because of the huge increase in the number and size of cities. The construction and operation of cities contributes to the destruction of the earth in many ways. It removes much of the best agricultural land from productive use, and vast resources, including energy, are used in the construction of cities. Moreover, heating and cooling and lighting of buildings uses a great deal of energy, as does transportation within cities. Finally, urbanization is virtually inseparable from industrialization, and industry is a major consumer of energy and a major polluter.

The change in agricultural practice proposed above would help by reducing the flow of population from rural to urban areas. However, the need to build more cities will not end. In China, for example, the surplus population of rural areas is enormous, and in the next few decades China will need to house hundreds of millions more people in cities. If these cities are like those of the West or those China has been building in recent decades, pressures on the earth will intensify terribly.

Another world, however, is possible. First, architects are now fully aware that buildings can be designed to use only passive solar energy for heating and cooling. This improvement will probably be forced on us as the cost of energy rises, so we may hope that little needs to be said about it. However, urban sprawl remains, with its twin consequences of occupying some of the best agricultural land and increasing transportation problems within the city.

The good news here is that other forms of urban habitat are possible. Today it is often thought that ecological considerations call for parks and other open spaces in the city along with wide boulevards capable of handling the traffic. Such designs, however, instensify the problems of urban sprawl. Urban habitat should be planned so as to use as little land as possible. The denser the population per acre, the more accessible are the facilities of the city, including employment opportunities. But such density can be nightmarish. We picture the tiny residences and crowded streets of many of the world's current cities, especially their slums, and we want nothing of this sort.

Density per acre, however, need not reduce personal living space if buildings are very tall. Population density is high in some of the most luxurious parts of Manhattan. If the total area of the city is small enough, then automobiles, buses, and trains are not needed to move people from one part to another, and streets, highways, and freeways within the city can be abolished. Today half or even more of the space in parts of cities is taken up by these facilities for moving people and goods from one part of the city to another. Their removal, therefore, greatly increases the space available for other purposes. What results is a whole city under one roof. Residences would be located on the outside walls. Factories would be located underground. Movement from one part of the huge building to other parts would be by elevator, escalator, moving sidewalks, and paths for walking and bicycling. In some designs, where the city is long and narrow, an electric train can be included. There would be small parks and other open spaces scattered around the city. Today's cities are up to sixty miles in breadth, so most urban dwellers are largely cut off from nature, but cities can be built so that in a few minutes one could get from any part of the city to the countryside.

Urban habitat of this sort is so different from that to which we are accustomed that it is difficult to imagine. Fortunately, Paolo Soleri has designs for many "architectural ecologies" or "arcologies." They are beautiful both without and within. He originally put them forward primarily because of his social and cultural concerns, but their contribution to resolving the problem of sustainable habitat are also great. He believes that arcologies can be so designed that they use no energy other than passive solar. Whether that is true should be tested, but even if his claim is exaggerated, the reduction of resource use and pollution as well as urban sprawl would be enormous.

There may be flaws in Soleri's designs, just as in specific plans for a sustainable agriculture. The point we are making is that instead of pouring all our efforts into technical solutions that assume the continuation of unsustainable agriculture and unsustainable cities, we should experiment with proposals for sustainable ones. We will learn from such experiments how to bring into being a sustainable world that is also truly livable and attractive.

OBSTACLES TO ACTION:
POLITICAL, ECONOMIC, AND CULTURAL

Although another world is possible, formidable obstacles to achieving this psychological and spiritual turnaround exist. Let us briefly evaluate four of these:

- Public misinformation
- The delays of democratic compromise and bureaucratic lethargy
- The embedded economic doctrine of perpetual growth
- The culture of egocentric individualism

Public Misinformation

The American public and other publics are aware of the need for environmental responsibility at many levels. A Pew Center poll in June 2006 found 74 percent of Americans saying either that global warming is "very serious" or is "somewhat serious." Similarly, a Zogby Poll in August 2006 found that 70 percent of Americans were concerned about global warming, generally saying that they had become more convinced of its significance in the past two years. The wide distribution of the Al Gore film *An Inconvenient Truth* in early 2006 apparently played a role in this change.

Sadly, this increased recognition that global warming is a problem is not accompanied by much understanding. By 1998 the problem of the ozone hole was well on its way to solution, but the majority of respondents to the Dunlap poll that year thought it was a greater problem than global warming. Only 41 percent of responders to the 2006 Pew poll agreed that global warming is to a significant degree the result of human activity.

Closely linked political and economic power can and do contribute to public misinformation by campaigns of disinformation. Oil companies have contributed millions of dollars to some forty different think tanks, opinion groups, and political groups disposed to question global warming. In 2004 Michael Crichton, MD, noted novelist and creator of the TV show *ER*, wrote a best-selling page-turner novel titled *State of Fear*, which made villains of environmentalists and portrayed them as bent on exaggerating the threat of global warming simply to increase their political power. Crichton toured for his book, appeared on television, and made a number of speeches. In January 2005 he spoke before an American Enterprise Institute (AEI) luncheon. He was introduced by the president of the AEI, a former Reagan administration budget official, who praised the "serious science" of the novel based on its use of charts, footnotes, and bibliography, unusual for a novel. Crichton sought scientific respectability by leaning heavily on a projection graph by NASA climatologist James Hansen, never mentioning that this graph was the earliest of three projections and the least valid, one that Hansen had repudiated on the basis of later evidence.

Powerful politicians such as James M. Inhofe (R., Okla.), who until 2007 chaired the Environmental and Public Works Committee of the Senate, cited Crichton's book in support of denial of the human contribution to global warming. In a speech on the Senate floor on July 28, 2003, Inhofe called global warming "the greatest hoax ever perpetrated on the American people." He reaffirmed this position in a similar speech on January 4, 2005.

The Delays of Democratic Compromise and Bureaucratic Lethargy

Democracy tries to allow everyone to have a say, and it is bent toward compromise, making for a slow process. American politicians of many stripes still talk about "energy independence," meaning the ability of the United States to go it alone, rather than reduction of *energy use*. Likewise, the more bureaucratized a society is, the slower it may be to change. It took the Environmental Protection Agency until 2008, for example, to declare the polar bear an endangered species and to acknowledge that the shrinking polar ice cap was a crucial factor in the endangerment. Democracies run on money as well as on votes; therefore short-term economic benefits can often override long-term societal interests, even to the point of threatening survival. Nevertheless, passionate majorities can sometimes bring durable changes to a democracy.

International efforts, though often frustrating, are essential and not to be disparaged. Many American leaders were surprised when on February 16, 2005, the signatories to the Kyoto treaty went ahead and formed a continuing international organization after the United States had withdrawn. Contrary to expectations, Russia's leaders, sensing a political opportunity, changed their position and by joining were instrumental in keeping the Kyoto momentum going.

To be sure, the political tide is turning in the United States. All the candidates for president in the 2008 election, Republicans and Democrats, are saying that something must be done about global warming. They are responding to public opinion if not to science.

The Embedded Economic Doctrine of Perpetual Growth

Bill McKibben in *Deep Economy* (2007) shows with clarity the degree to which not just America but much of the world has tied itself to the American dream of endless economic growth. Our economic system is predicated on perpetual expansion: higher production, higher income, higher employment, higher investment, and higher energy use. This system, called rather ingenuously "free-market capitalism," is deeply embedded in the thinking of most citizens of the West and is widely touted as the course of the future for the developing world.

Sir Nicholas Stern, head of Britain's Government Economics Service and former chief economist with the World Bank, wrote a seven-hundred-page report commissioned by the Chancellor of the Exchequer titled *The Economics of Climate Change*, which was released on October 30, 2006, and appeared as a book in 2007. A central conclusion is that 1 percent of global GDP will be required to cope with the effects of global warming and that failure to invest that much "could create risks of major disruptions to economic and social activity, later in this century and in the next, on a scale similar to those associated with the great wars and the economic depression of the first half of the 20th century." Compared to the worst-case scenarios previously cited, this projection seems quite optimistic. The world did, after all, survive the depression and the great wars. The author put this claim in terms familiar to economists: Global warming is an "externality" the cost of which is not taken into account when the price of gasoline and electrical power is calculated. "When people do not pay for the consequences of their actions, we have market failure. This is the greatest market failure the world has seen."[19]

Despite Stern's market approach, champions of "free-market" economics attacked his report with vigor. Professor George Reisman of Pepperdine University, author of *Capitalism: A Treatise on Economics*,[20] examines the report on the Ludwig von Mises Institute Web site:

> The report is a rehash of now standard environmentalist claims concerning alleged disasters that await the world if it continues its wicked ways of fossil fuel consumption. [Stern's allusions to] "runaway warming" come very close to conjuring up images of hellfire and brimstone as the fate of the world if it does not take Sir Nicholas's report to heart and repent of its ways. . . . The only safe response to global warming [says Reisman] . . . is the maximum degree of individual freedom.[21]

Reisman's response, however, begs every crucial question. It does not represent a prevailing view, but we can expect much debate to occur between those seriously concerned with global warming and the beneficiaries of the status quo. The latter will evoke some of these vacuous but nevertheless influential arguments. Conservative columnists have mirrored this question-begging by first accusing environmentalists of "fearmongering," then claiming that a few degrees of heat ought to be seen as a small price to pay for the huge increase in America's Gross Domestic Product (GDP) in the past century. They do not mention the industrialization of China and India.

The Culture of Egocentric Individualism

The post–World War II generation has sometimes been called the "me generation," and the teens of the early-twenty-first century have been accused of "narcissism." These attributions may be unfair, but the wider culture has certainly fostered a consumerist mentality[22] that puts a high value on individual pleasure and the acquisition of material things, which a review of most advertising will illustrate. By contrast, appeals to the value of community and to sacrifice for others are a hard sell.

A culture of egocentric individualism interferes with our ability to take the steps that will be necessary to cope effectively with an overheated planet. It is easy, for example, to pretend to be more active in saving the earth than one really is. This hypocrisy is illustrated in Hollywood by show people who drive gas-guzzling Hummers in private but rent hybrid "ecolimos" for publicity events so that they will appear more environmentally correct than they really are. In show business, as in politics, the appearance of action often trumps action.

A CHRISTIAN RESPONSE

In 1967 Lynn White gave a speech to the American Association for the Advancement of Science,[23] "The Historical Roots of Our Ecological Crisis." In this lecture White argued that the roots of the crisis lay in the interpretation of the Bible in the West. This interpretation, he declared, was anthropocentric and dualistic and gave human beings the freedom to exploit the natural world.

Fortunately, few Christians responded by enthusiastically claiming that White was correct and that he described the proper Christian position. Most responses were to defend the Bible *against* this interpretation. Since White never argued that the Bible as such held the views that became dominant in its Western interpretation, this was not an objection to White's thesis, but the response nevertheless was useful in bringing to the fore better ways to interpret the Bible.

The influence of centuries of anthropocentric teaching, fully expressed also in the liberal Protestant tradition, is still with us and is a main obstacle to the needed changes. Most Christian worship continues to focus on humanity to the virtual exclusion of the natural world. This makes sustained attention to that world difficult and rare. For many Christians, concern for other human beings is central, and the call for peace and for justice gains immediate response, but ecological issues seem peripheral.

However, most church leaders are now fully committed to repentance with respect to those teachings that have contributed to the ecological crisis, and Christians of various convictions subscribe to the notion of human stewardship of the earth as expressed in Genesis. We want to be good stewards of God's bounty. Only a perverse minority still explicitly seeks to exploit the supposed loophole that the word "dominion" offers: "Fill the earth and subdue it; and have dominion over the fish of the sea and over the birds of the air and over every living thing that moves upon the earth'" (Gen. 1:28). The perversion comes in turning "dominion" into "domination," implying that humans have the right to take whatever they want out of the earth. That this is a questionable interpretation is suggested by some recent biblical scholarship noting that the Hebrew phrase translated "dominion over" can be better understood as "responsibility for." Humans have responsibility for the earth and its creatures.

The message of Genesis 1 is reinforced in the story of the flood. The flood was the result of human wickedness, but God did not will the destruction of the earth or of any species of animals. God did not preserve Noah simply because he was a righteous man, though he was. God gave Noah the responsibility to preserve all species. The covenant of the rainbow, declared after the waters receded, was not a covenant with Noah only but one between God and every living creature—creeping things and green plants. God said, "'I have set my bow in the clouds, and it shall be a sign of the covenant between me and the earth'" (Gen. 9:13). The flood came as punishment for the wickedness of human beings, but the human survivors of the flood were charged with the responsibility of taking care of the earth for the sake of the earth itself. The problem of global warming can be viewed in this light, though we may not want to know what the "flood" will be like this time.

Nevertheless, even though most Christians reject a "right" to dominate the earth, most of us in the developed world, with or without conscious reflection, act as players in a system that is despoiling the earth. The need now is not so much to change the beliefs Christians affirm as to make them real in our lives and to relate them to the wider realities in which we live.

The churches are in a unique position in our society. They are free, at least in prospect, from commercial greed and nationalistic bias. Popes and the Patriarch of Constantinople have spoken strongly and well on human responsibility to care for the earth. Among Protestants, evangelicals, however "conservative," are not indifferent to the crisis. Indeed, persons like Rev. Richard Cizik of the National Association of Evangelicals, Rev. Rick Warren of Saddleback Church, and Rev. Jim Wallis of Sojourners have been leaders in expressing environmental concern. Many old-line Protestant denominations have spoken well.

In February 2005 the National Council of Churches (NCC) issued a "Theological Statement on the Environment." It condemned the "false gospel" which holds that "God cares for the salvation of humans only and that our human calling is to exploit Earth for our own ends alone." It concluded, "In Christ's name and for Christ's glory, we call out with broken yet hopeful hearts: join us in restoring God's Earth—the greatest healing work and moral assignment of our time." The NCC has sponsored the Interfaith Climate Change

Network, which has a program called Protecting Creation.[24] In July 2004 it organized a "Religion and Science Together" call-in to support the bipartisan Climate Stewardship Act in the U.S. Senate.

The World Council of Churches (WCC) has wrestled with the problem of climate change for many years, publishing study papers and holding conferences. It sent a delegation to the continuing Kyoto process negotiations (the "Conferences of Parties" [COP]) in Marrakech, Morocco, in November 2002.

RESISTANCE AND HOPE

We have emphasized the critical urgency of ending those practices that lead to global warming, and we have considered the technological responses designed to enable the economy to continue to grow along the lines of the recent past. Recognizing that these can at most postpone catastrophe, we have pointed to a vision of a quite different way of organizing human life on this planet. However, we have seen that a realistic appraisal of the social, cultural, political, and economic situation in our nation is not encouraging.

Among major institutions in the United States, the churches have gone the furthest in calling for needed changes. Church leaders are making excellent statements and promoting promising actions. However, most church members are formed as much by the general culture as by their participation in the church, and the legacy of anthropocentrism in traditional Western theology and liturgy still shapes their habits of thought and action more than recent pronouncements of their leaders. Even small steps toward needed change are slow and difficult, and unless change occurs at the deepest level of conviction, perception, and habit—the level at which religious traditions operate—the realization of a hopeful future is hard to imagine. The change led by radical environmentalists is beginning among progressive Christians, but it has a long way to go.

The radical changes needed to offer a happy future for our descendants are not even on the table for discussion. Hence, in this area as in others, progressive Christians cannot be simply reformists. We will support whatever reforms move in the right direction, but we will oppose the notion with which these reforms are usually bound up: that the goal is to enable society to continue in its present rut. Accordingly, our stance will be to resist the dominant forces in our society.

To resist here as elsewhere is not simply to protest and oppose, although resistance includes that. Inwardly, it is to orient ourselves and to live by very different values from those celebrated around us. This new orientation will require our spiritual growth in freedom from bondage to "the world." Outwardly, it is to do what we can to change the character of public discourse both in the church and in the larger world. This will require organization and action. We will point out the inadequacy, even the absurdity, of discussing only options that will not avoid catastrophe. We will call as loudly as we can for recognition that another world is possible, and we will depict that world as a real and attractive option.

We will remember that Jesus announced as his mission the proclamation of the nearness of the *basileia theou*, which we usually translate as the "kingdom of God." Given Jesus' understanding of God as *abba* or "daddy" rather than as monarch, we suggest that "commonwealth of God" or "divine commonwealth" comes closer to what he taught. In the midst of the oppressive Roman Empire, Jesus proclaimed that this very different order was near at hand. God was at work in the world, and it was already possible for those who heard Jesus' message to live individually and collectively by God's purposes for them rather than by the values promoted by the empire. As they did so, others could join. The divine commonwealth could transform the values of society.

Something like that makes sense for us today. As Christians we will think of the other world that is possible as one that fulfills God's purposes—as, indeed, the divine commonwealth. We can live now from that vision rather than allow ourselves to be formed by the madness of the dominant culture. We can join with others in community. The communities that share this vision and live by it are growing.

Because God is at work seeking to save the world from the consequences of human madness, we do not despair when we find that we cannot control the course of events. Although the great breakthroughs of the twentieth century could not have occurred if the work of faithful people had not prepared the way, they did not result merely from well-planned and well-organized programs of change. The success of the struggle for the rights of African Americans could not have succeeded had there not been a heightened awareness of the gross injustice inflicted on them and an increased desire for its rectification. Advances would not have occurred apart from hard work on the part of civil rights activists, but much in the actual course of events—for example, in the Montgomery bus boycott—could not have been foreseen. These occurred as individuals such as Martin Luther King Jr., who already ordered their lives by the norms of a just society, responded to concrete situations. The ending of military rivalry and warfare among the nations of Europe was also not the result of a well-organized movement for a continental union. It came about when the leaders of France and Germany concluded that it was time to end the long period in which quarrels of the European nations dragged the world into war after war.

Other examples can be found in the democratization of South Africa and the self-dismantling of the Soviet Empire without bloodshed. Still another is the transformation of the relation of the Roman Catholic Church to Protestantism and other religious traditions in Vatican II. Each case is different, but none involved reforms of the sort that pundits discussed in advance and that gradually gained majority support. Instead, special circumstances made radical change possible, as did people of conscience and vision who were open to God's call and in positions of leadership. They responded, and the course of history was changed.

The enemies of change want us to believe that the direction in which they now lead is the only real option, that nothing else is possible. They claim that their way will somehow work out well for humanity, that the environmental threats are grossly exaggerated. They want our complacency and, through that, our complicity. We know that they are false teachers and false prophets.

The danger would be to accept the verdict that nothing else is possible even when we know that their way leads to catastrophe. That would lead to hopelessness, and hopelessness disempowers as thoroughly as does complacency. Hope is, in itself, resistance. It is a theological virtue because it is an expression of the faith that God is working in ways that are impossible for us alone. We do not know whom God will call for decisive action or whether those who are called will respond. But we do know that God is calling all of us to live for and out of the divine commonwealth and not the American Empire. And we know that as we do so, we make it a little more likely that God will be able to lead humanity through the time of trials in which we live.

DISCUSSION QUESTIONS

1. Do you feel that a world ecological disaster during the twenty-first century is impending? Why or why not?
2. Do you think you have a reasonable, basic understanding of the scientific evidence that explains both global warming and the human contribution to global warming? Do you know where to find reports of such evidence?
3. Are most of your friends and fellow church members concerned about global warming, or do most of them think the problem is too distant or too complicated for them to be concerned? Does your congregation have an environmental program? How is it working?
4. What have you and your family done to conserve energy and reduce carbon dioxide emissions? What more might you do?
5. Do you think that many Christians have been culpable of confusing stewardship of nature with the domination of nature? Have we humans exploited the earth and other species? How? Is a fundamental change in the way we think about nature required?

FOR FURTHER READING

Brown, Lester R. *Plan B 2.0* . New York: W. W. Norton & Co., 2006.
Cobb, John B. Jr. *Sustaining the Common Good.* Cleveland: Pilgrim Press, 1994.
Daly, Herman E. *Beyond Growth.* Boston: Beacon Press, 1996.
Dow, Kristin, and Thomas E. Downing. *An Atlas of Climate Change.* Berkeley: University of California Press, 2006.
Flannery, Tim. *The Weather Makers.* New York: Grove Atlantic, 2006.
Gore, Al. *Earth in the Balance.* New York: Penguin Books, 1993.
———. *An Inconvenient Truth: The Crisis of Global Warming.* New York: Viking Press, 2007.
Houghton, John T. *Global Warming.* 3rd ed. Cambridge: Cambridge University Press, 2004.
Intergovernmental Panel on Climate Change (Working Group #3). *Third Assessment Report, Climate Change, 2001.* New York: Cambridge University Press, 2001.
———. (Working Group 1). *Fourth Assessment Report, Climate Change, 2007.* New York: Cambridge University Press, 2007.
Lovelock, James. *The Revenge of Gaia.* New York: Basic Books, 2006.
McKibben, Bill. *Deep Economy: The Wealth of Communities and the Durable Future.* New York: Times Books, 2007.
———. *The End of Nature.* New York: Random House, 2006.
Speth, James Gustave. *Red Sky at Morning: America and the Crisis of the Global Environment.* New Haven, CT: Yale University Press, 2004. See 203–38 for extensive review of information sources and useful Web sites.

PART 3

Theologies of Resistance

Latin American Liberation Theology

George Pixley

A BIBLICAL DISCUSSION IN A BASE COMMUNITY

The following is a fragment from a discussion of the Gospel reading of Matt. 26:69–75 in the fishing community of Solentiname, Nicaragua, in the late 1960s. The "I' is Father Ernesto Cardenal, the pastor:

> *"Meanwhile, Peter was seated outside in the courtyard, and a servant approached him and said, You also were with him in Galilee. But Peter denied it before all, saying, 'I don't know what you are saying.'"*
>
> I: "The 'meanwhile'means that while Jesus was being tried within, and afterwards while he was being beaten, Peter was denying him outside."
>
> A woman: "Before Peter had been showing off; he felt very brave with his sword, but when the moment came to give up his life, he was a coward."
>
> Some young fellows:
>
> "I don't see anything wrong. It was tactics."
>
> "If someone of the *Frente* is questioned, he does not confess."
>
> "Yes, maybe he wasn't a coward, but acted like a revolutionary, because if he turned himself over he could not have fulfilled what Jesus had commissioned to him. I think he is doing the same as Jesus, who did not wish to say publicly that he was the Christ because that was dangerous. It wasn't until the very last that he admitted to being the Christ."
>
> I: "But the Gospel doesn't seem to approve the denial, the way you are doing. It says that afterward he cried bitterly."
>
> The woman: "I think, Ernesto, that the boys are right, that Peter denied so as not to sell his master; he saw that they had him but thought that maybe they wouldn't kill him; and he denied so that they couldn't get anything from him. But when Peter saw that it had done no good, that they were going to screw Jesus, he cried."

I: "Then did Jesus also not accomplish anything by turning himself over?"

A young fellow: "He was redfaced. . . . He didn't turn himself in but was trapped."[1]

INTRODUCTION

The previous chapters have been written by North Americans about the Bible's challenge to us to resist some of the most powerful currents in our society. We are calling on those who benefit from consumerism, American imperialism, and the policies that bring about poisonous inequality to resist. We are also calling for resistance to scientism, and above all to those policies and practices that are threatening the habitability of the planet. However, we must acknowledge that this new emphasis in the North American liberal tradition might never have arisen if we had not learned it first from those who suffer from our activities.

Liberation theologies are, almost by definition, theologies of resistance. Once the context has been identified as oppressive, the response must be either acquiescence or resistance. Liberation theologies also find in the Bible the call to resist, and they have taught us to do so as well. Their resistance calls us to recognize that the context of all of our lives is one of oppression. This recognition is harder for those of us who belong to the oppressing group and benefit economically from the oppressive system. Yet without our participation in resistance, the struggle of the oppressed becomes very hard indeed. Nothing is more important than our genuinely hearing the voices of the oppressed and seeking to be in solidarity with them. Without them our own reading of the Bible is severely impoverished. Indeed, the authors of this book acknowledge that the chapter on the Bible with which this book begins and which sets the tone for the whole would have been quite different had we not first discussed this chapter on liberation theology.

Looking back from the first decade of the twenty-first century, we may judge that the most important theological development in the second half of the twentieth century was the rise of a theology of the oppressed. In principle there are as many theologies of the oppressed as there are oppressed groups in the world, and the number of such theologies has become quite large. Such theology arose among blacks in the United States and among peasants in Latin America or among those who identified themselves closely with these peasants; it has spread around the world primarily from Latin America.

Liberation theology is theology that (1) discovers the transcendent in the earthly and hence reflects on earthly realities, expecting to find there revelations of the divine and salvation; (2) reflects from a situation of oppression among a people who struggle for their liberation; and (3) reads its tradition and its social reality in order to promote that struggle.

In the last four decades various forms of liberation theology have emerged on the ecclesiastical scene. Black theology irrupted in the 1960s with a strong presence on the U.S. church scene, compelling even liberal theologians to recognize that they for the most part had paid no attention to the enormous role that race played in American society. Such was true even of the social gospel writers, who took racial segregation for granted without protest. Even the recognition of the evils of segregation forced on American society by Martin Luther King Jr. and the support of white churches for his work did not awaken a full recognition of the deeply embedded racism of most white Christians.

Powerful theological voices such as James Cone and Gayraud Wilmore were recognized by mainstream theological schools, but coinciding as they did with the presence of the Black Power movement and its threatening leader/martyr Malcolm X, they sent a shiver through the church establishment. As time has gone on and the prosperity of the seventies succeeded the questioning of the sixties, the presence of black churches with a legitimate cry of long-standing and continuing oppression was recognized, and hence the need for a continuing presence of black liberation theology was acknowledged.

During the second half of the seventies the first systematizing books of Latin American liberation theology were brought to an English-reading public by Orbis Books and gained immediate recognition by the dominant theological schools. But in the cold-war spirit of the time, the response of many church people and of the U.S. government was hostility to persons and ideas seen as fellow-traveling infiltrators in the Latin American churches. More recently, this response has been softened as Latin American liberation theologies have incorporated a wider range of concerns.

At about the same time another form of liberation theology, feminist theology, appeared on the scene. The feminist challenge to patriarchal structures hit the North American churches directly, and many churches responded. The issues it raised were less about public policy and more about the internal life of the church and the family, that private space which is a refuge for all of us. Feminist theologies thus hit close to home and will be needed for generations to come. We examine their influence in the next chapter.

Because the original forms of Latin American liberation theology and of black theology were shaped by men, and the women who developed feminist theology were of European background, new forms of liberation theology have crossed these boundaries. Latin American, Asian, and black women have found their distinctive voices. Indeed, once it became clear that theology should be done by each oppressed group, a wide range of liberation theologies arose. One of the most important was Minjung theology in Korea. African theologians and Dalit theologians in India also contributed significantly to the conversation.

In the United States, the new context allowed those Christians who were sexually oriented to members of their own gender also to find their voices. We have been made aware that divergence from the cultural norm in this respect has been a source of intense oppression even for those who in other ways belong to the elite. For those who belong to otherwise oppressed groups, it has added yet another layer of oppression, sometimes the most painful of all. Gay and lesbian liberation writers have further compelled us to recognize that more than any other group, gays and lesbians look to the church as the special source of their suffering. Their call for recognition and full acceptance has engendered some of the most intense and divisive struggles in our churches.

The movement to preserve the natural environment is also a form of liberation that has gained expression in theology. The environment is oppressed and destroyed just as much as poor people, and it is the poor who suffer most as a result of environmental degradation. We have discussed the need to resist this oppression and destruction in the preceding chapter, focusing on the threat and reality of global warming.

We make no attempt in this book to examine the full range of liberation theologies. Instead we deal with only two. In this chapter we look at the most political of these theologies, Latin American liberation theology. The chapter is divided into two parts. The first deals with Latin American theology in three sections: (1) its history; (2) its main focus, by which it justifies its claim to be a new way to do theology; and (3) the biblical movement spawned by this theology and feeding back into it. The second part asks, In light of the truth that we progressive Christians in North America recognize in this liberation theology, what positive role can we play? The answers point back to topics dealt with in the preceding chapters but focus here on the limitations caused by the nature of our society and the steps we can take to break out of them.

THE EMERGENCE OF LIBERATION THEOLOGY IN LATIN AMERICA

The World Council of Churches, founded in 1948, was part of an ecumenical movement that seemed promising not just in industrialized nations but also in those sectors of the third world that were touched by the modern world. There were mainline Protestant seminaries and Christian student movements in universities. The first signs of theological reflection in the line of what was to become liberation theology emerged in ecumenical student groups in Brazil.

Here Protestants and Catholics came together for Bible study and also to discuss the political problems that agitated all of the universities in Latin America at the time.

Early in his papacy, Pope John XXIII called on the U.S. church to tithe personnel and money to evangelize Latin America. It was a region with a large number of Catholics, many of whom were baptized but not evangelized, and one in which the increasing presence of Protestant churches was a threat to Catholic religious monopoly. The result was a wave of missionaries, both male and female, in the 1960s. Most of these were assigned by local bishops to regions where native priests did not want to serve: large, dispersed, rural parishes and populous urban slums. Many of these missionaries were shocked at the depressed conditions they discovered and at the correlation they often saw between poverty in Latin America and the actions of North Americans. These include the American policy of supporting "friendly" governments even when they were corrupt and allowing U.S. corporations to exploit labor in inhuman conditions at subhuman wages.

Often far away from episcopal supervision, the pastoral work of these missionaries was centered in small discussion groups. Some of these groups received sympathetic encouragement from higher authorities, as in the cases of Hélder Câmara, bishop of Recife; Leonidas Proaño of Riobamba; Sergio Méndez Arceo of Cuernavaca; and Samuel Ruiz of San Cristóbal de las Casas. The work with small groups was conducted especially by nuns, who were prevented by church regulations from providing the sacraments to their people. In their place, these women led services of the Word. In indigenous regions, such as those of Proaño and Ruiz, discussion in native languages opened many Christian groups to new levels of enthusiasm about Scripture and the exploration of social problems.

Other events contributed to the new climate. The Cuban revolution showed that social change was possible, and Marxism presented itself as a powerful engine of social analysis and transformation. Altogether, it was a heady mixture.

More or less simultaneously in the middle 1960s in the conferences of ISAL (Church and Society in Latin America) and of the JEC (Catholic student movement) the expression "liberation theology" emerged. In ISAL, pastors such as Julio de Santa Ana and Emilio Castro wrote in their journal *Cristianismo y Sociedad* about liberation in the Bible and in Christian social practice.

In the famous San Marcos University of Lima the chaplain was a parish priest named Gustavo Gutiérrez, who had studied in Lyons, France. He was also the pastor of a parish in Rimac, a depressed area of Lima. At the continental meeting of bishops in Medellín (1968), Gustavo Gutiérrez was an advisor, and and several Protestant leaders were included as visitors with full rights to share in the debates. The meeting began in a way that was new for a bishops' pastoral gathering: for three days the bishops heard from political scientists and economists who laid out the Latin American crisis. The subsequent pastoral debates took place under that cloud, and though liberation was not mentioned in the final document, the method of "seeing, judging, acting" (*ver, juzgar, actuar*) of the base groups changed the nature of the pastoral recommendations. The church had to address the world with its voice and its action. The resultant documents have had a greater impact on church action and reflection than any others in the history of the Latin American church.

Also in the 1960s, Paulo Freire was director of literacy programs for the archdiocese of Recife and, later, minister of education and culture for the Brazilian government. His method of educating for freedom sent shock waves through Latin America, and his educational work in Brazil was thus cut off in March 1964 by a military coup that drove him into exile. But his books written in exile, especially *Pedagogía do Oprimido*,[2] were widely read and influenced many theologians. Their power lay in their emphasis on freedom as subjectivity and on the necessity of community for freedom to be secure and humanly meaningful.

This theological and pastoral ferment was given formal expression shortly afterward. In 1969 Brazilian Presbyterian pastor Rubem Alves published his Princeton dissertation *Toward a Liberation Theology*. The U.S. publisher changed the title to *A Theology of Human Hope*. Shortly thereafter (1970) it appeared in Spanish at Montevideo as *Religión ¿Opio o instrumento de liberación?*[3] Here, in dialogue with Jürgen Moltmann and Karl Barth, the argument was presented that theology that did not lead to concrete social changes was sterile.

In 1971 three bombshell books appeared, one in Montevideo, one in Lima, and one in Mexico City. A Brazilian priest in exile who had worked with the JEC and was then working with ISAL, Hugo Assmann, wrote *Opresión-liberación, desafío a los cristianos*, which appeared in Salamanca in 1973 as *Teología desde la praxis de la liberación*.[4] In Lima, JEC advisor Gustavo Gutiérrez published his now-classic *Notas para una teología de la liberación*;[5] it appeared in Salamanca in 1972 as *Teología de la liberación, perspectivas*. And that same year Jose Porfirio Miranda, a Mexican professor of biblical studies at the Jesuit seminary in Mexico City, published *Marx y la Biblia: Crítica a la filosofía de la opresión*, which also appeared in Salamanca in 1972 with its original title.[6] These three books all appeared in English translation published by the press of the Maryknoll missionary fathers (Orbis Press) a few years after their originals.

With these four books the theology of liberation had become a full-fledged theological current. The proportion of one Protestant work and three Catholic ones, all by male clergy, is fairly representative of the original publishing situation, though not the pastoral one, where women religious had a major role. Perhaps it is also representative that one of the the original three priests was a Jesuit and two were secular (that is, directly under a bishop and not members of a religious order). Later, members of the religious orders and Protestant theological professors dominated the scene—still exclusively male until the 1980s.

The 1970s and 1980s were a period of steady growth both of the pastoral work and theological publishing of this new current. Feminists, both Catholic and Protestant, were challenging both the male and the clerical domination of the movement, though the assimilation of the challenge was spotty among the leading authors and pastors.

❧❧❧❧❧

Liberation theology was, and still is, dependent on the Marxist analysis of capitalism, although it has rethought Marx dramatically. It reads his critique of religion as a critique of idolatry; it appropriates his flexible reading of economic history over and against Stalin's five necessary stages; and it stresses the voluntary elements in class struggle against the reading of Marx as an economic determinist. Its reading of Marx and Marxism was thoroughly explored by Enrique Dussel and Giulio Girardi in several erudite books.[7]

Even though the philosophical bases of liberation theology were not the same as those of the orthodox Marxism of the Communist parties of Eastern Europe, they were brought into question by the end of the cold war. The movements symbolized by events in 1989 and 1992 brought dramatic changes. In 1989 the Berlin wall fell, and Eastern European Communism showed the unravelling that was in process. The collapse of European Communism called for some major rethinking on the part of liberation theology, because the political program of revolutionary struggle depended on the bipolarity of the cold war.

The net result was a lessening of interest in further philosophical explorations that, indirectly, was a boost to the spirituality of liberation theology and its biblical aspects. Talk of taking over the state by revolution became largely irrelevant, resulting, first of all, from a recognition that the liberation movement had to be democratic from its beginnings to avoid the temptation of becoming oppressive itself should it achieve power. In a movement that had previously found much of its dynamism from its revolutionary politics, this position produced a period of political uncertainty.

Already in the 1980s, in the early years of the pontificate of John Paul II, the Vatican reacted negatively to liberation theology, and it lost the official status it had gained. Liberation theology was never declared heretical, but it was accused of using an unacceptable Marxist philosophical instrument and of not respecting the hierarchy in its ecclesiology. Although the first accusation was more prominent in the two documents that came out of Cardinal Ratzinger's Commission for the Defense of the Faith, the timing suggests that in much of the curia it was the latter that was the major concern. In September 1984 Leonardo Boff was called to Rome to defend his collection of articles published as *Igreja: Carisma e poder*, and he was silenced the next year. The opposition of the Vatican since then has had a dampening effect on theologians who are also priests, as a majority of Catholic theologians are. At the same time, care has been taken by the Vatican not to appoint bishops sympathetic to this theology, thus making it difficult for communities who cultivate it in their daily spiritual lives.

The massive movements surrounding the 500th anniversary of the beginning of the conquest of the "new world" by Columbus brought a major commotion in Latin American liberation theology. The Native Americans and the African Americans gave the anniversary its decisive twist. It was celebrated as five hundred years of the struggles of peoples against oppression, both European and Christian. Liberation theologians had thought of themselves as "Latin Americans," and suddenly they realized that they really were only "Latins" and that this made them exclusive of many of the peoples of this vast region. Suddenly the ecological demands of the indigenous peoples were put on the theological agenda, and the religions of the Haitians, the Afro-Brazilians, and Afro-Cubans became important dialogue partners in a common struggle for liberation. Liberation struggles had to become Latin-feminist-Afro-eco-indigenous struggles.

It thus became clear that the cultural arena of struggles was more important than Marxist social science had led liberation theologians to believe. Unless the Afro-Brazilian cultures were respected and indigenous and Afro-Brazilian peoples recognized as having their own rights as peoples, they would not join any struggle. And the same was true of Aymaras, Quechuas, Guaraníes, Tarahumaras, Tzoltziles, and dozens of other original peoples of these lands. Culture became a significant factor of the struggle for liberation and had to be factored into the theology.

The changed situation also required some fundamental rethinking in the biblical foundations of liberation theology. The exodus, so central to this theology, is a threatening story for Native Americans because of its sequel in the conquest of the "promised land." These are not easy issues and have not been adequately resolved.

A final stage of liberation theology is that related to the jubilee year (2000) and the simultaneous movement for "another world." Preparations for the year 2000 centered on the demand from many parts of the third world for a cancellation of international debts. These debts have become instruments for putting poor nations in slavery to the banks of the rich nations. In one sense the Jubilee 2000 campaign accomplished little. Although there were some cancellations, the bulk of the debts remain in place. But in another sense much was achieved: first, a growing solidarity of the poor peoples of the world, expressed by the major gathering at Gauteng, South Africa, in 2000; second, the jubilee movement, which continues to campaign against the enslaving debts. Some important bishops, notably Cardinal Oscar Andrés Rodríguez of Tegucigalpa, have joined the movement and provided leadership.

Perhaps more important yet is the movement that expresses itself in the annual January gatherings in Porto Alegre, Brazil, of the World Social Forum under the slogan "Another world is possible." The slogan is a reference to Margaret Thatcher's famous dictum "There is no alternative [to the global market system]," a dictum known as TINA. The timing of these events coincides with the meeting of the leaders of the wealthy world at the World Economic Forum in Davos, Switzerland, to plan the control of the world within the global market. Tens of thousands of people gather at Port Alegre and, through hundreds of workshops, explore the possibilities for dreaming and for building a different world.

The importance of this topic can hardly be exaggerated. It is no longer possible in the third world to think of transforming society for justice and peace from above. In the context of the global market, governments have ever less power over the real dynamics of society. Change must come from below. But people need to know where they want to go and how to get there if legislation and decrees will not do it. And that is what the debate at Porto Alegre and at many other locations is about.

This topic is necessary for liberation theology if it is to maintain its relevance. Today it is the subject of many a theological meeting and many a publication. It is already clear that there is no *one* new world. The present world system is unacceptable because it destroys life, human and other, on a massive scale never before imagined. The alternatives must be built up from below, respecting the divergent cultural demands of the many peoples of the world and giving participation to citizens in the control of local affairs, as a new global system is slowly constructed in a manner that cannot be predicted. It is the major challenge faced by those struggling for liberation today.

A NEW WAY TO DO THEOLOGY

Liberation theology claims not to be another topic of theology like ecclesiology or eschatology, but rather a new approach to doing theology as a whole. Let us look at this claim:

1. *Liberation theologians affirm that theology comes after*. It is a second act. We first must live our faith, and then reflect on its meaning. Liberation theology usually lives in communities of believers who are poor and who believe that salvation cannot be referred solely to another life. Their present living conditions

are unacceptable because they truncate human life, denying adequate food, hygienic possibilities, schools, and medicines. Their spiritual lives must reflect these facts. The usual way of speaking about the Christian life in this context is to call it following Jesus, living like Jesus, who was poor and who lived and died with the poor.

When we speak of liberation theology, we are really speaking about Christian communities who live their Christian lives by following Jesus in his option for the poor and in his proclaiming the gospel as good news for the poor. This theological reflection is aimed at social liberation and not primarily at intellectual satisfaction. Faithful action and reflection on that action belong together. We call the relation of action and theology *praxis*, by which is intended that their relation is dialectical. It is like magnetic poles, for no field is created unless there are two poles. Theology can not exist without Christian living, nor can Christian living exist without reflection.

The Christian life of following Jesus is the practice of an option for the poor. Even the poor themselves must make this option theirs. They must recognize their human dignity as the persons for whom God has given the life of God's Son. There are in fact many poor individuals who feel that because their poverty makes them less than fully human, they must escape and leave the community behind. To make an option for the poor, on the contrary, is to recognize their full human dignity, to reject the degradation to which they are subjected in broader society, to affirm and celebrate this dignity in the festivities of their communities, and to join in struggle to overcome poverty. Paulo Freire said it famously, "No one liberates himself. No one liberates anybody. We liberate ourselves in community."[8] Prayer and action need theory (social and theological) to become effective. Contrariwise, theory (theology) dissociated from spiritual life and action is sterile.

2. Already implied in the situation in which liberation theology lives is "the option for the poor," seen as that of God and of Jesus. This expression was given legitmacy when it was included in the final documents of the Latin American bishops at their meeting in Medellín in 1968. But of course it is evangelically necessary with or without episcopal endorsement. Jesus made his option for the poor quite clear in the conversation with the rich man in Mark 10:17–25, summarizing it negatively in saying, "It is easier for a camel to go through the eye of a needle than for someone who is rich to enter the realm of God" (Mark 10:25). This difficult saying is given some flesh in the vision of the last judgment in Matt. 25:31–46. At the hour of judgment one's relation to Christ will not be judged a matter of belief or of taking the bread and wine but rather of contact with and service for the poor.

Jeremiah makes clear the theological centrality of the option for the poor when he says of King Josiah,

He judged the cause of poor and needy;
  then it was well.
Is not this to know me?

(Jer. 22:16)

Josiah was not poor but his life was, at least according to this text, lived out in relation to the needs of the poor. And this was counted as knowledge of God! Josiah may help us in the United States understand that we know God in the measure in which we respect, and expose ourselves to, the persons of those deprived of their basic needs. The novelty of liberation theology is its recognition that to be Christian, theology must begin with an option for the poor. If one wishes to follow Jesus, an option of solidarity with the movements of the poor to overcome their oppression and/or exclusion is not optional.

The option for the poor does not require poverty, but it does require a living presence with the poor. If one is living in the third world, this is no problem. One need not go far from one's house to come upon a grouping of self-made houses inhabited by crowds of defenseless people. If one has a car, as one drives down the streets of most cities in the world one will be accosted at major stoplights by children and handicapped adults begging, and by healthy adults selling anything from cold water in plastic bags to hubcaps or umbrellas. One is thus made aware daily that he or she lives in an island of comforts in a sea of poverty.[9]

3. The title of a book by Leonardo Boff expresses well the ecclesiology of liberation theology: *A Church Which Is Born from the People*. Already in the Second Vatican Council, the Constitution on the Church, *Lumen gentium*, began with a section on the people of God, before proceding to one on the hierarchy and then one on the laity. Because liberation theology grew and is sustained to this day in small communities of believers (base communities), *its understanding of the church is not so much institutional as communal*. The church does not become church by being appointed from above. It becomes church by the belief and practice of the people. Although these believing communities always claim to be loyal to church authorities and to hold to orthodox belief, there is undeniably a permanent tension here. For the authorities, the hierarchy itself is the font from which the true church takes its being, the channel the Holy Spirit has designated to govern God's people. The base communities accept the governance of church authorities, but they deny that they can be fully the church only where there are such authorities.

4. To opt for the poor means also *to struggle against systems that reduce people to poverty*. For Christians the founding story of the Bible is the story of the exodus from Egypt. Not only did the people of God escape from a system that practiced generalized slavery under the headship of a god-king; they also

received a law from YHWH their God that excluded kingship or, rather, recognized only God as king. The book of Judges attempts to re-create what life was like before Israel succumbed to the temptation of having kings "like the nations."

Here we need to take a slight detour into biblical studies to clarify how the exodus is understood in most base communities. Even before Norman Gottwald had launched his impressive treatment of early Israel in his *Tribes of Yahweh* (1979), the communities were talking about slavery in Egypt as a global system and observing that the exodus/Sinai event was the establishment of a system without systematic slavery. It was a revolution because it was a system change. A reading of the book of Exodus with this assumption shows that Israel became a people after the exodus and not before. It was a mixed multitude (Exod. 12:38) whom YHWH, the God of the poor, freed from slavery. It was this mixed multitude who became Israel, the people of YHWH. Those who were willing to follow YHWH and Moses his prophet accepted YHWH as God-king, excluding human kings with their slave systems.

The Sinaitic law is given with this introduction: "I am the LORD your God, who brought you out of the land of Egypt, out of the house of slavery" (Exod. 20:2). In all the laws of Exodus, Leviticus, and Numbers there is no mention of a human king. The only law in the Pentateuch that deals with a king is the seventeenth chapter of Deuteronomy, part of which is generally agreed to be a sixth-century revision of Israelite law originally formulated in the seventh century BCE during the reign of King Josiah.

The current global market, which reduces millions of people to poverty and powerlessness, is to be resisted now just as the people of God resisted the system of universalized slavery to the kings of Egypt. It is clear, therefore, that those, poor or not, who opt for the poor will seek by some means the transformation of this system into something more fair and human. It is at this point of analyzing the system and seeking means for its transformation that Marxist social science remains useful.

5. One of the more controversial aspects of liberation theology has been *the suspicion that it is "Marxist,"* with all the negative connotations that term carried during the cold war. In fact, Karl Marx's scientific works have proved to be most useful to liberation theologians, who have made their own study and interpretation of them. The importance of Marx for liberation theology can be summarized under four headings.

    a. *The holistic approach that refuses to separate economics, sociology, and political science.* Marxism is a study of society as a whole. In more recent times it has been seen that culture, which includes religion as really practiced, is a fourth factor to be considered in a truly holistic scheme.

b. *The recognition that the modern theological problem is idolatry and not atheism.*
Karl Marx believed that in his time the real God of European society was
Capital, that is, value which gives the appearance of generating more value
out of itself. Marx considered this belief "fetishistic," and Christians identify it with the biblical term *idolatry.* Atheism is an intellectual position
with few implications for daily life, whereas idolatry runs through all of
daily living. We do not need research to conclude that most people in the
United States spend more time shopping than praying. A look at any
major newspaper shows more space devoted to advertisements and to
stock market quotations than to synagogues, mosques, and churches.
Need more be said?[10]

c. *The analysis of how capital really grows* (over against the appearance that it
multiplies itself). In his view, the source of all value is socially necessary
labor. For some, this view is refuted by later economic developments, but
for many it requires only some new formulations. According to Marx, the
value of anything is the total amount of socially necessary labor incarnated
in it, both the immediate labor in its production and the past labor frozen
in the factory installations and machinery used in the production process.
The implication of this theory of value is that all value is seen as generated by humans.[11] Capital cannot create more value without the addition
of human labor.

d. *Affirming that all social interaction is to be judged in terms of its usefulness
toward human life values.* It makes no sense to speak of a healthy economy
when the people are starving, as is often done today by economists who
do not look at the whole of society.

Almost all base groups of Christians accept this more-holistic, social-
scientific analysis, obviously with different levels of sophistication. Does this
really mean that liberation theology is Marxist? As the term is loosely applied
by the press and by the church censors, the answer must be no. Nobody associated with liberation theology accepts orthodox Marxism as defined by Communist parties. Of course, if Marxism is used in the sense in which Platonism
or process theology are used to refer to ideas derived from particular thinkers,
the answer is yes. Many of the expressions of liberation theology do derive
from Marx. His theories make possible a social-scientific analysis that is more
sensitive to human values than are most economic- or political-scientific or
anthropological analyses. Just as important, liberation theologians share with
Marxists a commitment to radical social transformation.

THE ROLE OF BIBLE STUDY

One of the most notable characteristics of liberation theology as a movement
is the importance of the study of the Bible. In Latin America are tens of

thousands of small Bible study groups that read the Bible as a guide to their social situations. The largest number of these are in Brazil, many of them in rural areas. Usually they are accompanied by a trained pastoral agent, in most cases a woman of a religious order. Many have been prepared in "intensive Bible courses" given in different countries over the last twenty years. These courses last from one to six months, and the longer ones include an introduction to biblical languages. For English readers a glimpse of this movement can be gained from Ernesto Cardenal's *The Gospel in Solentiname*.[12] Cardenal is a priest, formerly a Trappist monk, who lived with a fishing community in Solentiname in Nicaragua in the late 1960s, recording their group discussions and later transcribing them for publication. Of course, the local situations produce considerable variation. The dictatorship that existed in Nicaragua at that time colored much of the debate and influenced the reading of the Gospels. Most groups today have a different political context, but the effort to relate Scripture to community problems, whatever the political situation, is a decisive feature for the interpretation of Scripture.

The situation with respect to the Bible differs for Catholics and Protestants. For most Catholics, reading the Bible is a discovery of a book previously unknown. They approach it with great reverence and are amazed to find the social sensitivity of the founding exodus event, the Sinai laws, the prophets, and the preaching of Jesus. Protestants have studied the Bible in Sunday school, and it has become a familiar book. However, they have read it as a book of theological truths that has little to say about their living conditions. This past experience creates a theological blockage that is difficult to overcome.

Liberation theology is often part of the program of Bible study in Protestant theological schools, but pastors find it difficult to use this approach in their churches when they graduate. In rare instances Sunday schools have become centers for reading the Bible from their social context. A spectacular example is Iglesia Bautista Emanuel in San Salvador, where a middle-sized urban congregation has given up some fifteen martyrs over the past twenty-five years in their troubled nation. Some of them were labor leaders; others, human rights workers; others, journalists; and some, student leaders. All were murdered for living their faith as they came to understand it through their Bible study.

So far we have said little about the content of Bible study that is inspired by liberation theology. The most important single feature, the exodus foundation story, has been mentioned. Closely related is the biblical concept of the realm of God. In the preaching of Jesus in the Synoptic Gospels, it is an organizing concept, the center of the whole of that preaching. It is also present in the Gospel of John and in Paul's theology, though with a less central role. When the realm of God is seen as a utopian vision of social transformation for Galilee and Judea, the groups get an idea of what they too need. Often the relationship is drawn between Jesus' preaching and the social practice presupposed in the Sinai laws and in the book of Judges. Here the realm of God meant that there could be no human kings who enslave people; the land and other resources were equitably distributed. Whether there ever was a time when the tribes of Israel rejected kingship and proclaimed themselves God's realm is not important, though most readers assume this was the case. Some more sophisticated readers believe that both in the laws and in the stories in the book of Judges, we have projections from the days of Ezra and Nehemiah. In either case, it is Scripture and would have been known to Jesus and have informed his preaching.

An important instrument for Bible reading in Latin America is the journal called *Revista de Interpretación Bíblica Latinoamericana* (RIBLA). This journal appears three times a year simultaneously in Spanish and Portuguese. Its articles are written by Protestant and Catholic biblical scholars, most of them professors in theological schools, who attempt to bring the latest scholarly discussion to the pastoral agents who accompany Bible groups of the liberation theology variety. The authors must make a deliberate effort to keep in touch with people's Bible-reading groups in order to address the problems that concern them as they present essays on different biblical subjects.[13]

LESSONS FOR PROGRESSIVE CHRISTIANS IN THE UNITED STATES

To have any success in the struggle to transform the global market, poor people who are the victims of exploitation and/or exclusion will need the support of progressive people who are themselves not poor, both in the third world and in rich countries. The project is daunting, and it will not be accomplished without all possible allies. Liberal Christians in the United States see great failings in the present global system and believe that their best bet at changing it comes from seeking political power within existing structures. They do not, however, intend to overthrow those structures. Liberals have too much stake in the system to risk destroying it, with all the chaos that would create. On the other hand, even though liberation theologians have rejected, at least for now, the usefulness of violent revolution, most third-world victims of the global system believe that a crisis of destruction and rebuilding is unavoidable, because it is the capitalist system itself that has produced our crisis and continues to generate poverty for the benefit of the rich.

Progressives are still largely shaped by their liberal heritage. However, as earlier chapters indicate, we have learned from liberation theologians that we are participating in an inherently unjust and oppressive system, and we are trying to find ways to resist it. As temporary beneficiaries of this system, we know that our economic situation is sufficiently different from that of Latin American peasants that our resistance will also be different from theirs.

Nevertheless, despite these differences, the two groups need each other. As long as we do not allow our social contexts to divide us, we are natural allies. The question of how drastic the changes needed will be should be postponed as we work together to face the current crisis.

Our response to liberation theology cannot be only a practical alliance, however. Its theological message is not important just for third-world countries, that is, the countries on the periphery of the global economy. The poverty of peripheral countries is directly related to the unprecedented accumulation of wealth in central countries. We in the wealthiest of the central • countries must come to terms with this reality.

Bible study with an understanding of social contexts and implications is both necessary and challenging for U.S. Christians. It is especially challenging because so many Euro-American Christians in the United States have little or no understanding of history as a struggle to oppose unjust social structures. Technological progress dominates the feeling for history in this sector of the U.S. population. As long as this is so, the past becomes no more than a prelude to the present period, in which we have automobiles, computers, precision bombs, and wonder drugs. African Americans and third-world immigrants know history differently. And so does the Bible! The challenge for biblical study is to make both biblical and current history live.

The *necessity* of liberation-oriented Bible study in U.S. churches comes from the urgency to change a world whose economic system condems 75 percent of humans to lives of permanent scarcity of basic vital needs. It is also a system that slowly destroys the environment. And in the United States, and to some extent elsewhere, it isolates classes through residential stratification. It drastically reduces mobility for those who do not have cars and reduces access to health care for those who do not have insurance. There are many imperatives for liberating social change!

Liberation theology claims to represent the gospel message as a whole and not just one aspect or topic among others. For that reason, those of us who acknowledge its basic truth are called to adopt it. On the other hand, our situation in the old-line churches of North America is so different from that out of which Latin American liberation theology arose that efforts to adopt it directly or wholesale are doomed to failure. In this concluding section, we struggle with the question of what this "alien" theology means for us. We will consider this in two sections, one focusing on an option for the poor and the other on liberation/salvation.

THE OPTION FOR THE POOR
FOR PROGRESSIVE CHRISTIANS

Let us begin by recognizing that when we speak about both liberal and progressive Christians, we are speaking about believers who are mostly well-to-do by global standards. In other words, in terms of our class situation we are not neutral or above the fray. If class warfare in today's world is primarily the war of the rich against the poor, we, as members of the "rich" class, are taking control of the means to assure life away from others of God's children. Whether we like it or not, this puts us on the side of the oppressors and requires that we approach the gospel call for an option for the poor from that starting place.

We must also recognize that our churches are voluntary communities and not natural ones. Most Latin American liberation theology flourishes in villages or depressed urban areas where all the participants have the same economic and political problems. If the source of water—a spring, well, or faucet—is far away and requires a lot of carrying, it is a problem for all. If there is no local school, or if the one that exists is poorly staffed and furnished, that is a problem for all. The same is true when there are deficiencies in transportation or health care or when political bosses act oppressively. The so-called "popular" reading of the Bible in Latin America depends to a considerable extent on this common perception of community problems. Our North American churches face a somewhat different problem, that of creating a real sense of community among persons who do not live together and most of whom have their vital needs easily provided.

We noted that in Latin American cities middle-class people are daily made aware that they live in an island of comforts in a sea of poverty. But in the daily life of the average U.S. churchgoer, there are no occasions to enter poor communities. Beggars and homeless people can survive only in the downtown streets of big cities, where they are largely invisible except at night when suburban people are ensconced in their homes and neighborhoods. Most church people in the United States do not know by name even one person who lives in makeshift quarters and who does not know from one day to the next where food will come from. In this environment, where cities have been so built as to isolate classes from each other, the option for the poor, which means not being just *for* the poor but also *with* the poor, can hardly be realized for believers as a group.

In this very different context, how can we make an option for the poor, an option that is not optional for Christians? Our suggestion is that the pastoral response to this issue is twofold: Our churches should make an important part of their activities to be programs that bring believers into contact with the poor in ways that are not paternalistic but promote solidarity. Built into these programs should be reflection on the causes that generate the kind of poverty that plagues our world in this twenty-first century after Christ. Social solidarity with the poor and reflection on the causes of poverty should be dialectically related. Solidarity should feed reflection, and reflection should deepen and improve solidarity.

What programs of contact and solidarity are feasible for our congregations?

1. Experience has shown that *work camps* in the inner cities or in impoverished rural areas can provide Christians from privileged areas an opportunity to share with the impoverished people of the United States and other countries. Projects should be so organized that the outsiders to the community come to share in doing projects decided on and led by the community leaders. This is often difficult, but we must assume that people in an impoverished location know their real needs better than visitors from outside. The reflection on the experience should be done, at least in part, by both groups together. If both groups are Christian, the natural way to do this is through common Bible study. Naturally, it is important to have an experienced leader who knows the Bible and, ideally, understands both communities.
2. *BorderLinks* is a program based in Tucson that helps people share in and reflect on the special problems suffered by the poor who live on the border between Mexico and the United States. This and similar programs, such as *Global Education in Central America*, have proved effective for many Christian groups. Borders are places where the conflictive relations between the center and the periphery come to the surface more than elsewhere. In the BorderLinks programs local groups have a long experience in receiving those who come in solidarity to share their lives with them.
3. *Pastors for Peace* is a program that organizes caravans of trucks with medical, housing, and other supplies for impoverished communities in nearby countries. The trucks as well as the supplies are usually left for the programs of the receiving communities in places like Chiapas, Cuba, or Guatemala. The pastors and others who collect these goods and deliver them also stay with the receiving communities long enough to find out what their lives are like through living in their homes.

There is always something artificial about these experiences, since one group is permanently living in poverty and the other is composed of visitors who can seek little more than a tourist experience to broaden their views of the world. Nevertheless, in a world divided so radically by class differences, the option for the poor among the well-to-do must be programmed and worked at in ways like these.

It is important that our congregations learn not only about the economic chasm between central and peripheral countries but also about the pervading class problem that corrodes U.S. society. The various programs that churches can and should carry out to bring the issue of poverty home to them should be followed by reflection on the ways our transportation, tax, housing, health, and other social systems reflect and deepen the class division between the wealthy and the poor within the United States. Unless Christians become quite clear about the mechanisms that are deepening our class divisions, they will never get serious about facing up to the difficult decisions necessary to effect real change.

Perhaps the most important goal for churches that want to take to heart the spiritual dynamics of liberation theology is to work among their membership at raising the awareness of the very existence of this class struggle, which our news media try hard to ignore. When the capitalists of this country can come so close to convincing a majority that tax cuts just for themselves will benefit us all, it is clear that we have a class struggle from above against those who are exploited. When politicians can even dare to suggest that the social security system or parts of it should be privatized, that is, handled by the wealthy, we are greatly in need of learning to see the class struggle that is going on in this country. The outcome of the programs we have mentioned for bringing church people into contact with the poor should contribute to creating this consciousness.

Proclaiming Salvation to All

It is unnecessary to argue that our world is divided between those who have a surplus of the goods of life and a majority who must live with a daily deficit. This was also true in Jesus' days, though much less visibly so. Faced with this fact, the Gospels seem to speak with two voices on the question of salvation. On the one hand, Mary of Nazareth can celebrate the overthrow of the powerful and the coming hunger of those who are now satisfied (Luke 1:46–55), and Jesus can tell John that his mission is to preach good news *to the poor* (Luke 7:21–22). On the other hand, we hear from John the evangelist that all who believe, regardless of social class, will be saved (John 3:16). This is less contradictory than it might seem. In a world where there are some who are enriched by excessive accumulation of the goods of this world and others who are impoverished by the same excessive accumulation, liberation/salvation for all must begin with the poor, the victims. This can be achieved only in solidarity with those who will join them, struggling for a new world in which nobody goes to bed hungry and no child dies of readily curable diseases such as measles and diarrhea.

For progressive Christian congregations it is important to have contact with poor groups and to grow in understanding the interrelatedness of all on our planet earth and the injustices created by the current global economy.

But it is not enough. Our churches must engage in actions that will chip away at the wrongs that afflict our world. On this planet, either we are all saved or we are all damned. It is one world.

Liberation theology in Latin America began with economic analysis. It gradually recognized that issues of gender, ethnicity, and ecology are also crucially important and moved to a holistic view of the problem and of salvation from it. In the progressive churches of the United States, we have dealt more with issues of gender, ethnicity, and ecology than with issues of economic class. Hence, in this chapter we have emphasized the latter. But there is much still to be done on all these fronts, and here, as in Latin America, what is needed is a holistic view.

From this holistic perspective progressive North American Christians will find much to do. Our book *Progressive Christians Speak*[14] includes sixteen chapters dealing with areas in which we are called to work. In general the focus is on possible reforms, but even that book deals little with the issues of class that Latin American liberation theology highlights. It also deals too little with issues of race, which in American history have been inseparable from those of class.[15]

Responding to racism in American society calls for many reforms, some of which we discussed in *Progressive Christians Speak*. But it also calls for resistance of a more fundamental kind to the deep-seated racism in which we as part of the American people are fully involved. One form that such resistance may take is the movement for reparations, especially for African Americans who have suffered so long from slavery and legal segregation and are even now too often second-class citizens. Currently, success of this movement is only a remote possibility, but its promotion is a means of forcing a deeper consciousness of the wrongs under which American blacks have lived and continue to suffer. Like other forms of resistance, this one may ultimately result in practical reforms.

The case for reparations is primarily based on the need to recognize that all of us share in the victimization of our fellow citizens of African origin. The United States, in spite of language about the rights of all in the founding documents, was built on the expropriation of the lands of the native peoples and on slave labor. Then, when slave labor was no longer profitable, African Americans were turned into sharecroppers and often kept permanently in debt, restricted to undesirable neighborhoods, limited in their access to good schools and jobs, and in general treated as ex-slaves with lesser rights.

The reparations movement is designed to create consciousness and recognition of how Euro-Americans have benefited from the oppression of African Americans and are collectively responsible for creating and maintaining a racist system. The amount of the reparations and how they would be used to reduce the negative consequences of discrimination suffered by descendents of slaves remains to be discussed, but we should be able to get together on the moral imperative to find ways to confess our guilt and to make amends, so that this racial issue does not continue to plague the nation. We need to recognize that it is more a white problem than a black one, so Euro-Americans have the responsibility to lead in changes.[16]

As we seek to hear the voices of the oppressed of the world and to work in solidarity with them, progressive Christians in the United States need to keep abreast of the discussions at Porto Alegre as to how, working from below, the common people of the world can resist their economic enslavement. We need to ask how we can join their resistance and what role we can play, as citizens of the world's only superpower, in supporting them in their efforts.

Liberation theology claims that it is a matter of faith, of spiritual life, to struggle against oppression. This struggle is not an ethical second step after salvation. It is a matter of being, or not being, a Christian. Do we believe that? And if so, are we ready to follow Jesus in this situation of crisis? This is the challenge that liberation theology poses to progressive Christians.

DISCUSSION QUESTIONS

1. Would reading the Bible in small groups in churches help Christians in the United States understand the gap between the rich and the poor?
2. Would it help us to understand the need to rebuild community for a better future?
3. How can the "unsafe" feeling we get in poor neighborhoods be translated into helping us understand the desperate need for community there and between those neighborhoods and our own neighborhoods?
4. Does this chapter convince you that we need to understand Christianity and society from the bottom up?

FOR FURTHER READING

Boff, Clodovis, and George V. Pixley. *The Bible, the Church and the Poor*. Maryknoll, NY: Orbis Books, 1989.

Brown, Robert McAfee. *Liberation Theology: An Introductory Guide*. Louisville, KY: Westminster/John Knox Press, 1993.

———. *Spirituality and Liberation: Overcoming the Great Fallacy*. Louisville, KY: Westminster John Knox Press, 1988.

Freire, Paulo. *Pedagogy of the Oppressed*. New York: Continuum, 1970.

Gutierrez, Gustavo. *A Theology of Liberation*. Maryknoll, NY: Orbis Books, 1973.

9

Feminist Theology

Rosemary Radford Ruether

ONE WOMAN'S STORY

I grew up Christian, but in my 20s, something about my traditional faith was chaffing me. It just didn't fit. It was the late 1970s, I was a young professional woman, trying to find my place in the world and in the Church. I thought I might have outgrown Christianity, when I fell into the company of a group of "uppity women" who were "nobody's brothers in Christ, thank you very much." In the years that we shared our lives, we read Ruether's *God-Talk* and Walberg's *Jesus according to a Woman* and Alice Walker's *The Color Purple*, among other books. I remember clearly—right down to the time of day and the color of the sky—when that old grey god on the ceiling of the Sistine Chapel, to whom I'd always directed my prayers, blew up. Utterly blew up. And suddenly, though there was no one image to take the old guy's place, God seemed ENORMOUS, more mysterious and wonderful and BIG than I had ever imagined. I had to do theology differently from that day on. I had to do everything differently because I understood God, myself, my companions on the journey and the whole of creation differently.

Now I'm fifty-something. When my 18 year old niece told me recently she thinks feminism is old-fashioned and Christian women would be happier without it, I realized the story has to be retold. We have to help a new generation discover for themselves the power of the liberating Word.

Anonymous

INTRODUCTION

In the previous chapter we saw that although Latin American liberation theology has much to teach us, its role in Latin America cannot be directly imitated in the United States. Our context is too different. We learn from it, and this whole volume is deeply indebted to it. But it cannot as such be our theology. We belong to the segment of the global population that oppresses those who speak through this theology, and even the kinds of solidarity with the poor for which it calls are only partly realizable by most of us.

Black theology speaks to us Euro-American progressive Christians more directly because it focuses on an oppression from which we as a group have more obviously benefited and for the continuation of which even today we are more blatantly responsible. We can acknowledge its truth and recognize the importance of changing. But white Americans cannot claim to become black theologians. It is our task to be white theologians in light of the truth of black theology.

Furthermore, it is possible to go about our business day by day without giving much thought to the relation of either of these theologies to what we are doing. We do not say this happily. We know that such a relation exists and that we need repeatedly to bring it to mind. But we will do so only as we make a special effort.

With regard to another form of liberation theology, feminist theology, the situation is quite different. When we gather as progressive Christians, half of us are women, and most of these women identify, at least to some degree, with feminist theology. As progressives, the men are also supportive of this theology even if they cannot claim it as theirs in the same sense. In our families and at work, we face every day in our relations across lines of gender many of the issues discussed in feminist theology. They relate quite immediately to our worship on Sunday morning and to the way our congregations function throughout the week. As progressive Christians, both men and women, we are committed to the realization of the vision provided by feminist theology.

As a movement of *reform*, feminism has had remarkable success in old-line Protestant churches. Many of our pastors and other leaders at all levels are now women. Our hymnbooks have been changed to avoid, or at least greatly reduce, the dominance of masculine language about both human beings and God. Some improvement has been made in biblical translations. A lectionary has been developed that avoids patriarchal language in the translation of the selected biblical passages. A fair number of preachers at least try to use neutral language. Of course, only a minority of congregations work hard at these changes, and even they find it easy to slip back at times. Constant reminders are needed. But reform continues and still spreads within these churches.

However, feminist theology is also a theology of *resistance*. Reform can accomplish much of importance, but patriarchy is deeply entrenched in all the major world cultures and in the psyches of both men and women. The change to a feminist vision is a profound conversion, as the story with which the chapter begins makes clear. Nothing remains quite the same. Sadly, the very success of reform in opening up new opportunities for women reduces the pressure for deeper changes. Indeed, as the story that begins this chapter also makes clear, women who have grown up in the Reformed context often do not understand the need for feminism or want to identify themselves as feminists. The deeper struggle against patriarchy has just begun.

Both men and women are psychologically confused by efforts to rid themselves and their culture of patriarchal assumptions and habits. There are frequent backlashes against changes that have already been made so that even at the level where reforms can take place, deep-seated patriarchal attitudes reassert themselves and seek reversals. There is much to resist, and we can engage effectively in this resistance only as we remind ourselves, again and again, of the full feminist vision.

WHAT IS FEMINIST THEOLOGY?

Feminist theology is not just women doing theology. Women have done and continue to do theology that does not question the masculinist paradigms of traditional theology. Nor is feminist theology simply the affirmation of "feminine" themes in theology. What has been called "feminine" in Western thought has been constructed to complement the construction of masculinity. Sexism in patriarchal anthropology is a system of stratified relationships. Both masculinity and femininity are constructed as part of this same system. Thus to make the feminine side of this system explicit in religious symbolism does not undermine but empowers the masculine side while restricting women to what is defined as "feminine."

Feminism seeks to deconstruct this whole system, both symbolically and socially. Feminism rejects the patriarchal gender paradigm that associates males with human characteristics defined as superior and dominant (rationalist, power over others) and women with those defined as inferior or auxiliary (intuition, passivity). The goal is a redefinition of both men and women as fully and equivalently human.

Christian feminist theology applies feminist critique and reconstruction of gender paradigms to Christian theology. It rejects patterns of theology that justify male dominance and female subordination, such as exclusive male language for God, imaging God after social roles of male dominance, viewing

males as more like God than females, and asserting that only males can represent God as leaders in the church and in society while women were created by
God to be subordinate to men and sin when they reject this subordination.

Feminist theology seeks to reconstruct all the basic symbols in the theological system: the concept of God; humanity as male and female; the meaning of creation, sin, and redemption; the person and work of Christ; and the
church itself, with future hope in a gender-inclusive and egalitarian way. Feminists not only deconstruct misogynist and male-dominant themes in the tradition but also search out the more egalitarian themes in Scripture and church
tradition to reenvision the whole system of theology.

For feminist theology to develop, certain cultural and social conditions are
necessary. There needs to be a stance toward knowledge that recognizes that
all human symbols, including theological symbols, are human social constructions, not fixed truths eternally and unchangeably disclosed from beyond
history. Many of our cultural symbols have been constructed by those in power
to validate their own dominance and the subjugation of those they wish to
dominate: women, inferiorized social classes, and those of other races. Such
symbols can be rejected and changed.

Not all social symbols, however, are simply expressions of the will to power
of some against others. There are also human quests for harmony, justice, and
mutual affirmation of the other equally with oneself. Feminist theology, like
all liberation theologies, seeks criteria for differentiating between symbols of
dominance and power over others and symbols that arise from the prophetic
quest for justice and mutually affirming human relations. It seeks to critique
the first pattern of symbolism while creating renewed theology around the second type of symbolism. The fundamental assumption of all such renewed theologies is that the basic message of Christian theology should be about
redemption from evil, from unjust relations between humans, not the perpet-
uation of injustice.

Why didn't feminist theology arise before the late 1960s? The shifts of consciousness that give birth to feminist theology depend on certain social conditions. Women must gain agency in the institutions of the church. Women's
cultural agency in the church must be organized as a movement and a community of discourse that supports women's and men's critique of the dominant
gender paradigm. Women must acquire the educational credentials that
enable them to be recognized as theological teachers in and for the church.
These social conditions did not exist adequately before the late 1960s and still
do not exist fully today.

Yet feminist theology is not left without historical witnesses. There were
glimmers of feminist insights in medieval women mystical theologians, such as
Hildegard of Bingen and Julian of Norwich. There was a debate about the

nature of women that raged from the fourteenth into the seventeenth century
in which defenders of women, beginning with Christian de Pisan in France and
extending into the Reformation with Marie Dentière in Geneva, criticized negative interpretations of biblical passages about women and offered alternatives.
There were more fully developed feminist theological critiques in seventeenth-
century church leaders, such as Quaker foundress Margaret Fell in her 1666
treatise *Womens Speaking Justified* and Anglican Mary Astell in her 1694 book
A Serious Proposal to the Ladies. The nineteenth-century U.S. women's rights
movement generated several critical feminist theologians, such as Sarah
Grimke, Lucretia Mott, and Elizabeth Cady Stanton.

Yet these proto- and early-feminist theological writings were largely buried
and forgotten. It is feminist theology today that has rediscovered and repub-
lished them. Thus feminist theology is possible not simply when a few women
manage to write feminist thoughts that escape oblivion but when this earlier
and contemporary work becomes a part of a teaching tradition in the theological seminaries and churches. This began to happen only in the late 1960s
and 1970s in the United States, and now, increasingly, around the world, as
women have gained both theological education and ordination and have
become teachers in theological schools and pastors in churches.

Yet feminist theology has still not gained a secure foothold in the churches
and theological schools. Continual backlash movements in the churches seek
to invalidate feminist theology. This backlash misinterprets feminist theology
as mere hostility of women against men that seeks to reverse the relations of
dominance and subordination, and as totally contrary to the gospel. Other
more-moderate church leaders accept the inclusion of some women in ministry and theological education but wish their presence to be merely token.
Feminist theology is allowable as an occasional "specialized" course in the theological schools, not as a revision of the main lines of the theological memory
and vision that must become the basis of the theological training for everyone,
not just for a few "feminist" women and men.

Others construe feminist theology as a 1960s "fad" or as a corrective that
has done its work, with many women now present in theological education and
the church, and is now passé. Thus feminist theology is in danger of falling
well short of its goal of a deep and thoroughgoing revision of theology. It may
be pushed to the side, marginalized and forgotten by those who see it only as
a passing and "special interest" perspective that does not need to be absorbed
into the thinking of the whole church. Feminist theology needs to broaden its
base in order to be heard by all Christians. This means not only constant correction of the misinterpretation of feminism as reverse sexism (by some feminists as well as by antifeminist men and women), but also continual
restatement of the basic vision of feminism in new and diverse contexts.

THE METHODOLOGY OF FEMINIST THEOLOGY

In the rest of this chapter I will lay out the basic methodology of feminist theology and its hermeneutics (interpretive method) of both recovery and reinterpretation of Christian Scripture and tradition. Feminist theology is done through a continual renewal of a basic hermeneutical process. This process has three interrelated aspects: (1) critique of the misogyny, that is, negative attitudes toward women reflected in the biblical and theological tradition as well as their androcentrism, that is, their almost exclusively male point of view; (2) recovery of alternative, prophetic, egalitarian traditions in our heritage; and (3) reenvisioning all the theological symbols in an egalitarian, justice-making way.

Feminist theology usually begins with the critique of misogyny. This misogyny is expressed most explicitly in negations of women, typically for the purpose of justifying some restriction of their activities. A classical example is 1 Tim. 2:13–14's interpretation of Gen. 1–3: "For Adam was formed first, then Eve; and Adam was not deceived, but the woman was deceived and became a transgressor." The point of this interpretation is made clear in verse 12: "I permit no woman to teach or to have authority over a man; she is to keep silent." One starts with such misogynist passages, because they are what "stick out" in the tradition. They are the passages constantly reiterated to reinforce women's renewed silencing. One has to deal with their claims to authority before one can get on to further questions.

As the Christian tradition has understood this passage, woman was created by God to be second and subordinate in the order of creation. Therefore, by God's intent and her very nature she is to have no public authority. But women also became insubordinate, and this insubordination of women is the cause of the entry of sin into the world. Therefore, women must be resubordinated, both as a reaffirmation of her original and subordinate place as normative in society and to punish her for her inveterate tendency to insubordination, which is the root of evil.

This passage thus sums up the classic double bind of the definition of women in church and society in the Christian tradition. Woman is seen as both naturally subordinate and sinfully insubordinate. Her subordination must be doubly affirmed as both her nature and her due punishment.

The critique of such misogynist passages in the Bible presupposes a critical shift of consciousness that has major implications for the authority of the Bible. By naming such a passage as "misogynist," one rejects it as authoritative for revealing the will of God and the true nature of God's will for humanity and creation. Classical Christian tradition has regarded this passage as definitive and final, as revealing God's original intent in creating humanity as male and female, their fallen or distorted state, and the path to restoration of humanity according to God's redemptive will.

A feminist renaming of this passage as misogynist rejects this authoritative status. The passage is redefined as expressing a prejudiced view of women by a male shaped by social ideologies and systems unjust to women. This redefinition does not mean that everything in the Bible is rejected as lacking authority. Rather this passage is shown to contradict other touchstones that Christians have taken to be revelatory of what is true and good, such as Gen. 1:27, which speaks of both genders as created in the image of God without one being subordinated to another. Above all, it contradicts the revolutionary, egalitarian teachings of Jesus to which the Gospels testify, in whom the mighty are put down from their thrones and those who have been oppressed are lifted up (Luke 1:52).

Feminist hermeneutics begins with a shift in consciousness that questions the inerrancy of the Bible and the classical Christian traditions based on it. The Bible comes to be seen as ambiguous. It has many expressions of loving and justice-making insights, but it also has some statements that reflect prejudiced human opinion that mandate and seek to reinforce unjust relations, such as sexist views of women, or ethnocentric and militarist views of other people. Christian feminist theology and hermeneutics makes another foundational assumption: namely, that the true God is a God who is good and wills good. Therefore any cultural and social constructions that mandate what is unloving and unjust in human relations are not of God and do not reflect the true nature or will of God.

This criteria for sorting out what is normative and what is not normative in the Scriptures and Christian tradition is stated in my 1983 book *Sexism and God-Talk*:

> Whatever denies, diminishes or distorts the full humanity of women is . . . appraised as not redemptive. Theologically speaking, whatever diminishes or denies the full humanity of women must be presumed not to reflect the divine or authentic relation to the divine, not to reflect the authentic nature of things nor to be the message or work of an authentic redeemer or a community of redemption. This negative principle also implies a positive principle: what does promote the full humanity of women is of the Holy, it does reflect true relation to the divine; it is the true nature of things, the authentic message of redemption and the mission of the redemptive community.[1]

We should add to this definition an awareness that women exist in many class, race, and cultural contexts. Feminist theology is concerned with and is in solidarity with the oppressed in all contexts, but it looks at theology from the particular lens of gender, just as Latin American liberation theology looks at theology from a Latin American lens. As is the case in this chapter, different class, race, ethnic, and cultural contexts are addressed in feminist theology, with the focus on gender in each of these contexts.

In my exposition of this theme of "full humanity of women" there is a need to indicate that we don't know what "full humanity of women" would mean in any particular context, since we have experienced various distortions in our historical experience. In some sense, it is an eschatological hope. But we have touchstones of what this would mean in healing, loving, and just experiences with one another. I also assume that we have some inherent capacity or good potential for this, which reflects our created relation to God, or what has traditionally been called "the image of God." Furthermore this good potential for women's being cannot be defined against men. Full humanity of women by definition cannot be based on negating the full humanity of men, any more than men's full humanity can be defined as negating that of women. Human good potential is relational; so any negation of another person or group diminishes ourselves as well.

This judgment that any biblical passage that is misogynist is not authoritative, not redemptive, and not of God needs to be put in the larger context of androcentrism. As Elisabeth Schüssler Fiorenza has rightly asserted, the Bible as a whole is androcentric; it is not just selected passages that are explicitly misogynist. The entire Bible was written by men (actually by a dominant class and race of men) and, therefore, from a male point of view. It assumes that males are the normative human beings. This means that women are generally absent or silent. They are usually mentioned only when they are seen as a problem. Explicit mandates about women are typically articulated only when men want to prohibit women from doing something, to define them as less than men, or to confine them to stereotypic activities presumed to be particular to women, such as the anointing women of the Gospels. At other times women become visible only because all the men have left the scene, such as the women at the cross and the tomb.

Even passages that define women as "equal" are androcentric. This applies both to Gen. 1:27, where women are included in the image of God only within a male-defined and male-headed collective "Adam," and to Gal. 3:28, where the difference of male and female is negated in the context of a male-defined Christ. Only rarely do we seem to hear a woman's own voice, such as Hagar's poignant reply to the angel of the Lord in the desert in Gen. 16:8: "'I am running away from my mistress Sarai.'" Sadly, this only sets the stage for the command "'Return to your mistress, and submit to her'" (Gen. 16:9). As Schüssler Fiorenza has said, we have to read all of the Scripture from the underside, in the context of women-identified communities of interpretation, imagining what this experience might have been like for the woman herself.

This pattern of misogyny and androcentrism in the Scripture is not acci-
dental. It reflects a male-dominated society where women are legally and culturally marginalized. They are not autonomous persons in their own right but
dependents in various relations to dominant men, whether as wives, daughters, or mothers of such men, or as doubly or triply subordinated people, such
as servants or slaves of dominant males or females. In classical patriarchies of
the kind reflected in the Bible, women are denied elite education and access
to the circles where dominant men expound and pass on the culture.

Even where a few women have partially broken free from this control, by
having gained some education, a prophetic voice, economic means as entrepreneurs, or political power as queens, their stories are censored or preserved
according to the interests of men. We may hear of a foreign queen because she
is defined as a purveyor of idolatry or of a queen mother in Israel because she
championed the son who won the throne. We know there was a woman
prophet and teacher in the church of Thyatira only because the writer of the
Revelation of John defines her as a Jezebel, who beguiles his servants "to practice fornication and eat food sacrificed to idols" (Rev. 2:20). She is then threatened with gang rape and the striking dead of her children (Rev. 2:22–23).

The stories of women are read from men's interests both in the scriptural
account and in the subsequent interpretations of these accounts. Thus the
midwives who defy the orders of Pharaoh to save the child Moses may be seen
as too independent for proper femininity by subsequent male interpreters,
who read into their stories assumptions about their timidity or fear that are
not in the original accounts, or the male interpreters may tell the story in a
way that ignores the role of the midwives altogether. Thus we receive our traditions with many misogynist and androcentric overlays.

Androcentric overlays include class and race overlays. A foreign queen is
assumed to be an idolater because she is foreign and brings another religious
culture. An Egyptian woman slave is triply marginalized as female, slave, and
foreigner. These gender, class, and race biases, which are already in the Scripture, are added to by subsequent interpreters who read them out of their own
gender, class, and race assumptions.

This does not mean that there have been no women-identified women and
sympathetic men in past generations of the biblical and Christian community.
Indeed, I assume that every girl-child is born woman-identified, and every boy-
child, with a capacity for empathy with his sister. It takes intentional and continually enforced socialization to beat that self-affirmation out of women and
that empathy out of men. Those who don't learn their lessons get harsh treatment. Yet this capacity for creative potential and empathetic relations wells up
irresistibly in every generation. Again and again, breakthrough communities
arise, imagining a new human society and questioning the dominant system.

Schüssler Fiorenza believes, and I agree with her, that there was such an incipient woman-church as the roots of the Jesus community out of which the Christian church arose. Traces of their vision remain in the New Testament stories, despite layers of censorship and reassertion of patriarchal commands.

FEMINIST THEOLOGY IN CHURCH TRADITION

Again and again through church history, subversive ideas sprout: in circles of widows and virgins, in women's religious communities, in moments of church renewal such as the Quaker meetings of the seventeenth century, or perhaps at times when just two or three women talk together in their homes. Texts such as Acts 2:17, "Your sons and your daughters shall prophesy," are accessed to imagine the Holy Spirit pouring out her power on women and giving them voice to speak their grievances and hopes. In prophetic writings by Baptist and Quaker women in mid-seventeenth-century England, this text from Acts appears over and over again. One can only stand in awestruck horror at the enormous energy it has taken for ruling-class, male-dominated cultures to assure that such thoughts are stillborn in most women and that those few women who act them out are severely punished.

Only with great effort and special luck do the occasional women theologians such as Hildegard of Bingen and Julian of Norwich obtain the favor of a few supportive men to articulate their visions and have them written down. Even more extraordinary is the process by which these rare texts managed to be preserved and to come down to us. Julian's revelations were carried from England by monks fleeing from monastic closures in the sixteenth century and preserved only because they were seen as part of their monastic tradition. It was only in the twentieth century that they were read, translated, and then, with the rise of a new women's movement, studied from women's point of view.

This overwhelming overlay of androcentrism and misogyny poses severe problems about how we can hope to find any genuinely liberating woman-identified touchstones in the Bible and theological tradition. I believe that there is liberating tradition in the Hebrew Scripture and Second Testament, but it is limited and ambiguous, as indeed are all of our finite liberating efforts. To me, the two bodies of religious literature that we have inherited from our Christian ancestors and their Jewish ancestors before them are defined by a deep struggle between two tendencies: the prophetic tendency that sides with the poor and oppressed and critiques the systems that oppress them, understanding this critique as the Word of God; and the tendency to establish social and religious systems of male, race, and class domination and to validate these systems as God's revealed law.

This struggle is a continually renewed process. One generation's break-through to critical questioning of forms of domination may generate language and texts that are then used by the next generation to validate their systems of controlling power, as happened with the apostles of Jesus. Moreover, every prophetic breakthrough to critical questioning and new vision is limited by the context of the questioners, or rather the context of those whose questions are accepted as texts for others to hear and receive. When the Hebrew prophets denounced the appropriation of the land of the poor farmer by rich landown-ers and the arrogance of the priests in the temple, they ignored the oppression of women and children in the family. These are mentioned only when they become widows and orphans due to the oppression of other more-powerful men. Prophetic denunciations in biblical texts are often couched in a way that reinforces ethnic and religious discrimination against the non-Israelite or the Jews who do not accept Christ. Occasionally we may hear of a man who loves another man or a woman another woman, but heterosexism is assumed as normative.

These limits of what can be heard and accepted as prophetic means that the liberating vision of the questioner is rooted in particular contexts: for exam-ple, a Jewish male of middling economic status, who may be marginalized as a hill country dweller by the rich landowners of the plains or as a Jew by Assyr-ians, Persians, or Romans, but who has little insight into what it means to be a woman, much less a slave woman, not to mention a gay or lesbian slave in his own culture. When he speaks for the liberation of "his people," he means a group of men like himself, with their women, slaves, and children included under them, but with those social systems that keep these dependent people in bondage unchanged.

The reading of critical prophetic texts as inclusive of ourselves is thus a con-tinual process of interpretation and reinterpretation that Jews call "midrash." This is especially true for those of us who search the Scripture for a liberating word for women, even more so for women of oppressed classes and races. We take texts that reflect some questioning of oppressive conditions within one limited context in the past and transfer them to our context. We apply them not only to a historical time that was unimagined by those who originally fash-ioned them but also to social conditions that they did not intend: for example, to women oppressed by patriarchy, class, race, and heterosexism.

We may take the powerful words of Mary in the Magnificat, a midrashic appropriation of the song of Hannah, into the first-century Jesus movement: "He has brought down the powerful from their thrones and lifted up the lowly" (Luke 1:52), and we read our own oppressions and hopes into it. In one context the mighty might mean the bureaucrats of the World Bank and the World Trade Organization and the lowly, exploited women workers of free trade zones. In another context the mighty might be arrogant, homophobic churchmen who deny the possibility of blessing of unions and priestly ordination to gay and lesbian people.

It is appropriate to use Scripture this way, for this is the way Scripture uses itself. But we need to be clear that this is midrash, not exegesis (recovery of what it meant originally). Texts with a liberating vision are applied to a new context, used to critique a different situation and to imagine a liberating alternative. We also need to realize that our context also is limited and our vision has its blinders. We are aware of who is stepping on us, but not of those on whom we are trespassing, until they too gain critical voice to call us to task. Then the parameters of our vision become visible and are tested.

Short of the reign of God—and we will ever be short of the reign of God—we will never reach the fully inclusive vision, where everyone is included equally, where justice reigns for all, where no one buys redemption at the expense of others. The best we can do is to keep the process going, to keep questioning the powerful and seeking to include those more marginalized than ourselves. For example, African American women, now present with some voice at some seminaries, speak for the marginalized among marginalized women in this context. But when a group of African American women from Garrett-Evangelical Seminary journeyed to South Africa for the World Parliament of Religions in December of 1999, they became very aware of their affluence and privilege as educated, middle-strata Americans whose income puts them in the wealthiest 20 percent of the world's population. They spent much time discussing this experience and how they should take responsibility in relation to the desperately poor and AIDs-afflicted black South Africans whom they met there.

This is not to discredit our cries and criticisms, but simply to ask, How do we keep the process going? How do we keep empowering the others and not joining the establishment? This means that the third step of feminist theology is always a work in progress, contextually limited and never definitive. We tell a hopeful tale of good news for a moment, for a particular circle of people in a particular time and place. We don't speak for anyone else. We barely and only momentarily speak for ourselves. We can only hope that our reconstructions of liberating symbols don't implicitly exclude others and that they carry sparks that others can carry over into their context to give light to their situation, just as we have been able to use texts generated by critical and hopeful movements preserved in the Bible. We join the stream of witnesses that carry on the process of critical questioning of oppression and hopeful dreaming of promised lands and beloved communities.

We also need to gain some perspective on that stream of witnesses connecting us to a biblical text that we may appropriate as liberating for ourselves today. What were its context and limits? What are our contexts and limits? Who are the parents, grandparents, and great-grandparents whose reimaginings of this text link us to its scriptural expression? But there is more than a stream of witnesses. There is also the living Spirit, present now as much as in any past moment, to set us free to critique injustices and to imagine new worlds not imagined before. The goal of interpretation of hermeneutics is not historical exegesis; it is liberating midrash, liberating storytelling and proclamation. Hermeneutics is about preaching in communities of faith. We will never be freed to imagine what a text can/should mean today at this time, at this place, as long as we are bound by the odd idea that hermeneutics has to do with discovering what a text meant originally. It is a useful beginning point in the process but a deadening end point.

Take, for example, two favorite texts for feminist theology: "God created humankind in his image; . . . male and female he created them" (Gen. 1:27); and "There is no longer Jew or Greek . . . slave or free . . . male and female . . . in Christ" (Gal. 3:28). Each of the pairs of these texts have somewhat different problems. The male-female pair very likely existed by itself and had a different philosophical base and development than the other two pairs. The focus here is on the male-female pair. We may wish to read from these two texts the glad news that women, equally with men, were created by God in God's image, and that in Christ all hierarchical domination of male over female has been overcome to restore us to our original equality in God's image. It is a good modern feminist midrash, but it can't be derived directly from what was probably its earliest meaning. Rather it is itself the product of a long historical process of interpretation.

Careful exegesis of the Genesis text by Phyllis Bird has made it clear that the first half of this phrase was not identified with but separated from the second half. The "image of God" did not include but was differentiated from "male and female" in the thought of the male priestly writers that constructed this text. "Image of God" was understood not as sharing God's divine nature but rather as representing divine sovereignty on earth. Although this was given to all humans collectively, it was assumed that it was the males of the ruling class that exercised this representation of divine sovereignty over the rest of creation, a sovereignty that includes dependent humans, women, children, and slaves. Second, "male and female" does not refer to the "image of God," for God is not male and female, but rather to those characteristics that humans share with animals but not with God, namely, gender, sexuality, and reproduction.

It was the Greek Platonic tradition that read into the phrase "image of God" a different meaning, namely, a sharing in the divine nature of God. Our souls participate in the divine Wisdom or Logos of the Creator, and this iconic sta-

tus gives us both dignity and the promise of immortality. But did women possess this image of God equally with men? Here Paul's statement in 1 Cor. 11:7
restricts the possibility of attributing the image of God to women equally: "A
man ought not to have his head veiled, since he is the image and reflection of
God; but the woman is the reflection of man." Here Paul assumes the Hebrew
view that "image of God" contains the representation of divine sovereignty
and rule over creation. Women do not possess this sovereignty in themselves
but are under male sovereignty or headship. Women are secondary reflections
of a humanity whose norm is male.

Galatians 3:28, "no more male and female . . . in Christ" also poses problems for a feminist, egalitarian appropriation. Probably lurking behind this
statement, perhaps originally a baptismal proclamation, is a concept that orig-
inated with the Hellenistic Jewish philosopher Philo of an original spiritual
androgyne (male-female union), in which the separation of male and female
did not exist. The separation of the female from inclusion under the male represented a fall into sin and mortality, necessitating sex and reproduction. Genesis 1:27, the creation of humans as male and female, was understood not as
the original creation but as a fallen state. What was proclaimed, then, is that
in Christ, the creation/fall into male and female has been overcome. There is
no more male and female. We have been subsumed back into the spiritual
androgyne, Christ, in whom we may rise in a spiritual body to immortal life.
The price for this transformation is the rejection of our somatic, gendered
bodies and their sexual expression, a price to be paid much more deeply by
women than men, since it is women who are identified with the sexual body,
whose "difference" from the male, spiritual body is to be overcome.

The church fathers wrestled with the dichotomies between these different
views of gender in relation to creation, fall, and redemption. Some opined that
women lacked the image of God, lacking sovereignty, but this idea contra-
dicted the assumption that women could be baptized and share in immortal
life. Augustine came up with the solution that would be normative for Western theology through the Reformation, to be repeated in slight variations by
Luther and Calvin.

Augustine affirmed that woman was created in the image of God, in the
sense of possessing a nongendered spiritual nature in her soul capable of
redemption. But as female she lacks the image of God and represents the body,
created subordinate to the male as her head. This subordination of the female
to the male was part of the original order of creation, not something that
appeared only with sin. Rather, the first sin was woman's refusal of her proper
subordination, to which the male acceded, losing original immortality and pre-
cipitating humanity into sin and death, and also concupiscence, through which
sin and death are passed to the next generation through the sexual act.

Because woman took the initiative in sin, she was insubordinate to God and hence to the male as her head. This can only be corrected by a coercive reinforcement of her original subordination. Women who are redeemed in Christ accept this subordination and its reinforcement as punishment for the primal sin of woman. Redemption thus does not overcome women's subordination, but rather redeemed women internalize its sanctions. Only in heaven, however, after mortal life has been overcome, are women freed of subordination and become spiritually equal with men according to the merits of their virtues.

This view was transmitted with some adaptations as Christian orthodoxy through the centuries. Calvin, for example, believed that women had the same image of God as men in their spiritual capacity but lacked "that part" of the image of God that has to do with dominion, that is, authority for rule. The Christian Right today has revived the view that women are both guilty for primacy in sin and by nature under male "headship." But alternative understandings of these scriptural texts, minority views at first, have gradually become assumed by Christians with a liberationist perspective. Ascetic women and their monastic daughters from the early church understood themselves as spiritually equal, believing that this equality was restored in Christ and was expressed in women's celibate communities, where women are autonomous persons. Medieval women mystics also took over a Jewish tradition of the divine as woman-identified Wisdom and saw women as especially imaging this aspect of God.

In the sixteenth century the Catholic humanist Cornelius Agrippa, as well as the Society of Friends in the seventeenth century, pioneered a fundamental shift in the interpretation of gender in creation, sin, and salvation. In their view, original spiritual equality was unmodified by any doctrine of original subordination of women. Moreover, subordination of women is not from God but originates in the tyranny of dominant men. As the Quakers put it, disobedience to God is expressed in the "usurpation of power of some over others." Thus the onus of origination of sin is shifted from the victim to the perpetrator. Relations of domination/subordination are defined as themselves sinful, not expressions of a divinely decreed order of creation reinforced on women as punishment for sin.

Nineteenth-century abolitionist feminists, such as Sarah and Angelina Grimké, assumed this interpretation of original nature, sin, and salvation. As Sarah Grimké put it in 1837, "The lust of domination was probably the first effect of the fall, and as there was no other intelligent being over whom to exercise it, woman was the first victim of this unhallowed passion." Grimké goes on to say, "But I ask no favors for my sex, I surrender not our claim to equality. All I ask of my brethren is that they will take their feet from off our necks and permit us to stand upright on that ground which God has designed for us to occupy."[2] The Grimké sisters developed this egalitarian reading of the image of God first in their antislavery work, insisting that the image of God was given equally to all and no domination was given to some, as masters, over others, as slaves. After having developed this reading to combat the theological arguments for slavery, they then applied it to gender relations.

Thus an egalitarian view of the image of God and the new humanity in Christ does not come to us simply from accessing ancient Hebrew and Greek assumptions behind these scriptural texts, but rather through a stream of midrashic rereadings that come to us from our female (and male) ancestors who interpreted these texts out of a basic faith in a God who loves all persons equally and whose work in history is to restore and renew this equality in a new community of love and justice. As feminist theologians we are heirs of a long line of witnesses to a liberating vision, and we do our own work of extending and developing this reading out of our relationship to them.

NEW CONTEXTS FOR FEMINIST THEOLOGY TODAY

As exciting as it is to discover them, it is not enough to rest on these ancestresses. We need to continue the process with new insights and in new contexts. The Grimké sisters were sensitive to class and race as well as gender injustices in their own time, but their voices cannot substitute for the inside perspective of African American women themselves. Womanist theologians and ethicists have claimed their own line of witnesses and foremothers, in African American freedom fighters such Sojourner Truth, Harriet Tubman, and Ida B. Wells Barnett, and in literary texts from such writers as Zora Neale Hurston and Toni Morrison. African American women's history and culture of resistance and survival is the authoritative touchstone of truth.

Today women's critical and prophetic theologies are growing in Africa, Asia, and Latin America. Often, after having been spurned by their brothers in African, Asian, and Latin American liberation theology, women in these worlds are finding their own voices. For African and Asian women particularly this not only means cultural contextualization of a Christian women's theology; it also means that this theology must break from Christian exclusivism. It must take the many religious of their communities, in some contexts, including Islam, as resources for their theological articulation.

Asian women are very aware that, with the exception of the Philippines, Christianity is a minority Western religion in Asia, often still looked on with suspicion as the religion of the Western colonialist. To make Christianity a vehicle of liberating hope they must first make it Asian by connecting it with the great Asian faiths: Hinduism in India; Buddhism, Confucianism, and

Shamanism in Korea; and Taoism in China. An Asian women's liberation theology must address the Asian women's experiences of oppression: dowry deaths in India, the mass rape of comfort women of Korea, domestic violence and sex tourism, the contradictions of wealth for a few and extreme poverty for the many throughout Asia. Who can bring a healing touch, a word of hope to the garbage pickers and child prostitutes of Metro Manila? Bangkok? Calcutta?

Ecofeminism is also a growing perspective of feminist theologians of so-called first and third worlds. Without necessarily using the term, more and more groups of women (and men) know that there can be no justice for the oppressed of the human community without a sustainable relationship to the nonhuman world in which we are embedded: the ecosystems of air, water and soil, plants, birds, and animals. The Grimké sisters in 1837 confidently claimed equality of black and white, men and women, based on their belief that God had made all humans equally in the image of God. God had given all humans shared sovereignty over the earth and no sovereignty of some, white males, over others, women and slaves.

The ecological issue has raised the question about a concept of the image of God rooted in an anthropocentric domination of humans over nonhuman nature. It has challenged us to think of the whole creation as one shared community of life rather than as a divine domination over nature that humans share and represent. If the whole creation is God's body, as Sallie McFague would have it, must we not encounter the divine presence in the winged, the finned, and the four-footed races, as well as in the two-footed we have grandly dubbed *Homo sapiens sapiens*?

Are there any limits to this continual reinterpretation and recontextualization of theological symbols? Are there any norms to discern good from bad midrash? There is no once-for-all perfection, no infallibility in our interpretations any more than there is in past Scripture or decrees issued from the Holy See. But there are many touchstones to be found in that line of witnesses from the communities reflected in the Hebrew Scriptures and the Second Testament and their heirs through the centuries, in liberators and wise ones in our and other cultures. These we can consult. Finally it comes down to a continual reach for faithful discernment of what makes for living and justice-making community and what does not.

The completion of that hope lies in a yet-unrealized future, not a perfect and normative past. Our capacity to keep up the process rests in the presence of the Holy Spirit, which is ever with us, keeping us restless with what is less than good, stirring us up to new resistance and new vision. In the words of our brother Paul, "We do not know how to pray as we ought, but that very Spirit intercedes with sighs too deep for words" (Rom. 8:26b).

DISCUSSION QUESTIONS

1. According to this chapter, "feminist theology is not just women doing" or "women present in theological education and churches" or "the church's giving temporary attention to this 'special interest.'" Rather, feminist theology calls for a deep and thorough revision of theology. Do you agree? What would this entail?
2. How does feminist theology view God? Church authority? Scripture? Jesus?
3. Do you find these views threatening? Why or why not?
4. What are the standards by which feminist theologians distinguish good theology from bad theology?
5. How might your church be different in its overall tone, preaching, teaching, service, use of religious and social symbols, and selection of leaders if it reconstructed its theology along feminist and ecofeminist lines?

FOR FURTHER READING

Fabella, Virginia, and Mercy Oduyoye. *With Passion and Compassion: Third World Women Doing Theology*. Maryknoll, NY: Orbis Books, 1988.

Isasi-Díaz, Ada Maria. *En la Lucha: Elaborating a Mujerista Theology*. Minneapolis: Fortress Press, 1993.

Johnson, Elizabeth. *She Who Is: The Mystery of God in Feminist Theological Discourse*. New York: Crossroad, 1993.

Kwok, Pul-Lan. *Introducing Asian Feminist Theology*. Cleveland: Pilgrim Press, 2000.

McFague, Sally. *The Body of God: An Ecological Theology*. Minneapolis: Fortress Press, 1993.

Ruether, Rosemary Radford. *Gaia and God: An Ecofeminist Theology of Earth Healing*. San Francisco: Harper & Row, 1987.

———. *Sexism and God Talk: Toward a Feminist Theology*. Boston: Beacon Press, 1983.

———. *Women and Redemption: A Theological History*. Minneapolis: Fortress Press, 1998.

Russell, Letty. *The Church in the Round: A Feminist Interpretation of the Church*. Louisville, KY: Westminster/John Knox Press, 1993.

Schüssler Fiorenza, Elisabeth. *In Memory of Her*. New York: Crossroad, 1983.

Williams, Delores. *Sisters in the Wilderness: The Challenge of Womanist God-talk*. Maryknoll, NY: Orbis Books, 1993.

PART 4

Parameters of Resistance

10

The Church and Politics

Lee C. McDonald

Everything begins in religion and ends in politics.
Charles Péguy (1873–1914)

INTRODUCTION

Early in the twenty-first century, America and the world are in crisis. That crisis is both social and ecological, with the global growth of poverty, on the one hand, and the degradation of the earth, on the other. As progressive Christians, we believe there is much wisdom in the Christian tradition that could go far to save the world from the worst consequences of its present policies and practices. But we also see that the actual public impact of the Christian faith is often more harmful than helpful.

One problem is that those Protestant denominations that have engaged in the most serious study of their heritage and of the world situation are declining in membership and influence. As a public expression of Christianity in the United States, they are being replaced by TV evangelists, parachurch organizations, and fundamentalist or "evangelical" "megachurches" often led by charismatic and somewhat independent pastors, who together lead the "Christian Right." This movement is closely connected with the now-popular apocalyptic vision of the Left Behind series of books.

Although many traditional evangelicals do not follow the Christian Right, the shift in the public image of Christianity has been radical. It reflects a response by the Christian Right to what it calls "secular humanism," on the one side, and international terrorism, on the other. The Christian Right generally sees itself as defending Christianity against external threats and, as part of this stance, as defending America as a Christian nation.

We as progressive Christians are trying to offer an alternative understanding of what Christianity is and what it offers to a wounded world. Thus far in this book we have exercised our right to speak as individuals and as a group, and to do so we do not require the support of the institutional church. However, we are committed to the church, and we would like for our churches to respond more relevantly to the crises of our time.

We do not expect local congregations to take stands on all the political issues that we as progressive Christians address. Congregations have important roles to play that would be destroyed if they involved themselves in normal political activity, that is, in supporting candidates for office and taking stands on numerous issues on which its own members are divided. Ordinarily the church should not support one party or the other or take sides on the central issues that divide them. For example, one party might emphasize the value of governmental regulation of business while the other argues that government should give more freedom to business, and individual Christians may have strong views on such questions. The church, however, should not take sides.

On the other hand, the congregation should certainly put forward its own ethical convictions even when they have obvious relevance to current political issues. It should also help its members become thoughtful about the relevance of their faith to their individual political positions. Moreover, there are extraordinary circumstances when the church as an institution is called to speak and act even at great cost.

It is not easy to draw the line for congregations and denominations between the ordinary politics they should avoid and their profound responsibility to relate the gospel to the political sphere. The churches to which we belong typically err on the side of avoiding political involvement of all sorts. This chapter attempts to bring some clarity to this difficult question and thus encourage churches to accept their responsibilities in this crucial sphere.

WHAT IS POLITICS?

If the word *politics* is itself a cause of upset and confusion while the process of politics is, for most of us, inescapable, then building a spirit of intelligent cooperation requires a common understanding for which definition may be helpful. Politics begins with a community. The word *politics* comes from the ancient Greek word *polis*, or the community of free citizens formed by the ten tribes of Athens. Between the extremes of coercion and freedom is the overlapping of power and morality, for power is never absent, and every political judgment is, in its way, a moral judgment. From the beginning, politics is, or ought to be, a welcome alternative to war.

Politics may best be conceived as a community deciding what it *shall* do. Political ethics is the subject of deciding what a community *should* do. Ideally the ethics and the action converge, but in populations of any size divergent opinions about threats to the community, divergent understandings of what is possible, and a wide variety of moral positions make such ideal convergence rare. A political decision is a decision *for* other people. That is the sense in which politics is a moral enterprise, even when the consequence of the decision turns out badly.

No phrase is heard more often in American political debates than "what the American people want." Most speakers using the phrase are appealing to a higher authority: *vox populi, vox Dei.* The phrase is a talisman suggesting that what is being proposed is more than what the proposer happens to want at the moment. If "the American people," however, literally means everybody, then no one knows exactly what the American people want, not even the most artful pollsters.

The viable narratives of politics, like those of religion, cannot be literal but are more like myths. There are "dead" myths that we see as mere stories and also "live" myths that we may recognize as myths but that nevertheless penetrate our conscious awareness of what the world is and where it is going. "The American Dream" is one of these myths, one that can be confirmed in some lives and made hollow in others. It is nevertheless powerful, and politicians may either manipulate such myths or be manipulated by them. Good myths convey truth even or especially if they transcend literal truths. That the people rule may not be a literal fact, but it is part of the mythical context capable of making some leaders more powerful or more responsible than they otherwise would be.

Politics governs a society but requires a community. A society is a network of material interdependence, but a community requires the sharing of common understandings, values, myths of identity, as well as a sense of shared history. An ant colony is a society but not a community. Humans may be unique by virtue of living in communities, though perhaps elephants, whales, dolphins, and baboons could also qualify as community dwellers. "America" is clearly a society *and* a community, though other communities within the society may have a stronger hold on the psyche of individual persons than America as a community. Globalization in its many manifestations, including new racial, ethnic, and religious contacts and conflict, is having a complexifying, and maybe weakening, effect on the community character of the United States as well as other nations.

One might expect that the church of Christ would be a deeper community than the national community. But disagreements within congregations over support for a war, or over the place of the national flag in the sanctuary, or over criticism of national leaders suggest that even in the church the subordinate position of the national community cannot be taken for granted. That national governments still are granted the largely unquestioned authority to send young men and women to die in battle may suggest that some lingering residue of kingly divinity resides in our national soul.

Democracy is the term usually applied to our politics. Because democracy as an ideal form is inclusive and tries to respect the opinions of as many persons as possible, it is messy, noisy, and inconclusive. Just as Americans take politics for granted, they may also take their democratic liberties for granted. In public rhetoric almost everywhere, democracy is seen as desirable. Even despots claim to favor it.

Yet when rulers rule by fear rather than consent, whatever the form, democratic politics can scarcely begin. Critics of democracy (and they are many) generally invoke the necessity of law and order in the face of threatening anarchy. A democracy may well exhibit anarchic tendencies whenever a minority, however small, whose voice is not represented in prevailing policy, does not shut up and go along but instead insists loudly and persistently on its rightness. Throughout most of history and still in much of the world, the rigidity of coercive authority makes criticizing the government dangerous.

Democratic process can also be slow. Democratic leaders must learn to wait until as many as possible who wish to speak can be heard. Unfortunately, such patience is unlikely in the face of natural disasters (tsunamis, earthquakes, hurricanes) or artificial disasters (wars, stock-market crashes, airplanes hitting skyscrapers).

Throughout history the word *justice*, like the word *democracy* in modern times, has become identified with the struggle between the haves and the have-nots. What is clear is that the Bible, both the Hebrew Scriptures and the New Testament, and especially the words of the Hebrew prophets and the words of Jesus, overwhelmingly come down on the side of the have-nots against the haves. The question is whether Jesus approached this issue politically. Older scholars tend to see Jesus as nonpolitical because they defined first-century politics rather narrowly as gaining Jewish liberation from Rome. Others believe that Jesus' eschatology, his expectation of the end of the world, transcended any politics. More recent biblical research has found that "Jesus both challenged the existing social order and advocated an alternative. . . . It is in this broader sense of the word 'politics' that contemporary scholarship is increasingly affirming a sociopolitical dimension to Jesus."[1]

HOW SHOULD THE CHURCH RELATE
TO ORDINARY POLITICS?

We are calling for Christian resistance against much of what is going on in the world today, and for reform where that is possible. Much of what we call for is political, and progressive Christians as individuals and groups will find ways to act that are not appropriate for most congregations as congregations. Nevertheless, there is a sense in which the *church* should *not* be "political," and congregations need clarity in this regard.

For example, that the U.S. Internal Revenue Service (IRS) may deny a religious body a tax exemption if it crosses the line from religious activity to political activity is a practical but less than inspirational reason for a congregation to avoid politics. Some believe the church should forswear tax exemption in order to maintain its freedom from any governmental ties, but the situation is complex. Tax exemption for churches is an expression of general sympathy for religion in our society and a perception that churches are good for the wider polity. It also represents the belief in the separation of church and state. Some theorists have claimed that this principle has been America's greatest contribution to democracy. A look at post-Saddam Iraq or present-day Iran may underscore the value of this principle. American churches, judged by weekly attendance figures, seem to have benefited from a "free market" in religion.

The U.S. Supreme Court has refused to define religion on the grounds that to do so would be an "establishment" forbidden by the First Amendment. Religion (which comes from *re-ligare*, being bound together, as in *ligament*), in its most general sense refers to the beliefs of the group, those that bind the members together. *Religion* also connotes devotion or reverence; thus one might speak of people making football or fame or family their religion. In this sense nationalism has a religious character that is surely part of our political heritage. Thus the IRS accepts, to a point, the self-definition of religion of every church, temple, mosque, or sect. The IRS's limiting rule therefore is that self-financed organizations may call themselves religious, but those deriving the bulk of their revenue from persons outside the fold may not. This rule has been the basis of the long-standing legal battles between the IRS and the Church of Scientology.

Were the IRS to disappear, it would still be wrong for churches to endorse candidates for public office—for both practical and theological reasons. Given the majority view in America that religion is a good thing, the competition for church endorsements would become intense, cheapening the reputation of the church in the eyes of *all* citizens. Moreover, the church should respect the opinions of its members on matters not fundamental to the faith. As in families, divergent political views should be tolerated as a matter of right and as a sign of trust in the autonomous judgment of its members. The church can stand as an example that people do not have to agree on everything to be members of an affectionate family.

More basic is that church endorsement of candidates would imply that it knows the soul of its candidate so well that he or she can be sent into the secular world to lead others in the political sphere as an agent of Christ. But God alone is the Lord of conscience. It is difficult enough to claim special godly authority in the process of ordination *within* the church. The assumption would be that those loyal to Christ would *have* to vote for the endorsed candidate, a terrible constraint to put upon church members.

Hence, there is validity to the belief that the church is *in* the world but not of the world (John 17:16). It should not cling too tightly to the ways of the world if it is to act as a saving remnant for the world. Its independence from everyday "petty politics" gives weight to its words when the church finds it necessary to take a political stand.

WHEN SHOULD THE CHURCH OPPOSE THE GOVERNMENT?

Traditional Teaching

Ordinarily the church should support the government as such even when it disapproves of many of the government's policies, and it should not involve itself directly in ordinary politics. But this does not mean that the church should never confront the government. Its greatest theologians have consistently indicated a role for the church in this respect. Even when many rulers were acknowledged tyrants and democracy was unheard of, churches have spoken out against the "principalities and powers" (Rom. 8:38; Eph. 1:21) that abuse their responsibility to protect human life.

Among the circumstances under which theologians have thought that the church should act, the clearest has been when the state oversteps its proper boundaries. In medieval and Reformation times, this was clearest when it usurped the prerogatives of the church, preventing it from carrying out its proper functions. Another circumstance is when rulers are not able to fulfill their duties, for example, if they are insane.

In Augustine's *City of God*, the distinction between the city of God and the city of man was sharp. The church was not identified wholly with the city of God, but it could speak in its name; the state could speak only for the often-corrupted city of man. The idea of these two separate realms has been influential down to our own day and has contributed to the often-ambiguous status of the idea of a Christian politics. Despite Augustine's adherence to Paul (Rom. 13:1–7) early and his admiration for the Christian emperor Theodosius I, he could say with a touch of sarcasm, "So then, if the Emperor enjoin one thing and God another, what judge ye?"[2] Thomas Aquinas affirmed that the church could punish unbelief in professed Christian rulers by depriving them of "the allegiance of their subjects."[3] Although somewhat naive in neglecting the need for restraints on secular rulers, Martin Luther in principle gave those men blessed with Christian freedom the right to challenge both kings and pontiffs.

John Calvin, however, did not regard civil government as a realm set apart with little occasion for interference from the church: "No virtue is so rare in Kings as moderation and yet none is more necessary."[4] His pessimism about personal virtue led him to a reliance on collective decision making in politics, and to *libertas* as a political as well as a spiritual concept. Calvin also saw that lesser magistrates could be agents of civil resistance. If they wink at "the fierce licentiousness of kings, . . . I declare that their dissimulation involves nefarious perfidy, because they dishonestly betray the freedom of the people, of which . . . they have been appointed protectors by God's ordinance. . . . We must obey God rather than any human authority."[5] All of these church leaders emphasized the distinct roles of church and state, but none of them concluded that the church should always leave the state alone.

Contemporary Application

The church has good reason to condemn tyranny. In proper historic usage a tyrant is a ruler who acts beyond the law. A "despot," often carelessly used as a synonym of "tyrant," historically meant something else: a ruler who was a bad man, typically one who took a perverse delight in cruelty. In ancient Greece some nondespots were in emergencies empowered to act as tyrants. Tyranny can be given many other meanings, but let us hold to this narrowest of definitions as a standard for testing where we are. By this test, President George W. Bush is probably not a despot, but he has acted as a tyrant.

Wrong policy is not tyranny. The official administration pretense until 2007 that there was no problem of global warming is not itself tyranny, only calculated ignorance of monumental proportions. In a case of this kind the church certainly has the responsibility to educate its people on issues, to help find ways in which individual Christians and congregations can make adjustments in their lives, and to urge its members to act politically in terms of the truth. Policy disputes, however serious, are part of the "normal" politics in which the church, as church, should not be involved. However, the abuse of constitutional authority is another issue. Traditionally the church has taught that it does have special responsibility to confront a government that has become tyrannical.

It is reluctantly but increasingly conceded by scholars, independent thinkers, and reasonable journalists that President Bush and Vice President Cheney have acted beyond the law. For the United States, that means beyond the Constitution. A president is required to execute the laws of Congress faithfully, whether he is pleased or displeased with them. The Bush administration subverted the laws of Congress.

In 1978, responding to the Supreme Court's unanimous rejection of President Nixon's secret wiretapping, Congress enacted the Foreign Intelligence Surveillance Act (FISA), setting up a special court to grant warrants for domestic wiretapping in the interest of national security. To cover emergencies, it included a three-day period (or fifteen days after a declaration of war by Congress) for warrantless taps, provided the executive would get the court's approval ex post facto. Until the Bush administration the special court had worked well. The Bush administration, however, through the National Security Agency, ignored this law, did not seek warrants, and secretly wiretapped numbers of people, including American citizens. After these actions came to light, the executive claimed that Congress had been kept informed, but few Congresspeople had in fact been informed, and even these, not fully. If the administration was unhappy with the existing law, seeking an amendment from Congress would have been the proper course to follow. Attorney General Alberto Gonzales admitted that some Congresspeople advised the administration that amending the law would be difficult if not impossible, so the administration chose simply to ignore it.

The justification was invariably the "War on Terrorism," an ill-defined, apparently interminable, and almost metaphorical "war," not exhausted by or confined to the boundaries of conventional warfare, for it is not a war that can be ended with a peace treaty. The president's position was that even discussing this topic was helping the enemy. How discussions of constitutional procedures help the enemy was not made clear, but not surprisingly, the unknown bureaucratic leakers and the newspapers who printed their reports were accused of what amounted to treason. Finally, after the November 2006 election that brought Democratic majorities to both Houses of Congress, Attorney General Gonzales announced that the administration would no longer secretly eavesdrop on international calls of suspected terrorists without first getting a court order as required by the FISA law. Even with this change, the new chair of the Senate Intelligence Committee said that the refusal of the attorney general to publish wiretap guidelines raises serious questions about the degree to which the announcement is meaningful.

A similar fate was inflicted on Senator John McCain's (R., Ariz.) antitorture amendment to a defense appropriation bill after revelations of the "extraordinary rendition" of terrorism suspects to third countries where torture was a common official practice, and of mistreatment of prisoners at Guantanamo, many of whom were turned over by Afghan bounty hunters for U.S. dollars. Vice President Cheney tried to persuade McCain to water down his amendment and failed. It passed the Senate 90 to 9, and the House, 308 to 122. Through the device of a "signing statement," however, Bush declined to be bound by it. These actions violated direct constitutional requirements of habeas corpus, the rights of trial by jury, a speedy trial, the right to counsel, not to mention the new statutory prohibition on torture.

Previous presidents have rarely written "signing statements" and have done so usually only to clarify how a particular detail of legislation is to be enforced. The Bush administration, however, developed new theories of a "unitary executive" and the constitutional authority of the president that have turned "signing statements" into a way of circumventing the division of powers established by the Constitution. The Bush signing statements are deliberately general and vague, designed to allow the president virtually unlimited discretion: for example, one of President Bush's signing statements reads as follows: "The executive branch shall construe [the provision—in this case against torture] in a manner consistent with the constitutional authority of the President to supervise the unitary executive branch and as Commander in Chief, and consistent with the constitutional limitations on the judiciary."[6] Rebuffs to the president's position by the lower federal courts were ignored pending appeal after appeal.

Bush has the constitutional prerogative of vetoing legislation to which he objects, and until close to the end of his term he had exercised this right only once. For the constitutional veto he substituted the unconstitutional view that a president can sign legislation without being bound by it. According to *The Boston Globe*, as of April 2006 Bush had claimed the right to ignore more than 750 laws enacted since he became president.[7]

It would be appropriate for churches as institutions to speak out against this abuse of power, for it is not a partisan issue but a constitutional one, and responsible conservatives are at least as concerned to preserve the Constitution as are responsible liberals.[8] In February 2006, after the McCain amendment episode, the bipartisan and nonprofit Constitution Project issued a statement of deep concern about unchecked presidential power and the president's assertion that he "may not be bound" by congressional statutes. The conclusion was that "we face a constitutional crisis." Among the signers were the chair of the American Conservative Union, former members of President Reagan's state department and justice department, and the director of the FBI under George H. W. Bush. Grover Norquist, a major strategist of the conservative movement, said that if you can ignore the laws, "you don't have a constitution, you have a king." Senator Charles Hagel (R., Nebraska) said, "There's a very clear pattern of aggressively asserting executive power, and the Congress has essentially been complicit in letting him do it."[9]

In May 2006, the libertarian Cato Institute published a twenty-eight-page document written by Gene Healy and Timothy Lynch of its staff, titled *Power Surge: The Constitutional Record of George W. Bush.* It documented "a federal government empowered to regulate core political speech . . . [and] a president who cannot be restrained through validly enacted statutes from pursuing any tactic he believes to be effective in the war on terror." It castigated the president for claims of "authority to arrest American citizens . . . [and] strip them of any constitutional protection and lock them up without charges."[10]

The failure of the American public, including Congress and the American churches, to confront the president's flagrant violation of constitutional division of powers will have long-term consequences. Most scholars of the presidency say that no matter who is elected to succeed President Bush, the new theory and practice of an unchecked presidency will encourage executive misbehavior for years to come. The church's silence is not justified by the proper separation of church and state and the avoidance of normal politics by the church.

IS AMERICA A CHRISTIAN NATION?

Clearly the United States has no established state church. Our Constitution prohibits any religious test for office (art. VI), the First Amendment forbids the "establishment" of religion, and freedom of worship is guaranteed. There is clearly no official endorsement of Christianity.

Nevertheless, many argue that this *is* a Christian nation. A number of Americans believe that quite apart from the Constitution, American society and American tradition are fundamentally Christian. This view has even been expressed in opinions, usually dissents, written by justices of the Supreme Court. The Christian Right has garnered considerable publicity by claiming that "secular humanists" have long been attacking Christianity itself in the public sphere, and they thus argue that the American Christian tradition requires a vigorous defense in public schools and elsewhere.

But is the Right right? Americans are certainly a religious people. For example, a higher percentage of Americans regularly attend religious services than do Western Europeans, and "In God We Trust" appears on our coins. A majority do think of themselves as Christians, but does that make us a "Christian nation" whose basic character is under siege by secular humanists? In fact, many, perhaps most, of the critics of the Christian Right on this point do not march under the banner of secular humanism; instead they represent vocal elements of Protestantism, Catholicism, and Judaism. Moreover, the growing number of Muslims in America can hardly be called secularists.

As for American tradition, the nation's founding fathers were religious but not all were orthodox Christians. George Washington was Anglican; John Adams was Congregational; and John Witherspoon, a Presbyterian, was the only clergyman among fifty-six signers of the Declaration of Independence. The author of the Declaration, Thomas Jefferson; his Virginia compatriot

James Madison ("Father of the Constitution"); and Benjamin Franklin, the senior eminence of the Declaration's signing, were all deists. So was Tom Paine, author of the incendiary popular pamphlet *Common Sense*. They believed in God as the author of nature but took an unorthodox view of Jesus. Franklin at one time proposed that Moses be on the great seal of the United States, and in his later years, Jefferson reedited, and almost rewrote, the four Gospels to emphasize the ethics of Jesus without reference to atonement, crucifixion, and resurrection.

Churches, corporations, schools, and service clubs often adopt mission statements, and one might call the Declaration of Independence America's mission statement. When we celebrate the nation's birthday on July 4, our most nationalistic holiday, it is the Declaration of Independence we read. It invokes "the Laws of Nature and of Nature's God" and urges a "decent respect for the opinions of Mankind." Its "self-evident" truths are that "all men are created equal" ("equal" meaning, of course, more than sameness). They are "endowed by their Creator with certain unalienable Rights" including "Life, Liberty, and the Pursuit of Happiness—That to secure these Rights Governments are instituted among Men, deriving their just powers from the Consent of the Governed." These words are so familiar that we have to make a deliberate effort to think about their meaning.

These days some who think about the words of the Declaration have become negatively critical of their literal meaning. They point out, for example, that "the governed" in 1776 included slaves, Native Americans, and women, none of whose consent was asked for and few of whose "unalienable" rights were heeded. Others have said that "the pursuit of happiness" is nothing but an encouragement to unbridled hedonism, leading to the undisciplined individualism and commercial consumerism that our chapter on that subject deplored. Pursuing happiness, it is said, reflected the Enlightenment of the seventeenth and eighteenth centuries with its naive faith in a natural law discovered by human reason and a natural science that could easily replace ancient theologies. For Jefferson, however, the happiness we were entitled to pursue was not hedonistic self-gratification but "public happiness," the sense of well-being arising from participation in a common community endeavor. The goal was not twenty-first-century consumerism, but one closer to Aristotle's well-being (*eudaemonia*). Indeed, the loss of Jefferson's meaning for this phrase can be seen as a national tragedy.

Focusing on Jefferson's deism tells us little about the actual value of the Declaration in giving us a direction to follow. Despite valid criticisms of the Enlightenment, the fact that the Declaration was an Enlightenment document does not diminish its significance as a democratic credo. Without the Enlightenment, modern democracy would not have come into being. Moreover, the metaphor of the light of God that illuminates our path is not alien to the Enlightenment: indeed it was its original stimulus. Voltaire and the latter-day French philosophes may have been skeptics, but Enlightenment progenitors such as Pierre Bayle and John Locke were writing from an assumed harmony between Christianity and modern science.

Yes, our founding fathers owned slaves, often referred to Native Americans as savages, and generally regarded women as inferior to men. We now feel confident in calling those attitudes unenlightened. But the ideals in the Declaration are in part what made it possible for us to arrive at that judgment. The fact that the Fourth-of-July ideals of the Declaration can call us forward, can spur us to challenge the denial of rights in our own day, is a sign of its power and importance. Martin Luther King Jr. could have made the impact he did only by showing that his dream was part of the American dream and by drawing on both the Bible and the Declaration of Independence to do that.

Likewise, the antislavery movement in America and the social gospel that criticized the excesses of Manifest Destiny at the end of the nineteenth century drew on both the Bible and the Declaration of Independence. We need both, not to go backward but to go forward. Hence, although the United States is not a Christian nation, some of the ideals of its founding fathers can be internalized by progressive Christians today and employed to further efforts for needed reform and even resistance.

OBSTACLES TO EFFECTIVENESS
IN THE POLITICAL ARENA

We have said that the church should stay out of normal politics and that while the majority of the people think of themselves as Christians, the United States should not be considered a Christian country. In this context, church leaders and church institutions have a responsibility to speak on many matters of importance for the well-being of individuals, the nation, and the world. For example, the church should respond to the relentless march of consumerism, the growth of poverty, American imperialism, the teaching of scientism, and the decay of the physical environment.

The restriction on church political action and the limitation of confrontation with the government to such issues as tyranny in no way mean that the church should not teach its distinctive morality, oppose corruption at all levels, and encourage its people to do what they can to prevent governmental actions that harm people. We hope that the chapters of this book constitute responsible church teaching. Further, when there is sufficient consensus at a local church or in a judicatory or ecumenical body, Christian convictions can and should be vigorously asserted. The hope and intention are often to influence the political order even while avoiding direct political action.

This kind of activity is currently taking place, but its effectiveness is severely limited for two main reasons: First, negative attitudes toward politics among church members severely restrict needed instruction and discussion. Second, especially since 1980, the media have been silent about the progressive leadership of the old-line churches. Progressive Christians need to understand and respond to these obstacles to effective church work for progressive causes. The following sections deal with these problems.

Popular Attitudes toward Politics

The very word *politics* seems to be in bad odor these days. People disdainful of politics tend not to think of its broader meaning but instead think of *partisans*, of divisiveness, of disharmony, of hypocrisy. Many Americans are now saying, "I hate politics." Teachers of political science are familiar with the frowns of citizens who are surprised that teachers would devote their lives to studying such a sordid subject. Such citizens perhaps do not realize that their sweeping disdain contributes to the sordidness. Disrespect for politics and politicians precedes, as well as follows, the rise of disrespectful politicians.

Perhaps the only pure lovers of politics are the few philosophers of Aristotelian persuasion who hold an elevated view of political activity as the master art of leading humanity to the fulfillment of the highest earthly good. But if so, they love a definition, not daily reality. There may be, nevertheless, among progressive Christians a tincture of Aristotelian aspiration: not just to live but to live well and in community.

Progressive Christians must deal with the common negative perceptions of what "politics" means and with the fact that the negative content of those perceptions has, in the last thirty-five years in the United States, enlarged alarmingly. In the 1960s a clear majority of Americans felt that most of the time our government worked for the benefit of most of the people. According to the polls, by the turn of the twenty-first century that figure had fallen to one-third.

One reason for the decline of respect in the political order is found in the political order itself. The heightened polarization of the two parties has bred incivility. The dominant influence of corporate donors in political campaigns and the gerrymandered protection of incumbents makes ordinary voters feel that voting is pointless. Cynicism also is a natural response to the government's unusual ruthlessness in punishing whistleblowers, its so-far largely fruitless effort to cloak major decisions in secrecy while hypocritically speaking of our "democracy of transparency," and its use of "antiterrorism" to justify torture, invasions of privacy, and even inefficiency.

Nevertheless, what is astounding in twenty-first-century America is the number of professed Christians who find it convenient to ignore the deep concern of the Hebrew prophets and of Jesus for the structure of society. One hesitates to pick on any one example, but the highly respected Alban Institute will serve. It is an independent, nonprofit publisher of books "grounded in faith and devoted to helping congregations be vital communities of faith, health, and leadership in the world today." It lists 163 books in its 2006 catalog. Only two come within a furlong of politics, and neither uses the word in title or description.

Rabbi Michael Lerner in *The Right Hand of God* has argued that the religious Right in America has used scriptural references to an angry, fear-inducing God in ways that perversely subvert images of a loving, hopeful, forgiving God. Theologically, old-line church pastors, reflecting their seminary education, are more conversant with critical New Testament scholarship than they are usually willing to share with their congregations. Politically, they are often more "liberal" than their congregations. Higher-echelon church officials may also favor more overt political action than local bodies. Such pastors and officials should be encouraged to speak the truth as they see it more boldly. Otherwise, given the clouded perspectives of both the unchurched and the megachurched, the name "Christian" is in serious danger of becoming in the public mind the exclusive possession of those who promote fear.

Meanwhile the general view of politics makes it very difficult to have serious discussions of politically controversial issues in the church. It leads congregations to discourage their pastors from preaching about such issues or participating in the formulation of statements. When church leaders make such statements, many congregants ignore them. Church "leaders" thus seem to have few followers.

The Silence of the Media

Christian humility and a decent respect for human autonomy forbid us to label any professed Christian as "not a Christian." Prudence suggests that there is some truth in all positions and the whole truth in none. Nothing prevents us, however, from using reason and good biblical scholarship to defend one position or one interpretation over another. Accordingly, leaders of the religious Right are entitled to state their views and be heard, and they do so effectively. Leaders of old-line churches have this same right, but what these churches rightly struggle against is that the media ignore them while giving major attention to the Right. In our society, being ignored by the media is tantamount to being silenced.

Leaders of old-line denominations have been trying to speak truth to power, but they are not heard. All of the old-line churches make official statements representing a Christianity that, we believe, is far more faithful to Jesus Christ than many of the pronouncements of the religious Right, but the only part of their work that receives media attention is their struggle over homosexuality. This media bias is leading to a distorted view of Christianity even among church members.

There are many examples of media bias, of which we offer two. For example, the president of the American United Church of Christ, attending the World Council of Churches Assembly in Brazil in February 2006, issued an apology to Christians worldwide for not doing more to prevent the American invasion of Iraq. No American news outlet covered it. When, however, shortly thereafter Jerry Falwell chided a Minnesota city for removing an Easter bunny from a public display, it instantly made the AP wire.

From 1997 to July 2006 Christian Right leaders such as Falwell, Pat Robertson, and Gary Bauer appeared on the major-network Sunday morning talk shows forty times whereas major leaders of old-line Protestant denominations appeared not once. Rev. Robert Edgar of the National Council of Churches and Rev. Peter Laarman, of Progressive Christians Uniting, among others, have attributed this news blackout in part to the political and economic power of the religious Right. Such organizations as the "neocon" Institute for Religion and Democracy (IRD) are trying to "take over"[11] the old-line denominations. For example, the IRD, founded in 1981, has subdivisions known as "United Methodist Action," "Presbyterian Action," and "Episcopalian Action," and the political backgrounds of their donors make the link between "conservative" politics and the Christian Right evident. The coalition formed between the Christian right and the Republican Party is, in Randall Balmer's words, "blasphemy, pure and simple."[12] He has asserted that the Christian Right, having gained political power, has used that power mainly to support the Republican platform and accuse those who don't of being unchristian.

The identification of Christians with the religious right has been affected by the actions of politicians and, in turn, has affected their actions. Beginning with the Reagan administration, representatives of ultraconservative forms of Christianity have had far more access to the presidents than have leaders of old-line churches. The close alliance of the religious Right with the Republican party too often subordinates distinctively Christian teaching to desire for political power in just the way that we previously warned against.

Fortunately, genuinely conservative Christians are distancing themselves from the politically motivated religious Right. The Baptist pastor of an evangelical megachurch in St. Paul, Minnesota, for example, got fed up with the pressure to preach a Republican line from the pulpit, and Rev. Gregory Boyd, a conservative, preached six sermons on keeping partisan politics out of the pulpit. He spoke against trusting in the sword rather than in the cross, against

a simplistic identification of America as a "Christian nation," and against the
nationalistic quest for power.

IS A NEW *KAIROS* STATEMENT CALLED FOR?

Despite the negative attitudes of many church members and the near silencing
of the old-line church by the media during recent decades, both here and on
a global basis churches have not ceased to speak prophetically. In our view, they
have often responded well to God's call. For example, chapter 1 noted the role
of the church and of Martin Luther King Jr. in the 1960s American civil rights
movement. It may well be the most promising model for us today, but there
are others. Beginning with the Barmen Declaration, churches and leaders
within them have sometimes addressed the political scene in effective ways that
have involved both statements and collective action.[13]

An important model emerged from the antiapartheid struggle in South
Africa. Beginning at least in mid-twentieth century, voices of church people of
several denominations inside South Africa and around the world called for
resistance to the increasingly oppressive apartheid laws. In 1972 the World
Council of Churches began advocating divestment from corporations doing
business with the apartheid regime of South Africa. Although many white
church people initially supported apartheid, particularly in the influential
Dutch Reformed Church, one of its daughter churches, the Dutch Reformed
Mission Church, created for people of mixed-race ancestry ("colored" people),
understood the implications of its Calvinist theological heritage very differently and offered strong leadership in resisting apartheid. This church turned
to the World Alliance of Reformed Churches for support, and in 1982 the
Alliance responded by suspending the membership of two South African white
denominations. It declared in a formal confession of faith that *"apartheid . . .*
is a sin, and that the moral and theological justification of it is a travesty of the
Gospel, and in its persistent disobedience to the Word of God, a theological
heresy."[14] The council also mobilized international support for Christians
resisting apartheid.

Among the documents coming from South African Christians were the Belhar Confession and the *Kairos* Document, which remain significant landmarks.
The Belhar Confession of the Dutch Reformed Mission Church in 1982 is a
clear, biblical, and irenic statement of the unity of the church as a result of
Christ's work of reconciliation and its incompatibility with the apartheid system. Like the Barmen Confession, it sharply contrasts authentic and false doctrine. It calls for resistance to all that threatens the unity of Christ's people of

diverse backgrounds, and it calls the church to witness and strive against all forms of injustice and to support the oppressed. The Belhar Confession asserts, "We believe that, in obedience to Jesus Christ, its only Head, the Church is called to confess and do all these things, even though the authorities and human laws might forbid them and punishment and suffering be the consequence. Jesus is Lord."[15] This became and remains an official confession of the new multiracial Uniting Reformed Church in Southern Africa and is in increasing use elsewhere in the world.

In 1985, a group of 156 pastors and laypeople from 20 South African denominations produced the *Kairos* Document,[16] a denunciation of the principle of apartheid. It included a critique of "state theology," the spurious justification of the status quo that relied heavily on Romans 13 and on "church theology," that is, the theology of church officials rather than that of the majority of the people. The *Kairos* Document presents a rereading of the Bible concerning reconciliation, justice, nonviolence, oppression, tyranny, and hope in the particular social context of South Africa, and it challenges Christians as a "moral duty" to take action "to resist oppression and to struggle for liberation and justice."[17] This effort informed the world community and contributed significantly to the 1994 election of Nelson Mandela as president of South Africa.

One symbol of the resistance movement in South Africa is Archbishop Desmond Tutu of the Anglican Church there, who at great risk led march after march of protest. Finally, after the end of legal apartheid, Archbishop Tutu headed the national Commission on Truth and Reconciliation, helping to facilitate the coming together of divided and alienated peoples in a new kind of nation.[18]

Also instructive is the critique of American capitalism in *Economic Justice for All*, the 1986 U.S. Bishops' Pastoral Letter on Catholic Social Teaching and the U.S. Economy. Among other things, it called for sweeping reform or replacement of the International Monetary Fund (IMF), the World Bank, and GATT, the General Agreement on Trade and Tariffs.

Still another resistance movement involving the churches is the protest against demands of payment by poor countries of debts that continually grew with interest that they could never pay off. Analysis of the circumstances by which the debt was acquired revealed that attempts to enforce payment were unjust and led only to deep impoverishment. The external debt issue became a significant concern at the World Alliance of Reformed Churches meeting in Seoul, South Korea, in 1989. By 1998 the "Jubilee 2000" movement to reduce third-world debt began, and many churches became involved. The World Council of Churches, meeting in Accra, Ghana, in 1996, issued its Accra Declaration, noting that the developed world, including the IMF and the World

Bank, was taking more money in debt servicing out of Africa than it was putting in by way of loans and grants.

Church bodies have called for debt cancellation, and representatives have met with the IMF and the World Bank to discuss their concerns, as have secular groups. These agencies now take the issue of alleviating poverty more seriously in their policies, and some measure of debt relief has been accorded to the poorest countries, though these issues are far from full resolution.

A still broader movement, calling for a confession of faith concerning justice in the global economy and justice for the ecology of the earth, was begun by the World Alliance of Reformed Churches meeting in Debrecen, Hungary, in 1997. It led to the Accra Confession at its next meeting in Accra in 2004, a call for churches to covenant together and join in this movement. Passages from the Accra Confession are quoted at the beginning of chapter 1 and the end of chapter 11.[19] The challenge of the Accra Confession has now also been taken up by the Lutheran World Federation and the World Council of Churches.

CAN FAITH JOURNEYS BECOME POLITICAL JOURNEYS? AN EXPERIMENT

A first step in generating within the church a larger following for its prophetic leaders would be to encourage reflection about the relation of faith to politics. Chapter 2 showed how prayer and spiritual formation can be fully integrated with prophetic thought and action. Here we propose an experiment in drawing more persons in our congregations into this sort of reflection.

"Spiritual direction" is a prominent emphasis in the Christian church these days, both Catholic and Protestant. Individual church members are quite used to being asked in retreats, Christian education classes, or even committees to tell their story of a "faith journey." If well conducted in a leisurely and nonthreatening atmosphere, and if auditors do not settle for merely superficial biographical data, this procedure can reveal the surprising depth of some, the shallowness of some, and the rich and varied experiences of many. Persons can learn from one another, be brought closer together, and even be inspired in new ways. These are obvious spiritual benefits.

Perhaps as a next step *after* faith-journey narrations, we propose experiments within congregations in which parishioners share their "political journeys" with one another in a kind of counterpart to their faith journeys. As with spiritual direction groups, the context must be open, nonthreatening, and skillfully led. The leader should make clear at the outset what the rules are: no arguing, pleading, booing, sarcastic snorts; no interruptions except for factual clarification. Genuine listening must be uppermost.

Initial prompting questions might be along the following lines: How have you been involved in politics and how have you felt about it? What is the source of your beliefs about the worth and possibility of genuine democracy in the United States? The worth of military power in the world? Respect for authority? The limits of individual liberty? Government regulation of business? The role of government in protecting the natural environment? What are your images of typical politicians, bureaucrats, judges, lawyers, lobbyists, feminists? What did you learn about political conviction and public duty from your parents, teachers, siblings, children, employers? When did you first identify with a political party? Which political leaders have you most admired and why? Most despised and why? What images arise in your mind when seeing words like "anarchism," "monarchy," socialism," communism," fascism," "theocracy," "church and state," "haves and have-nots," "Support our troops," "peace demonstration," "ideologue." How has your Christian faith influenced your views? Leaders should emphasize that the point is not to articulate or defend policy positions, but to find autobiographically the roots of basic political assumptions.

Why should churches undertake such experiments? There are both tactical and strategic reasons. Tactically, we know that American residential life is increasingly segmented along economic lines, which tend to produce enclaves of the politically similar. Churches are similarly affected, but they at least make the effort to cross class and ethnic lines. A group that has shared the faith journeys of its members often reaches a level of gracious acceptance of differences that sets it apart from other social groups. An effort should be made at the outset to set up small groups that reflect a diversity of political views.

It will not be easy. Congregations may be somewhat more politically diverse than other groups, but not by much. Moreover, "liberals," by and large, like to talk, and "conservatives" in general do not like to talk, at least about politics. The best defense of the status quo is often silence. In these discussions conservatives may feel that the deck is stacked against them and regard the whole enterprise as a "political" trick. This is why the procedure probably can only work in groups that have first gone through a satisfactory faith-journey exercise. Even if church members cannot speak with one voice, they may learn to speak with more informed and understanding voices. This exercise, we hope, is useful at any time.

The strategic goal is to help Christian citizens better understand both their Christianity and their citizenship, for they, the church, and the body politic will be better for it. One danger is that the passion appropriate to both religious faith and political faith will be diminished by its temporary suspension, which this exercise requires. We must hope, however, that reflection can chasten and improve action, not replace it.

Because these discussions take place in a church setting, members are more likely to become open to connect their political views to their professed faith. They might also become interested in how church leaders make these connections, so that denominational and ecumenical statements may become important to more of them. Perhaps in time the churches can falsify the assumption of our political leaders and the press that the efforts of old-line church leaders to speak truth to power express only their personal views and can be safely ignored.

FIVE CONCLUSIONS

We end this chapter by drawing five main conclusions: First, there is a strong consensus in the old-line churches that churches should help to inform the political world about problems involving moral issues, the most urgent being not matters of sexual behavior or personal rectitude, important though they are, but such communal matters as poverty, violence, discrimination, injustice, human rights, and degradation of the environment. Second, churches need to emphasize inclusiveness and to work with those most severely affected by these problems, to listen to them, and to support their efforts to deal with them. Third, resistance movements from the churches do not need to wait until everyone agrees on a full plan of action. Churches should listen carefully to the variety of voices and points of view, but only as church people become engaged with a problem and acquainted with the suffering of those affected will the needed consensus emerge. Fourth, where we or our churches or our nation are complicit in a wrong, we have a special responsibility to resist. And finally, if we are faithful to the gospel, we may be in a minority, but we will not be alone.

DISCUSSION QUESTIONS

1. Do you regard the United States as a Christian nation? Why or why not? In what sense?
2. How important is separation of church and state? How is this different from separation of religion and politics?
3. Do you see politics as a necessary evil? Is it sometimes a necessary good?
4. Is it realistic to apply Christian ethics to current American politics? Is it possible? If not possible, isn't this a counsel of despair?
5. In politics is there a difference in the aims of "secular liberals" and "progressive Christians"? What is the difference? What should be the difference?

FOR FURTHER READING

Balmer, Randall. *Thy Kingdom Come: How the Religious Right Distorts the Faith and Threatens America*. New York: Perseus Books, 2006.

Bennett, John C. *Christian Ethics and Social Policy*. New York: Scribners, 1946.

Carter, Jimmy. *Our Endangered Values: America's Moral Crisis*. New York: Simon & Schuster, 2005.

Chapman, John W., and William A. Galston, eds. *Virtue*. American Society of Political and Legal Philosophy NOMOS series. Vol. 34. New York: New York University Press, 1992. Esp. chap. 2, "Religion and Civic Virtue," by J. Budziszweski.

Cobb, John B., Jr., *Becoming a Thinking Christian*. Nashville: Abingdon Press, 1993.

———. *Lay Theology*. St. Louis: Chalice Press, 1994.

———, ed. *Progressive Christians Speak*. Louisville, KY: Westminster John Knox Press, 2003.

Dagger, Richard. *Civic Virtues*. New York: Oxford University Press, 1997.

Galston, William A. *Liberal Purposes: Good, Virtue, and Diversity in the Liberal State*. New York: Cambridge University Press, 1991.

Gamwell, Franklin I. *Politics as a Christian Vocation: Faith and Democracy Today*. New York: Cambridge University Press, 2005.

Lerner, Michael. *The Left Hand of God: Taking Back Our Country from the Religious Right*. San Francisco: HarperSanFrancisco, 2006.

Meyers, Robin. *Why the Christian Right Is Wrong*. San Francisco: Jossey-Bass, 2006.

O'Donovan, Oliver. *The Desire of Nations: Rediscovering the Roots of Political Theology*. Cambridge: Cambridge University Press, 1996.

Phillips, Kevin. *American Theocracy: The Peril and Politics of Radical Religion, Oil, and Borrowed Money in the Twenty-First Century*. New York: Viking, 2006

Rosenblum, Nancy L., ed. *Liberalism and the Moral Life*. Cambridge, MA: Harvard University Press, 1989. Esp. chapters by Shklar, Okin, Galston, Taylor, and Rosenblum.

Sweckler, Stephen, ed. *Hard Ball on Holy Ground: The Religious Right v. the Mainline for the Church's Soul*. North Berwick, ME: Boston Wesleyan Association, 2006.

Wallis, Jim. *God's Politics: Why the Right Gets It Wrong, and the Left Doesn't Get It*. San Francisco: HarperSanFrancisco. 2005.

11

Forgiveness and Reconciliation

Lee C. McDonald

A gentle, middle-aged woman in California had a bumper sticker on her car that reads "An eye for an eye and the whole world will be blind." This is a paraphrase of a famous saying of Mohandas Gandhi, but also a saying compatible with the Christian belief in forgiveness and the avoidance of vengeance. A few months after the September 11, 2001, attack on the World Trade Center, an angry, red-faced man approached this woman in a supermarket parking lot. In apoplectic, not altogether coherent language, he said something like "You want to be blind in both eyes?" She registered confusion (and no doubt some anxiety). He went on, "That's what you'll be if America doesn't fight back." At this point she saw some hope for an intelligent conversation and tried to explain that when nations simply act out feelings of revenge in foreign policy, the result is apt to be self-defeating. He was not interested in such explanations. Muttering something about her apparently not realizing that we are in a war on terrorism, he stormed off, leaving the woman a bit shaken.

INTRODUCTION

We have chosen forgiveness as the topic for this concluding chapter for several reasons. First, it is a Christian virtue that is needed particularly by Christians who are learning to resist perilous currents in our society. Second, as Christians committed to involvement in the political order, we need to reflect on the role that Christian virtues can and cannot play there. Forgiveness is a major test case. And third, rare and difficult as it is to bring the idea of forgiveness into the political order, it has played an important role there. We celebrate those rare occasions when it has made reconciliation possible.

We progressive Christians do not find it easy to forgive those whom we resist. Indeed, the story with which this chapter opens illustrates the obstacles to forgiveness. We like to say that what we feel toward wrongheaded people is "righteous indignation." We are made uncomfortable by Jesus' advice to forgive seventy-seven times because we know that this advice is central to Jesus' outlook, and yet we are angry with those who are destroying so much of what we cherish. Further, the world sees forgiveness as a sign of weakness, especially the political world, where the strong run over the weak with depressing regularity. Masses of people tend to rally around the strong and shun the weak. That movies and novels offering colorful plots of savage revenge are more popular than films and books that subtly portray the pain of forgiveness is no accident.

CHRISTIAN VIRTUE AND CIVIC VIRTUE

Like civic virtue, Christian virtue calls to mind a sense of justice, fairness, courage, and honesty but also other less-public, at least less-political, virtues: agapic love, compassion, generosity, humility, and forgiveness. These qualities are not irrelevant to politics, but they transcend the requirements of normal civic participation.

Humility is an important Christian virtue, but humility is not yet taken to be a civic virtue. As with compassion, politicians seek favor by striking poses of humility, often with self-deprecating humor. This is surely better than arrogance, but if genuinely humble they would shun the limelight, cancel photo ops, and not make pronouncements on burning issues about which they have little knowledge. Citizens expect their leaders to fight for them and to instill pride in their cause.

Christians are regularly tested by their capacity to forgive, but nations do not forgive. Unfortunately much of politics, even in the better democracies, is driven by a spirit of revenge. The aftermath of September 11, 2001, is only the most recent example of this. Relatives of victims of 9/11 were in many cases disappointed that Al Qaeda flunky Zacharias Moussaoui (who was already in jail when 9/11 occurred) was sentenced "only" to life in prison, in solitary confinement, without possibility of parole, rather than executed. Forgiveness as a Christian virtue can, one hopes, influence movements to diminish the public spirit of revenge, but doing so is a challenge of immense proportions.

Politicians like to use the word "compassion" since it has such warm connotations, but as a virtue it has little relevance to policies affecting millions of people. Slogans like "compassionate conservatism" or "compassionate liberalism" are likely to be empty. A "compassionate" tax policy, for example, is probably better called a fair tax policy. It is fairness for which progressive Christians properly call. General appeals to protect taxpayers have been politically effective because everyone pays taxes, but they are often the smokescreen that hides benefits for the wealthy.

Moral and physical courage, honesty, and hopefulness are both Christian and civic virtues, but they operate differently in the visible political order and the invisible church of Christ. Courage in the taking of risks may be similar, as may hopefulness in confronting daunting odds. But Christian courage bears a different relationship to truth telling. Christians are concerned with truths of the soul and, though obligated to be kind, tactful, and humble in the telling, aim not to shrink from difficult truths that may shock the complacent and offend the powerful.

Civic leaders almost always shade the truth for diplomatic and political reasons. The language of diplomacy includes a doublespeak of grand ideals and implies coercion if the political enemy acts wrongly. For powerless auditors, there are hints of rewards to come, and in democratic publics there is subtle flattery implying that the people's wisdom is guiding the policy. Christian truth telling does not make such concessions to power.

The psyche of the body politic showed itself all too clearly when President Eisenhower, after first denying our aerial spying, confessed to the Russians that it was our U-2 spy plane that they shot down. A clear majority of the American people objected not to our lies but to Eisenhower's honest confession, a response far from the Christian ethic "'Love your enemies, do good to those who hate you'" (Luke 6:27). The earth has not yet seen a pacifist nation-state, though anthropologists have identified some tribes of remarkable tranquility. In the aftermath of World War II, Japan adopted a pacifistic constitution, but under pressure from the United States it has found ways to circumvent its rejection of military force.

Many Christians in public office have modeled what a morally good politician or bureaucrat should be—responsible, fair-minded, and the rest—whereas others claiming to be Christian have been mean-spirited, deceptive, and vindictive.[1] To aspire to kindness and gentleness in the image of Christ is not to be neutral, and the fact that our national polity has been polarized does not mean each pole is equal in worthiness or equally responsible for the polarization. Of course, at a distance we cannot penetrate a politician's possibly hypocritical claims of loyalty to Christ, and we know that politicians and bureaucrats can be touched by grace like anyone else. We hear the warning "Do not judge, so that you may not be judged" (Matt. 7:1). We know that the sin of self-deception is pervasive in the human psyche, but we have too little respect for the morally good politician, bureaucrat, and citizen. It is as demanding to be the complete and good politician as it is to be the complete and good pastor.

WHAT IS FORGIVENESS?

Forgiveness is much more than saying, "No harm done. Forget about it." Telling someone else who has been deeply hurt to "forgive and forget" is easy, but it's not easy if you are the one who has been hurt. Merely saying the words "I forgive you," though they may calm troubled waters in the short run, may not count as forgiveness in the long run unless behind those words is a continuing disposition to be forgiving. For the forgiving person, what sometimes appear to be natural feelings of vengeance must be faced honestly and overcome.

For forgiveness to be meaningful, the offense must be real and must be an offense against the one for whom forgiveness is an option. That is, if we feel an offense has been committed that isn't an offense at all (we think the pastor deliberately slighted us, whereas in fact he didn't happen to see us), it is a misperception, and to take great offense because of it is a moral lapse on our part, not evidence of a moral lapse on the other person's part. Further, if we see Mr. A. physically abusing Ms. B, we can be morally outraged, and we can condemn Mr. A—we can even intervene to protect Ms. B—but forgiveness is not primarily our problem. It is Ms. B's problem. Indeed, "third-party" forgiveness may be something less than genuine forgiveness. In any case, the person in the best position to forgive is the person who has been hurt.

Offenses for which forgiveness may be appropriate are usually fairly serious. If I bump a person on the subway, I usually say, "Excuse me," not "Forgive me." To forgive is not to excuse or overlook or condone. If we condone the moral offenses of others too quickly and easily, we can rightly be charged with participating in the offense. We are encouraging the wrongdoer. From his point of view, the man in the parking lot perhaps thought that the bumper-sticker lady was encouraging terrorism.

We should probably overlook—without condoning—minor offenses. But if the offense is serious, and we say, "I forgive," and the offender goes right ahead doing the same thing, isn't forgiveness rather empty? Relatives of alcoholics have come to be called "enablers" when they do not practice "tough love." When there is no repentance at all, no acknowledgement of a wrong, our forgiveness turns into a condonation. Let us see what the Bible tells us about forgiving.

THE BIBLE AND FORGIVENESS

References to forgiveness in the Old Testament are, with few exceptions, pleas to God to forgive or thanks to God for forgiving (see Exod. 32:32; Lev. 4–5; Num. 15; Deut. 21:8; 1 Sam. 25; 1 Kgs. 8; 2 Chr. 6; Pss. 25, 32, 78, 85, 85, 130; Dan. 9:19; Amos 7:2.) Usually, of course, it is the people of Israel who need and seek forgiveness, but other peoples may be included (Ps. 99). God is sometimes seen as capable of forgiving but not always disposed to forgive, sometimes as an avenger of wrongdoing. Moreover, there may be pleas to God that he not forgive others: for example, those who bow down before idols (Isa. 2:9) or those who have been plotting against Jeremiah (Jer. 18:23).

That God is the one doing the forgiving, however, because God has the authority to forgive, is made evident even in stories of human forgiveness. The brothers of Joseph after their father Jacob's death remembered that their father had told them to beg forgiveness of Joseph for their crimes against him, and they do so. But Joseph's response was, "'Do not be afraid! Am I in the place of God?'" (Gen. 50:19). The clear implication is that ultimately only God has the right to forgive.

With the New Testament, the assumption that only God forgives changes in a very special way. In Mark 2, Jesus in Capernaum pronounces the sins of the paralytic lowered through the roof to be forgiven, and the scribes are scandalized, for this pronouncement appears to be blasphemy. "'Who can forgive sins but God alone?'" they ask (v. 7). Jesus responds by asking whether it is easier to say, "Your sins are forgiven," or to ask the paralytic to take up his mat and walk, which the paralytic promptly proceeds to do. All are amazed, we are told, and so are we. The same story is told in Luke 5:17–26 with the added words "'so that you may know that the Son of Man has authority on earth to forgive sins'" (v. 24). Matthew 9:2–8 tells the same story in a more abbreviated form, making clear how important the story was to the early church.

At one and the same time, Jesus affirms his own authority by suggesting that the forgiveness of God works through him and radically challenges the idea that human justice can be fulfilled by an eye for an eye and a tooth for a tooth. The possibility that through forgiveness God's justice can become human justice is set before us. In a way, the authority to forgive remains with God, and yet henceforth humans are encouraged to forgive each other, to reject the impulse for revenge. And so we have Jesus' answer to Peter when asked how often he should forgive "another member of the church" who is sinning against Peter: "'Not seven times, but, I tell you, seventy-seven times'" (Matt. 18:22).

The parable of the forgiven debt in Luke 7 is a link to the Lord's Prayer, which Christians pray every week: "Forgive us our debts, as we also have forgiven our debtors" (Matt. 6:12). In his Sermon on the Mount, Jesus makes the point even more forcefully: "If you do not forgive others, neither will your Father forgive your trespasses" (Matt. 6:15. Luke's version at 11:4 is "Forgive us our sins, for we ourselves forgive everyone indebted to us"). We are apt to forget the "as we forgive" part. We sometimes pray to be forgiven so that we may forgive, but that is not the direction the Lord's Prayer runs. We cannot expect the forgiveness of God unless we *first* forgive others. God is waiting for us to be forgiving; then perhaps we can expect our own divine forgiveness.

The political philosopher Hannah Arendt saw the human community as built by the promises we make to each other and the networks of trust we create. Yet not all promises can be fulfilled, for we cannot see the future. We misjudge what conditions are and what the terms of the promise imply; we make mistakes; we become self-protective when things go awry; we sin. We are then confronted with what Arendt calls "the predicament of irreversibility": everyone is stuck with their promises no matter what, even the well-intentioned ones; the course of history could get worse, not better. We are saved, however, by the capacity to forgive, the willingness to let others try again, and the ability to respond to new circumstances and do better the next time. We need the capacity to make promises if we are to control "the chaotic uncertainty of the future," and we need the capacity to forgive as a "remedy for unpredictability."[2]

One of the most nuanced treatments of forgiveness within the framework of an orthodox Christian outlook is that of Miroslav Volf in his book *Exclusion and Embrace*:

> "Forgiveness" sums up much of the significance of the cross—for Christians the ultimate symbol at the same time of the destructiveness of human sin and the greatness of God's love. . . . More than just the passive suffering of an innocent person, the passion of Christ is the agony of a tortured soul and a wrecked body offered as *a prayer for the forgiveness of the torturers*. No doubt such prayer adds to the agony of the passion. As Dietrich Bonhoeffer saw clearly, forgiveness itself is a form of suffering. . . . Forgiveness is the boundary between exclusion and embrace. It heals the wounds that the power-acts of exclusion have inflicted.[3]
>
> The cross is the giving up of God's self in order not to give up on humanity; it is the consequence of God's desire to break the power of human enmity without violence and receive human beings into divine communion.[4]

As such it is a scandal to a world filled with hostility, for this "good news" is too good to be believable by the perpetrator.

UNFORGIVING POLITICS

The world of politics is inescapable. If some people wish to insulate themselves from politics, they can do so only because of politics, for politics is a community deciding what it shall do (see chap. 10's discussion of the term *politics*). The *politēs* was the Greek citizen, the *politikos* was the statesman, and *politeia* was the constitution. These words are also the root of *police*, those who protect the community from internal threats, and *polite*, which is what diplomats must be if they are to protect the community from external threats without war. These are two ends of a spectrum. At one end, the wider end, politics is war prevention. At the police end, politics is anarchy prevention. In the middle, politics is managing common problems, the problems everybody cares about: getting water, disposing of sewage, getting enough to eat, protecting jobs, educating children, paving streets, ending an unpopular war, coping with global warming. The line between public and private concerns is always changing. We used to regard medicine as a private matter, but now with HMOs, drug addiction, epidemics, and the cost of prescription drugs being regarded as common problems, medicine has become a public concern, a matter of politics. However much people may think they can escape from politics, the fact is that no one escapes.

Ronald Reagan's Bitburg incident is a good example of how ordinary politics can intersect with the memory of hurt. It is a lesson in how difficult it is for political leaders to be—or even appear to be—forgiving. German officials had been excluded from the celebration of the fortieth anniversary of the Normandy invasion, and the German Chancellor invited President Reagan to visit Germany in May 1985 as a sign of reconciliation between the two countries. A visit to the Dachau death camp had been included in the suggested presidential itinerary, but the White House vacillated for four months on dates and itinerary. At a press conference in March, Reagan announced that he would not visit any concentration camps because it would cause "reawakening the memories" of the war, and in April the White House announced that Reagan would lay a wreath at the Bitburg Cemetery near the Luxembourg border as a gesture of reconciliation. This gesture seemed safe, for previous American-French-German ceremonies there had not raised a flap, and there had been good relations between Germans and the nearby NATO-American air base.

Researchers soon discovered that along with two thousand ordinary German soldiers buried at Bitburg were the bodies of forty-nine members of the Nazi elite Waffen SS. American war veteran groups and Jewish groups immediately protested loudly, and by April 18 fifty-three U.S. senators had signed a letter urging the president not to go to Bitburg. Reagan refused to back down, saying, "I think . . . there's nothing wrong with visiting that cemetery where those young men are victims of Nazism also, even though they were fighting in the German uniform. . . . They were victims, just as surely as the victims of the concentration camps."[5] This only launched another storm of protest, a protest that was not cooled by the speech of Elie Wiesel, recent Nobel Peace Prize winner, who, by chance, was to be honored at the White House two days later. Wiesel rose at 4:00 a.m. the day of the speech to revise his remarks. He praised the president's efforts at reconciliation and denied belief in collective guilt, but he also recalled that April 19 was the anniversary of the 1943 Warsaw Jewish ghetto uprising, the only underground movement not supported by the Allies. He described his concentration camp experience and asserted that "to build on ruins, . . . memory is the answer, perhaps the only answer. . . . May I, Mr. President, . . . implore you to do something else, to find another way, another site? That place, Mr. President, is not your place. Your place is with the victims of the SS."[6]

The president was said to be deeply moved but was still determined to stay on course. In volume of outrage the Americans exceeded the Germans. In Germany the parliamentary representative of Bitburg was "insulted" that the American president might *not* visit his hometown cemetery. Some German opinion conveniently overlooked the Jewish dimensions of the issue; other opinion was more overtly anti-Semitic. Press interviews with SS veterans found some saying they felt "rehabilitated" by the president's position. Chancellor Kohl, meanwhile, made a step forward by recalling the death of Ann Frank and saying that reconciliation is "only possible if we accept history as it really was, if we Germans acknowledge our shame."[7]

Reagan's visit to Bitburg was as brief and silent as possible. In his speech at the nearby U.S. Air Force base, he assured his hearers and the world that reconciliation does not mean forgetting, and he expressed hope for escape from the "cycle of destruction" that wars in the past have launched.

This incident teaches us that those who suffer most remember longest, and their obligation includes educating others in history. Unless such victims remind the apathetic majority of past negative events, there is "willed amnesia" about those events, for they make us uncomfortable and become an indictment of who we are. Individually and collectively, as Nietzsche suggested, when memory says, "I have done that," our pride still says, "I cannot have done that." The president inadvertently revealed to the nation how deep—or perhaps how close to the surface—passions from the past can be.

Such experiences can also qualify the axiom that only the injured victim is in a position to forgive—an axiom that can easily be used to justify indifference to truly common problems. Shared moral responsibility means that past hurts can to some extent be shared; non-Jews, for example, ought to be able to share with Jews resentment at the expressions of anti-Semitism that Bitburg stimulated. What causes resentment provides the opportunity for forgiveness, and though political forgiveness is not the same as personal forgiveness, there are nevertheless connections.

THE LIMITS OF VENGEANCE

From what has been said so far, it may appear that forgiveness in politics is either impossible or irrelevant. But this negative view is wrong. Politics is a substitute for war, not war itself, and those who move subjects by terror and force rather than by persuasion are not politicians at all but tyrants and dictators. If there is a touch of the would-be dictator in the dark heart of many politicians, healthy cultures manage to keep such impulses in check or even chastened. However bumbling and skewed, politics is a process of persuasion directed toward finding a *common* good, and politicians must be willing to compromise interests (not necessarily ideals) in order to achieve some part of that common good. Put another way, achieving any part of the common good requires the articulation of common ideals, ideals that people have but may not be aware that they have. The good politician, the one who—usually after death—is called a statesman, must be an educator, call forth the "better nature" of citizens, illuminate worthy aims, and inspire a public to seek them—one who can articulate the possibility of a better world and give people hope in that prospect. Overcoming instinctive feelings of revenge is part of this process.

A look at actual historic events reveals few cases of political actions that exemplify either "pure" forgiveness or "pure" revenge. The motives of historic actors are a tangle of competing and confused impulses. For example, one of the most tortured and painful stories of our time is the ongoing struggle for Israelis and Palestinians to find a secure and peaceful living space in their small corner of the world. The well-known story of the second intifada, which began in September 2000, is a story of Palestinian suicide bombers killing innocent Israelis in protest of the Israeli Defense Force having killed innocent Palestinians. Next come the IDF bulldozing and shelling the West Bank homes of the families of the suicide bombers and the buildings of suspected Palestinian militants, acts that lead to more suicide bombing, which leads to more retribution, and so on. The larger picture shares the same retributive dynamic: Palestinians say that Israel cannot be trusted because it refuses to grant genuine self-governing authority to the provisional Palestinian Authority and acts as an occupying power in the West Bank and Gaza. Israel says the Palestinians can't be trusted because they have not demonstrated the capacity to be self-governing by restraining terrorists, and recent experience with Hamas in a semi-free Gaza lends plausibility to this view.

This situation reflects a politics of revenge. As former President Clinton has said of the Middle East, it has not yet learned that when trapped in a hole, the first thing to do is to stop digging. Yet the story is not over. Religious and human rights groups exist on each side; some cooperate with groups on the other side, and all care about real peace. Ultimately, they may count for more than the leaders who hang on to power and popular support by playing on fear and who believe that violence is better than political compromise in solving political problems.

American Christians can take no comfort by dismissing Middle East conflict as simply a struggle between Jews and Palestinians, or dignifying it by calling it a "clash of civilizations." Although the Bush administration has been careful not to condemn Islam as a religion, against the advice of conservative and liberal experts alike, it has been uncritical in its support of Israel and has with single-mindedness expanded the "War on Terrorism," initially focused on Al Qaeda, to include war against the nation-state of Iraq on the false grounds that it had weapons of mass destruction and the irrelevant grounds that Iraq's dictatorial ruler was an evil man.

Coalition troops, largely Americans, have tried to be friendly with Iraqi citizens, giving candy to children and posing as liberators. Some Iraqis have received them as such but not a majority, for "liberation" suggests making life better, not worse. Meanwhile, deep-seated resentment between Shia and Sunni (partly from the ruthless domination of Shias by a minority government of Sunnis) has led to increasing violence and loss of life in a counterpoint of revenge and counterrevenge similar to that in Israel/Palestine. It is civil war regrettably encrusted with religious labels.

Some Christians ask in this and many other situations, "What would Jesus do?" The answer is not obvious, for the first century and the twenty-first century are very different times. The construction of a "Christian foreign policy" is not an easy task and is bound to beg a number of questions. Certainly it would need to take into account the tragedy of history symbolized by the cross and the participation of all of us in systems that manipulate, oppress, and destroy. But at a minumum it would include a list of preferences that would put foreign aid over military attack, saving lives over taking life, respect for diversity over self-righteousness, maximum consultation over secretiveness, and politics over war.

Where there is no justice, "taking justice into one's own hands" may seem morally required. The usual accompaniment, however, is impulsive action based on vengeful feelings, with no cooling-off period and no third-party impartiality. The validation of vengeful feelings requires a mental rigidity that the person or group to be punished is guilty or evil beyond any possible doubt. It is companion to a form of self-deceptive moral arrogance that puts all right on one side and all wrong on the other, bifurcating positions rather than elucidating issues. Even though once war has begun, terrible deeds may sometimes find a crude justification (e.g., taking a few lives to save many lives), normal human beings can do terrible deeds only in a psychological state of high emotional certitude. This generalization is connected to the familiar saying "The first casualty of war is truth." One must lie to the enemy because deception is one of the tools of warfare; one must lie to one's fellow militants to keep up morale; and one must lie to oneself to turn opponents into enemies and enemies into devils, and to help conceal from oneself the terribleness of one's own terrible deeds.

For its cruelty, casual deception, and mismanagement, the tragedy of the Iraq War will surely produce volumes of pained analysis for many years to come. As to the Israeli-Palestinian situation, which is not unrelated to the wider Middle East conflagrations or to American imperialist aspirations, we can say that Israelis, bound together by remembering their own historical pain in the Holocaust, have yet been too little able to identify with the pain their own policies have inflicted on West Bank and Gaza Palestinians. Second, there are no impartial observers left in power. Many in the press have courageously sought the truth but have encountered roadblocks thrown up by both sides. A United Nations team investigating the slaughter in the refugee camp in Jenin was turned back. It is hardly possible to talk with precision about forgiveness until the truth is known and persons are able to know *what* is to be forgiven.

RECONCILIATION

Political forgiveness is not the same as personal forgiveness and should probably be called "reconciliation." Whereas personal forgiveness occurs in the deepest recesses of the individual psyche, reconciliation binds together under one rubric, law, or practice the aggregate and mixed feelings of many people. Of course, if acts of public reconciliation only plaster over underlying personal feelings of revenge or come to be derided as mere "political correctness," the gains may be short-lived. Nevertheless, there is a continuing link between the personal and the political.

The pursuit of justice includes the pursuit of conditions where forgiveness might be possible. For example, some states and churches have programs that attempt to bring together victim and criminal offender in acts of reconciliation. The feelings of victims of crimes are often left out of the public equation, for in avoiding "vigilante justice" our system of criminal justice makes the state and not the victim the plaintiff against the accused. Victim-offender reconciliation programs transcend this distinction to some extent and have worked best, not surprisingly, when the crime is minor or the offender is a juvenile. But the delicate situation where each side has a chance to tell his or her story can sometimes lead to surprising examples of interpersonal healing without eliminating the need for punishment of wrongdoing.

In international relations, we have few examples of justice that approach the level of rectitude necessary to make talk of official forgiveness very meaningful. The Nuremberg trials after World War II were cases of "victor's justice," for no American or Soviet war criminals were brought to trial. The justice was retributive and also allowed ordinary Germans to live in a state of denial. The United States is still so self-protective that we have refused to join the United Nation's new International War Crimes Tribunal. The United Nations International Criminal Tribunal for Rwanda, in the years since the 1994 massacre of 800,000 ethnic Tutsis and moderate Hutus by Hutu mobs, has sought convictions, but only thirty or so have been charged and twenty-two convicted. The chief financial supporter of the genocide, tycoon Félicien Kabuga, is still on the run.

Though governments may apologize, governments do not forgive; forgiveness comes only from the inner pain and spiritual discipline of an individual person. After forty-some years the United States government apologized to the American citizens of Japanese descent who, on racist grounds, were shipped off to relocation centers in 1943. Modest reparations were paid, and many, but not all, of the victims forgave or had earlier forgiven their captors. The Japanese government has apologized for Pearl Harbor and for the earlier rape and pillage of Nanjing (Nanking), and though it apologized for the use of Korean women as sex slaves for the Japanese military, it backs away from acknowledging official responsibility. The U.S. government has never formally apologized for dropping atom bombs on Hiroshima and Nagasaki, nor for the fire bombing of Tokyo or the carpet bombing of Cologne and Essen in Germany. Many words continue to be written on the military "necessity" that is alleged to justify these actions, although objective historical research has more and more come to question the military benefits of large-scale killing of civilians. As Donald Shriver says, "War itself is atrocious human behavior; every side in a war commits atrocities in the eyes of its enemies. Yet, in their battles in the Pacific, both Americans and Japanese justified, enlarged, and glorified the death of enemies in ways that went far beyond military necessity."[8] The political theorist Michael Walzer has brilliantly shown how catchphrases like "All's fair in love and war" and "War is hell" and "military necessity" have been used to obscure the hard fact that every military decision is also a moral decision.[9]

Many works in Christian ethics have dealt with the problem of forgiveness, but the best recent work on forgiveness in politics is Donald W. Shriver's *An*

Ethic for Enemies, from which much of the previous discussion has drawn (see notes 5–8). Widespread and deep feelings of injustice prevent merely pro forma attempts at reconciliation and personal forgiveness from achieving the stated goal. For example, the democratization of Latin American regimes has produced various attempts to remedy past wrongs. One case is Peru, where in the fifteen years of internal war against terrorism that began in 1980 some 25,000 people were killed, of whom an estimated 13,000 had nothing to do with the Shining Path militants, who were the declared enemy of the military. Many victims were peaceful and legitimate critics of the government. When the struggle was over, the government passed a Law on Impunity, an amnesty law to free all those in prison for political offenses. In the debates over the law, one congressperson in support of the proposal appealed specifically to the Christian sense of forgiveness. The bill passed, but in the name of reconciliation it freed many, both military and rebels, who had violated the most basic human rights, such as summary executions and the murder of children. The result, says Rafael Goto Silva, although called forgiveness, actually worked against peace, for the law did not require that guilt be acknowledged or that repentance occur: "Legalized impunity institutionalizes evasiveness, the concealment of the offender, and contempt for the suffering of the victim."[10]

In the twentieth century the three most well-known protagonists of ultimately successful peaceful resistance have been Gandhi in India, Martin Luther King Jr. in the United States, and Nelson Mandela in South Africa. Peaceful civil disobedience is by no means the same as political reconciliation, but it can be a precious prerequisite for reconciliation. Each of these three examples provide lessons too rich in detail for summary here, so we will concentrate on a single aspect of the South African experience.

In South Africa, a government mechanism was developed specifically to make political reconciliation possible by means of the Truth and Reconciliation Commission (TRC), established after the presidency of Nelson Mandela succeeded the Afrikaner apartheid regime in 1994. Perhaps unique in history, the commission operated from 1996 to 1998, but the long-term outcome remains uncertain. Every political community is different, so we cannot presume that the experience of the TRC is easily transferable as a model for other societies. It did, however, provide the world with a hopeful glimpse of what might be.

Nelson Mandela spent twenty-eight years in prison as an enemy of the apartheid regime. His remarkable dignity, patience, strength, and diplomatic skill were essential elements in the TRC's coming into being, but a church conference in Rustenburg in 1990 was also a factor. The Dutch Reformed Church, earlier a supporter of apartheid, there joined with Methodists, Anglicans, and others who had opposed it in a common confession of sin, thus giving hope that healing between the races was possible. Legislation setting up the TRC was carried through parliament by Justice Minister Dullah Omar, a Muslim member of the African National Congress and a survivor of an attempt on his life by the segregationist security police. From six hundred nominees suggested by the public, a careful selection process produced the eighteen commission members finally named by President Mandela. He appointed as chair of the TRC Anglican Archbishop Desmond Tutu, who had received the Nobel Peace Prize in 1984. Alex Boraine, ex-president of the Methodist Church, became vice chair.

The Gross Human Rights Violations Committee of the TRC traveled about the country to hear the stories of those who had lost loved ones or who had themselves been victims of security-force abuse. In a concerted effort to be unbiased, the TRC interviewed those who had suffered at the hands of (liberation forces, i.e., extremist groups like the Pan Africanist Congress. Unlike the former government investigative unit, the TRC worked to confirm the evidence presented.) Most controversial was the Amnesty Committee, composed of judges and lawyers, which heard appeals for amnesty by those who had fully confessed to politically or racially motivated crimes against other persons. Perpetrators of ordinary or minor crimes were excluded. Of the 8,000 applications that came in by the May 1997 deadline, half were rejected. If disclosures before the committee were full and if amnesty was granted, the evidence presented could not be used in any subsequent court prosecution. Those who did not present themselves were to be subject to prosecution at any point in their lives. Vice President Thabo Mbeki, later to succeed Mandela as president, presented himself for an amnesty hearing. Former Afrikaner presidents P. W. Botha and F. W. de Klerk did not. The skill and stature of Archbishop Tutu was important for the success of the TRC. When passions became too heated, he would stop the proceedings for a prayer or a hymn, practices impossible to imagine in Western secular courts. Some thought that amnesty was a denial of justice whereas others criticized the absence of cross-examination procedures. Many thought the reparations provided were too scanty; however, even though requests for reparations were surprisingly modest, there was not enough money.

The aim was not to impose a code of retributive justice but to achieve reconciliation, to soften animosities that made civil war a constant threat. A police officer who had led the assault on a village resulting in the killing of several of its black residents testified, "I can never undo what I have done. . . . I have no right to ask your forgiveness, but I ask that you will allow me to spend my life helping you to rebuild your village and put your lives together."[11] A mother whose son had been dragged out of her house by security police and killed without trial testified about his accomplishments at school and her pride in him, and after a long pause she said, "I do not know if I can forgive. I must know who did this to my son. When I see the face of the one who killed him, and he tells me why, then perhaps I can forgive."[12]

Personal forgiveness is never easy, and the crude and fallible mechanisms of government cannot ease political reconciliation between hostile peoples. Still, the role played by some people of faith in South Africa gives us hope. Christians are called to be exemplars of those willing to confess, repent, and forgive—and in the right moments to protest and to resist.

As we have seen, forgiveness in international politics is even more difficult than in domestic politics, though our opening story shows how the two run together. The American popular response to September 11, 2001, was a mixture of awe, sadness, fear, outrage, and vengeance. If it is unrealistic or even foolish to expect masses of people to exhibit instantaneous forgiveness in such circumstances, it nevertheless is an essential expression of Christian faith to respect awe and sadness while discouraging the impulsive spirit of vengeance. The emotions of the American people might have been channeled into a serious effort to determine who was responsible for the attack and to bring those persons to trial rather than inflicting immense suffering on the largely innocent populations of Afghanistan and Iraq. With enough persistence, courage, and understanding of good politics, as opposed to narrow and superficial politics, Christians can at least move with others step by step in both small and large ways toward greater possibilities of human reconciliation.

CONCLUSIONS

We began this book with the call to resist as well as to reform. We end with the call to forgive and the promise of reconciliation. These differing actions and attitudes may exist in tension, but for one who would follow Jesus, they are each essential. Resistance without forgiveness can perpetuate the cycle of mutual suspicion and even hatred whereas forgiveness without resistance too often allows evil to have its way. There are, of course, violent forms of resistance. We have not argued that those are always wrong. But these are not forms of resistance of which we are speaking. Violent resistance, however, provokes violence, and for the most part, those who "take the sword will perish by the sword" (Matt. 26:52). Even when they succeed, the struggle leaves deep wounds that never fully heal. Even nonviolent resistance, when it is carried out with hatred and contempt for those who represent or embody what is resisted, has profoundly mixed consequences.

Insofar as we heed God's call, as we refuse to participate in consumerism, we will avoid contempt or even condescension toward those who do. As we reject those theories that generate practices leading to poisonous inequality, we will retain respect for those who sincerely affirm those theories, and we will understand those who make personal profit their goal. As we condemn the goal of American Empire, we will still view those who seek it as fellow human beings who, like ourselves, need to open their minds to a larger truth. As we oppose the domination of our educational system by a dehumanizing meta-physics, we will remember that those who teach it often do so with real con-viction of its truth. And as we struggle to redirect human activity away from its currently suicidal direction, we will not forget that many who promote this direction know of no alternative. As we resist, reject, and oppose, our ultimate goal remains reconciliation with those whose ideas and practices we resist, reject, and oppose.

We know that we repeatedly miss the mark of this Christian norm. Day by day we need the forgiveness both of those against whom we sin and of God. But the sin is not our resistance, which we cannot weaken. Our sin is our ten-dency to self-righteous and presumptuous condemnation of those against whom we struggle. It is only as forgiven sinners that we can enagage in Chris-tian resistance.

DISCUSSION QUESTIONS

1. How can political leaders be made more sensitive to the need for forgiveness?
2. How can the unforgiving be resisted without promoting violent reactions?
3. Why does the spirit of revenge seem so deep in the human psyche?
4. Have you ever practiced Walter Wink's defiant but nonviolent resistance? Was it a success or a failure?
5. Is our nation moving toward or away from a politics of vengeance?

FOR FURTHER READING

Adams, Marilyn McCord. "Forgiveness: A Christian Model." *Faith and Philosophy* 8 (1991): 277–304.

Bennett, John C. *Christian Ethics and Social Policy.* New York: Scribner's Sons, 1946.

Digeser, Peter. "Forgiveness and Politics." *Political Theory* 26 (October 1998): 700–24.

Erikson, Erik H. *Gandhi's Truth: On the Origins of Militant Nonviolence.* New York: W. W. Norton & Co., 1969.

Haber, Joram Graf. *Forgiveness.* Savage, MD: Rowan & Littlefield, 1991.

Hauerwas, Stanley. *After Christendom?* Nashville: Abingdon Press, 1991.

Horsley, Richard. *Jesus and the Spiral of Violence.* San Francisco: Harper & Row, 1987.

King, Martin Luther, Jr. *The Trumpet of Conscience.* San Francisco: Harper & Row, 1968.

Murphy, Jeffrie, and Jean Hampton. *Forgiveness and Mercy.* New York: Cambridge University Press, 1988.

Shriver, Donald W., Jr. *An Ethic for Enemies: Forgiveness in Politics*. New York: Oxford University Press, 1995.

Tutu, Desmond. *No Future without Forgiveness*. New York: Doubleday Image, 2000.

Volf, Miroslav. *Exclusion and Embrace: A Theological Exploration of Identity, Otherness, and Reconciliation*. Nashville: Abingdon Press, 1996.

Walzer, Michael. *Just and Unjust Wars*. New York: Basic Books, 1977.

Wink, Walter. *The Powers That Be*. New York: Doubleday, 1998.

Afterword

Forms of Resistance

Gordon Douglass

This book has called attention to a number of ways that the social-political situation in the United States and, indeed, in the whole world, is deteriorating. Many possible reforms are relevant to slowing or even stopping this negative movement, and though we favor reforms, encouraging efforts to effect reform has not been our focus for two reasons. First, reforms are already being widely discussed, and we are barraged with opportunities to support them by sending money to their proponents and writing to our legislators. Second, in relation to the main topics of this book, they do not go nearly far enough to resolve the problems.

We have therefore identified the alternative as "resistance," for we are all called to resist evils even when we do not know how to overcome them. We hope that our resistance may somehow, some day, help to change the situation; but even if it has no effect, we are called to resist.

We have written about some forms of resistance. We may, for instance, inwardly refuse to be drawn into attitudes and assumptions that support the policies and practices that now lead the world into disaster. We may join the World Social Forum in affirming that "another world is possible." We may also share in spelling out some features of what that other world would be like and doing what we can to evoke the popular desire for that world's realization.

We also encourage the church in all its dimensions to live out of its own convictions rather than the values of the enveloping society. This would mean listening to the Word of God as one hears it in the Bible. The church can also strengthen the capacity of individuals to live countercultural lives by providing them with support and helping them to pray both collectively in the church and privately in their homes. We have made further suggestions in chapters 8 and 10. In chapter 8 we discussed how the church can help its members attain

some sense of solidarity with the poor, a solidarity that Latin American liberation theologians have shown to be a central requirement of Christian discipleship. In chapter 10 we noted the critical failure of so many members of our
churches to reflect on the implications of their faith for their political thinking and action, and we suggested one way of responding to that situation.

For both adults and youth the church has unique opportunities for providing a perspective on the world that is different from the one that dominates
the U.S. media, which present the world only as it appears from the perspective of the United States. In this view, only places where Americans or American interests are clearly involved are important, and American lives are far
more valuable than others, especially those of the people killed by our troops
and our policies. The church can encourage Christians to keep in mind that
God shows no partiality and that for God every human life is important.

In the dominant perspective, increase of wealth is inherently good; indeed,
it is virtually the measure of the well-being of the society and of individuals
within it. The church can teach that putting wealth first is incompatible with
seeking first God's commonwealth. It can encourage its people to evaluate
developments according to their effects on relationships among people and
between them and other creatures.

The increasingly dominant worldview counts human beings as fully explicable by external and psychological forces and self-interest. To be rational is
now understood to be seeking one's own advantage and to view relationships,
including marriage, in terms of what each person gains. From this perspective,
love is understood to be sexual attraction. The church can help its members
to see that human beings are more than this; that love can be genuine concern
for others; that commitment to others, especially in marriage, calls for personal transformation and discipline; that service for others is personally
rewarding but also part of the life in community to which we are called even
when it demands real sacrifice.

Our churches can challenge their youth to subordinate the goal of wealth
to that of service. Too often service *for* others, and especially of the neediest,
is an appendage to success in the "real world" of consumerism. It is like the
payment of a tithe that has little effect on life's basic choices. Youth can be
invited to think seriously of their career choices as divine callings or vocations.
This entails placing the needs of society and the world first and giving secondary consideration to personal economic success.

Churches can also take the lead in responsible consumption. Their educational programs can focus more on the regenerative requirements of nature,
and institutional decisions about how to reduce bills for energy and water can
be occasion both for educating members and for modeling good practices. For
example, their conversations about styrofoam cups, substituting recycled

paper, and using drought-resistant plantings can raise consciousness about the complexities of good stewardship.

We have said less about the specific ways that other institutions and especially individuals can resist. These vary according to different roles in society. Since to a large extent the forces we are called to resist are bound up with the primacy now accorded to the economic order and the particular character that order has taken, we must give primary attention to our roles in relation to the economy.

Consider first what *consumers* already are doing to initiate a new form of American capitalism. Thanks to dozens of organizations that provide information about how products are made, who produces them, and how they affect the environment in which we live, millions of consumers favor "green" or environmentally sound products over those whose production or use harms the environment. Such products often cost more, representing an immediate self-sacrifice involved in resistance. Consumer groups continue to pressure the Food and Drug Administration to label eco-friendly products. Revelations about exploitative working conditions in some factories are also beginning to influence buying patterns.

As knowledge spreads about the environmental costs of transporting and refrigerating goods over long distances, many consumers are buying more local produce. With regard to products that cannot be produced nearby, such as coffee, chocolate, tea, bananas, and many kinds of handicrafts, responsible consumers avoid the exploitatively produced commercial forms and support instead fair-trade goods, which are produced in developing-country cooperatives under conditions more conducive to living wages and safe working conditions.

In addition to consuming more responsibly, consumers can live quite comfortably without consuming as much. This is so obvious in most middle-class households that we will not expound on it. One appropriate focus for change, especially for Christians, is Christmas, which has come to celebrate consumerism more than the birth of Jesus. Giving is a suitable way to celebrate the occasion, but most of the giving should be to those in need rather than to those who already have too much. Many churches now promote alternative Christmas giving—financial gifts to worthy, nonprofit service agencies in lieu of commercially purchased gifts. That is a start.

Next, consider what *workers* can do to model a new kind of American capitalism. To be sure, labor unions have now shrunk so much since their halcyon days following World War II that fewer than one in ten private-sector workers belong to unions. With so weakened an institutional voice, how can workers possibly help to redesign American capitalism? Despite recent losses, however, most American workers, whether union members or not, have savings in the form of pensions that amount to more than $6 trillion, the largest pool of investment capital in the country. In recent years, worker groups have tried harder to influence decisions about their pensions, and many have challenged corporate management through proxy resolutions to alter policies that undermine worker safety or harm the environment. Workers with influence over the sort of funds in which their retirement accounts are invested are opening the door to socially and environmentally responsible choices. In addition, a few examples of worker-owned cooperative enterprises in America are demonstrating how decisions can be made democratically about what to produce, by whom, and on what schedule, as guided by particular social and environmental values.

What can we do as *depositors and investors* to model a new kind of American capitalism? Many American households have learned to discriminate among banking and investment institutions according to their commitment to social and environmental values. Participation in mutual funds that avoid investments in companies with poor environmental or worker rights records, or that screen out alcohol, tobacco, or weapons-related companies, has been increasing rapidly. So, too, have deposits in banks and credit unions that have developed good records of investing in community development. Responsible depositors ask their banks for a copy of their Community Reinvestment Act Performance Evaluation to judge how they're doing.

A number of funds, some of which are church-related, specialize in microlending. Whereas most investments support large corporations that exercise vast power in questionable ways, microlending targets individuals, especially in the developing world, who are not served by normal commercial loans. For example, with very small amounts of capital many women are able to start tiny businesses by which they climb out of poverty, and they tend to be highly responsible in their repayment of the loans. Investment in these funds does not bring the highest return financially, but it contributes to the economic health of the world.

How can *business leaders* contribute to the search for a new kind of American capitalism? With so many recent examples of mismanagement and the abuse of power, even asking this question may seem pointless. Yet some of the nation's leading private-sector executives have joined the search for alternatives, with models variously called corporate social performance, corporate citizenship, stakeholder management, and corporate community involvement.[1] These business leaders suggest that under the right circumstances marketplace forces can help to direct corporations to the public interest. For example, electric companies have found that they profit more from encouraging customers to use less electricity than by building new facilities to produce more, usually in environmentally harmful ways. In general, data on corporations' social and environmental records should be made widely available, as should mechanisms to allow the marketplace to reward and punish corporations appropriately when they succeed or fail to achieve societal purposes. Cooperation by government, investors, consumers, and corporations themselves is essential to accomplish these goals.[2]

As *citizens* of a local community, state, nation, and world, millions struggle daily to hold our institutions of collective governance accountable. We affiliate with myriad community organizing efforts to implement real alternatives at home. We encourage and monitor state legislative initiatives that promise greater justice for those who are oppressed by the existing economic system. We support nonprofit organizations devoted to helping governments at all levels to better understand the negative consequences of existing policies and to plot changes in policies that mitigate them. We support voter education and registration efforts. We write our senators and representatives at both the federal and state levels, again and again and again. As resisters, we must never cease to be reformers.

Appendix

Covenanting for Justice in the Economy and the Earth

(As agreed by General Council)
The Accra Declaration of the World Alliance
of Reformed Churches—2004[1]

INTRODUCTION

1. In response to the urgent call of the Southern African constituency which met in Kitwe in 1995 and in recognition of the increasing urgency of global economic injustice and ecological destruction, the 23rd General Council (Debrecen, Hungary, 1997) invited the member churches of the World Alliance of Reformed Churches to enter into a process of "recognition, education, and confession (*processus confessionis*)." The churches reflected on the text of Isaiah 58.6, "Break the chains of oppression and the yoke of injustice, and let the oppressed go free," as they heard the cries of brothers and sisters around the world and witnessed God's gift of creation under threat.

2. Since then, nine member churches have committed themselves to a faith stance; some are in the process of covenanting; and others have studied the issues and come to a recognition of the depth of the crisis. Further, in partnership with the World Council of Churches, the Lutheran World Federation and regional ecumenical organizations, the World Alliance of Reformed Churches has engaged in consultations in all regions of the world, from Seoul/Bangkok (1999) to Stony Point (2004). Additional consultations took place with churches from the South in Buenos Aires (2003) and with churches from South and North in London Colney (2004).

3. Gathered in Accra, Ghana, for the General Council of the World Alliance of Reformed Churches, we visited the slave dungeons of Elmina and Cape Coast where millions of Africans were commodified, sold and subjected

to the horrors of repression and death. The cries of "never again" are put to the lie by the ongoing realities of human trafficking and the oppression of the global economic system.

4. Today we come to take a decision of faith commitment.

READING THE SIGNS OF THE TIMES

5. We have heard that creation continues to groan, in bondage, waiting for its liberation (Romans 8.22). We are challenged by the cries of the people who suffer and by the woundedness of creation itself. We see a dramatic convergence between the suffering of the people and the damage done to the rest of creation.

6. The signs of the times have become more alarming and must be interpreted. The root causes of massive threats to life are above all the product of an unjust economic system defended and protected by political and military might. Economic systems are a matter of life or death.

7. We live in a scandalous world that denies God's call to life for all. The annual income of the richest 1% is equal to that of the poorest 57%, and 24,000 people die each day from poverty and malnutrition. The debt of poor countries continues to increase despite paying back their original borrowing many times over. Resource-driven wars claim the lives of millions, while millions more die of preventable diseases. The HIV and AIDS global pandemic afflicts life in all parts of the world, affecting the poorest where generic drugs are not available. The majority of those in poverty are women and children and the number of people living in absolute poverty on less than one US dollar per day continues to increase.

8. The policy of unlimited growth among industrialized countries and the drive for profit of transnational corporations have plundered the earth and severely damaged the environment. In 1989, one species disappeared each day, and by 2000 it was one every hour. Climate change, the depletion of fish stocks, deforestation, soil erosion, and threats to fresh water are among the devastating consequences. Communities are disrupted, livelihoods are lost, coastal regions and Pacific islands are threatened with inundation, and storms increase. High levels of radioactivity threaten health and ecology. Life forms and cultural knowledge are being patented for financial gain.

9. This crisis is directly related to the development of neoliberal economic globalization, which is based on the following beliefs:

- unrestrained competition, consumerism, and the unlimited economic growth and accumulation of wealth is the best for the whole world;

- the ownership of private property has no social obligation;
- capital speculation, liberalization and deregulation of the market, privatization of public utilities and national resources, unrestricted access for foreign investments and imports, lower taxes, and the unrestricted movement of capital will achieve wealth for all;
- social obligations, protection of the poor and the weak, trade unions, and relationships between people, are subordinate to the processes of economic growth and capital accumulation.

10. This is an ideology that claims to be without alternative, demanding an endless flow of sacrifices from the poor and creation. It makes the false promise that it can save the world through the creation of wealth and prosperity, claiming sovereignty over life and demanding total allegiance, which amounts to idolatry.

11. We recognize the enormity and complexity of the situation. We do not seek simple answers. As seekers of truth and justice and looking through the eyes of powerless and suffering people, we see that the current world (dis)order is rooted in an extremely complex and immoral economic system defended by empire. In using the term "empire" we mean the coming together of economic, cultural, political and military power that constitutes a system of domination led by powerful nations to protect and defend their own interests.

12. In classical liberal economics, the state exists to protect private property and contracts in the competitive market. Through the struggles of the labour movement, states began to regulate markets and provide for the welfare of people. Since the 1980s, through the transnationalization of capital, neoliberalism has set out to dismantle the welfare functions of the state. Under neoliberalism the purpose of the economy is to increase profits and return for the owners of production and financial capital, while excluding the majority of the people and treating nature as a commodity.

13. As markets have become global, so have the political and legal institutions which protect them. The government of the United States of America and its allies, together with international finance and trade institutions (International Monetary Fund, World Bank, World Trade Organization) use political, economic, or military alliances to protect and advance the interest of capital owners.

14. We see the dramatic convergence of the economic crisis with the integration of economic globalization and geopolitics backed by neoliberal ideology. This is a global system that defends and protects the interests of the powerful. It affects and captivates us all. Further, in biblical terms such a system of wealth accumulation at the expense of the poor is seen as unfaithful to God and responsible for preventable human suffering and is called Mammon. Jesus has told us that we cannot serve both God and Mammon (Lk 16.13).

CONFESSION OF FAITH IN THE FACE OF ECONOMIC INJUSTICE AND ECOLOGICAL DESTRUCTION

15. Faith commitment may be expressed in various ways according to regional and theological traditions: as confession, as confessing together, as faith stance, as being faithful to the covenant of God. We choose confession, not meaning a classical doctrinal confession, because the World Alliance of Reformed Churches cannot make such a confession, but to show the necessity and urgency of an active response to the challenges of our time and the call of Debrecen. We invite member churches to receive and respond to our common witness.

16. Speaking from our Reformed tradition and having read the signs of the times, the General Council of the World Alliance of Reformed Churches affirms that global economic justice is essential to the integrity of our faith in God and our discipleship as Christians. We believe that the integrity of our faith is at stake if we remain silent or refuse to act in the face of the current system of neoliberal economic globalization and therefore we confess before God and one another.

17. We believe in God, Creator and Sustainer of all life, who calls us as partners in the creation and redemption of the world. We live under the promise that Jesus Christ came so that all might have life in fullness (Jn 10.10). Guided and upheld by the Holy Spirit we open ourselves to the reality of our world.

18. We believe that God is sovereign over all creation. "The earth is the Lord's and the fullness thereof" (Psalm 24.1).

19. Therefore, we reject the current world economic order imposed by global neoliberal capitalism and any other economic system, including absolute planned economies, which defy God's covenant by excluding the poor, the vulnerable and the whole of creation from the fullness of life. We reject any claim of economic, political, and military empire which subverts God's sovereignty over life and acts contrary to God's just rule.

20. We believe that God has made a covenant with all of creation (Gen 9.8–12). God has brought into being an earth community based on the vision of justice and peace. The covenant is a gift of grace that is not for sale in the market place (Is 55.1). It is an economy of grace for the household of all of creation. Jesus shows that this is an inclusive covenant in which the poor and marginalized are preferential partners, and calls us to put justice for the "least of these" (Mt 25.40) at the centre of the community of life. All creation is blessed and included in this covenant (Hos 2.18ff).

21. Therefore we reject the culture of rampant consumerism and the competitive greed and selfishness of the neoliberal global market system, or any other system, which claims there is no alternative.

22. We believe that any economy of the household of life, given to us by God's covenant to sustain life, is accountable to God. We believe the economy exists to serve the dignity and well being of people in community, within the bounds of the sustainability of creation. We believe that human beings are called to choose God over Mammon and that confessing our faith is an act of obedience.

23. Therefore we reject the unregulated accumulation of wealth and limitless growth that has already cost the lives of millions and destroyed much of God's creation.

24. We believe that God is a God of justice. In a world of corruption, exploitation, and greed, God is in a special way the God of the destitute, the poor, the exploited, the wronged, and the abused (Psalm 146.7–9). God calls for just relationships with all creation.

25. Therefore we reject any ideology or economic regime that puts profits before people, does not care for all creation, and privatizes those gifts of God meant for all. We reject any teaching which justifies those who support, or fail to resist, such an ideology in the name of the gospel.

26. We believe that God calls us to stand with those who are victims of injustice. We know what the Lord requires of us: to do justice, love kindness, and walk in God's way (Micah 6.8). We are called to stand against any form of injustice in the economy and the destruction of the environment, "so that justice may roll down like waters, and righteousness like an ever-flowing stream" (Amos 5.24).

27. Therefore we reject any theology that claims that God is only with the rich and that poverty is the fault of the poor. We reject any form of injustice which destroys right relations—gender, race, class, disability, or caste. We reject any theology which affirms that human interests dominate nature.

28. We believe that God calls us to hear the cries of the poor and the groaning of creation and to follow the public mission of Jesus Christ who came so that all may have life and have it in fullness (Jn 10.10). Jesus brings justice to the oppressed and gives bread to the hungry; he frees the prisoner and restores sight to the blind (Lk 4.18); he supports and protects the downtrodden, the stranger, the orphans and the widows.

29. Therefore we reject any church practice or teaching which excludes the poor and care for creation, in its mission; giving comfort to those who come to "steal, kill and destroy" (Jn 10.10) rather than following the "Good Shepherd" who has come for life for all (Jn 10.11).

30. We believe that God calls men, women and children from every place together, rich and poor, to uphold the unity of the church and its mission, so that the reconciliation to which Christ calls can become visible.

31. Therefore we reject any attempt in the life of the church to separate justice and unity.

32. We believe that we are called in the Spirit to account for the hope that is within us through Jesus Christ, and believe that justice shall prevail and peace shall reign.

33. We commit ourselves to seek a global covenant for justice in the economy and the earth in the household of God.

34. We humbly confess this hope, knowing that we, too, stand under the judgement of God's justice.

- We acknowledge the complicity and guilt of those who consciously or unconsciously benefit from the current neoliberal economic global system; we recognize that this includes both churches and members of our own Reformed family and therefore we call for confession of sin.
- We acknowledge that we have become captivated by the culture of consumerism, and the competitive greed and selfishness of the current economic system. This has all too often permeated our very spirituality.
- We confess our sin in misusing creation and failing to play our role as stewards and companions of nature.
- We confess our sin that our disunity within the Reformed family has impaired our ability to serve God's mission in fullness.

35. We believe, in obedience to Jesus Christ, that the church is called to confess, witness and act, even though the authorities and human law might forbid them, and punishment and suffering be the consequence (Acts 4.18ff). Jesus is Lord.

36. We join in praise to God, Creator, Redeemer, Spirit, who has "brought down the mighty from their thrones, lifted up the lowly, filled the hungry with good things and sent the rich away with empty hands" (Lk 1.52f).

COVENANTING FOR JUSTICE

37. By confessing our faith together, we covenant in obedience to God's will as an act of faithfulness in mutual solidarity and in accountable relationships. This binds us together to work for justice in the economy and the earth both in our common global context as well as our various regional and local settings.

38. On this common journey, some churches have already expressed their commitment in a confession of faith. We urge them to continue to translate this confession into concrete actions both regionally and locally. Other churches have already begun to engage in this process, including taking actions and we urge them to engage further, through education, confession and action. To those other churches, which are still in the process of recognition, we urge them on the basis of our mutual covenanting accountability, to deepen their education and move forward towards confession.

39. The General Council calls upon member churches, on the basis of this covenanting relationship, to undertake the difficult and prophetic task of interpreting this confession to their local congregations.

40. The General Council urges member churches to implement this confession by following up the Public Issues Committee's recommendations on economic justice and ecological issues

41. The General Council commits the World Alliance of Reformed Churches to work together with other communions, the ecumenical community, the community of other faiths, civil movements and people's movements for a just economy and the integrity of creation and calls upon our member churches to do the same.

42. Now we proclaim with passion that we will commit ourselves, our time and our energy to changing, renewing, and restoring the economy and the earth, choosing life, so that we and our descendants might live (Deuteronomy 30.19).

Notes

Foreword

1. We have a position paper reflecting on religious diversity that is available from the office of Progressive Christians Uniting, 1501 Wilshire Blvd., Los Angeles, CA 90017. Position papers may also be ordered by e-mail: admin@PCU-LA .org. It was also published as a booklet: *Christian Faith and Religious Diversity*, ed. John B. Cobb Jr. (Minneapolis: Augsburg Press, 2002).
2. See our position paper "Christian-Jewish Relations," by Eva Fleischner.
3. See our position paper "A Progressive Christian View of Islam," by Ward McAfee.
4. About the same time we were organizing, similar efforts were being made in other parts of the country. Today there is a visible movement of progressive Protestants nationally.
5. *Progressive Christians Speak: A Different Voice on Faith and Politics*, ed. John B. Cobb Jr. (Louisville, KY: Westminster John Knox Press, 2003). This was an expansion and a revision of our *Speaking of Religion & Politics: The Progressive Church Tackles Hot Topics* (Claremont, CA: Pinch Publications, 2000).

Chapter 1: The Bible's Call to Resist

1. The full text of the Accra Declaration is found in the appendix.
2. The inciting role of the Jewish authorities is variously pictured, but the Roman responsibility is never questioned: Jesus was executed by the instrument Rome used against rebellious slaves and against any who posed threats to the imperial authorities.
3. This is usually translated "kingdom," but given Jesus' understanding of the nature of God's rule, perhaps it is better translated as "commonwealth."
4. Enlightenment thinking, with its emphasis on the worth of individual liberty, was an important element in the rise of modern democracy, but the term "democracy" was not initially favored. Until well into the eighteenth century, "democracy" was often used as a synonym for mob rule. John Locke, the so-called "Godfather of Liberalism," defended the rights of individuals against arbitrary government and the right of a representative parliament against the authority of the king, and was later heralded for the phrase "consent of the governed." But

for him consent could be assumed from those who simply did not challenge the laws under which they lived. His defense of majority rule was eminently practical. A deliberative assembly "should move that way whither the greater force carries it, which is the consent of the majority" (*Second Treatise of Civil Government*, par. 96, 1690). It remained for Rousseau, by addressing the problem of will, to bring together the will of the citizen with the will of the community and make popular sovereignty, or democracy, a coherent if still difficult concept (*The Social Contract*, 1762). His imaginative vision of a modern small state, modeled on the ancient Greek *polis*, was often misinterpreted in the French Revolution, but it ultimately gave respectability to the term "democracy." By the nineteenth century, Enlightenment liberals were fully committed to the ideal of democracy.

5. See chapter 9 for a discussion of the role of women in Christianity and of women's perspective.
6. See Barmen Declaration at http://www.creeds.net/reformed/barmen.htm. The full text of actions at the Synod of Barmen, 1934, is in Arthur C. Cochrane's *The Church's Confession under Hitler*, 2nd ed. (Pittsburgh: Pickwick, 1976), appendix 7.
7. See chapter 6 for a fuller discussion of Christian faith and science.
8. Chapter 8 deals with liberation theology. Wrestling with that topic contributed greatly to our understanding of the Bible as developed in this chapter.
9. See the discussion of this resistance in chapter 10.
10. Chapter 3 discusses consumerism.
11. American imperialism is the topic of chapter 5.

Chapter 2: The Strength to Resist

1. Dorothee Soelle, *The Silent Cry: Mysticism and Resistance* (Minneapolis: Fortress Press, 2001), 205.
2. Description adapted from Bill Moyer, JoAnn McCallister, Mary Lou Finley, and Steve Soifer, *Doing Democracy: The Movement Action Plan (MAP) Model for Organizing Social Movements* (Gabriola Island, BC: New Society Publishers, 2001), 28–29. In the same work see also Moyer's diagram, "Eight Stages in the Cycle of a Social Movement," which identifies three stages in which the citizenry can be rallied to participate in a social movement, stages when and why political leaders move from resistance to co-optation, acceptance, and support of a proposed social change; and stages requiring that activists wait, act, train, and oversee a volunteer corps as well as celebrate change or maintain the vision when the issue cools and is supplanted by others.
3. Henri Nouwen, *Compassion: Reflections on the Christian Life* (Garden City, NY: Doubleday, 1982), 116–17; 27. See, for example, Gary Riebe-Estrella, "A Praxis-Oriented Methodology in Theological Formation," in *Dialogue Rejoined: Theology and Ministry in the United States Hispanic Reality*, ed. Ana Maria Pineda and Robert Schreiter (Collegeville, MN: Liturgical Press, 1995), 89–98. "I asked a Black Panther, 'What must I do for you to trust me?' He answered, 'Go up against the guns next to me.'" Jim Lamb, author's correspondence, October 22, 2006.
4. Nouwen, *Compassion*, 20, 68.
5. Walter Rauschenbusch, *Prayers of the Social Awakening* (Boston: Pilgrim Press, 1909; new ed., 1925), 9–13.
6. George McClain, *Claiming All Things for God: Prayer, Discernment, and Ritual for Social Change* (Nashville: Abingdon Press, 1998), 9.

7. Nouwen, *Compassion*, 139.

8. Marjorie Suchocki, *In God's Presence: Theological Reflection on Prayer* (St. Louis: Chalice Press, 1996), 33.

9. Ibid., 92.

10. Jim Wallis, addressing the Bishop's Convocation of the California-Pacific Annual Conference of the United Methodist Church, September 13–14, 2005, Palm Springs, CA; author's notes.

11. Marcus Borg, addressing the Tenth Annual Banquet of Progressive Christians Uniting, Pasadena, CA, February 19, 2007; author's notes.

12. Rauschenbusch, *Prayers of the Social Awakening*, 11.

13. John Wesley, "Sermon 26: Upon Our Lord's Sermon on the Mount (VI)," 1748, sect. 2.1.5; *John Wesley Sermons: An Anthology*, ed. Alfred C. Outler and Richard P. Heitzenrater (Nashville: Abingdon Press, 1991), 226–27.

14. G. Edwin Osborn, ed., *Christian Worship: A Service Book* (St. Louis; CBP, 1953), 243.

15. Cf. Harvey Pekar and Heather Roberson, *Macedonia: What Does It Take to Stop a War?* (New York: Random House, July 2007).

16. Douglas V. Steere, "Intercession: Caring for Souls," *Weavings: A Journal of the Christian Spiritual Life* 4, no. 2 (1989): 19.

17. Suchocki, *In God's Presence*, 49, 50.

18. Norman C. Habel, ed., *Readings from the Perspective of Earth: The Earth Bible*, vol. 1 (Cleveland: Pilgrim Press, 2000). The other volumes address the earth story from Genesis, the Wisdom traditions, the Psalms and Prophets, and the New Testament.

19. McClain, *Claiming All Things*, 63–64.

20. Soelle, *The Silent Cry*, 76.

21. Douglas V. Steere, *Dimensions of Prayer* (New York: Women's Division, Board of Global Ministries, The United Methodist Church, 1962), 95.

22. Soelle, *The Silent Cry*, 295.

23. Ibid., 230.

24. Ibid., 213.

25. Marcus Borg, address to Progressive Christians Uniting, Pasadena, CA, February 21, 2007; author's notes.

26. "Dark Night" differs from the experience of depression, with which it is often confused, in that the person can still carry on his or her daily functions throughout its duration.

27. John D'Arcy May, "'Rights of the Earth' and 'Care for the Earth': Two Paradigms for a Buddhist-Christian Ecological Ethic," *Horizons* 21, no. 1 (1994): 55–56.

28. Martin Luther King Jr., *A Testament of Hope: The Essential Writings and Speeches of Martin Luther King, Jr.*, ed. James M. Washington (New York: Harper Collins, 1986), 323; in Soelle, *The Silent Cry*, 273.

29. Soelle, *The Silent Cry*, 136.

30. Ibid., 47.

31. Ibid., 282.

32. Ibid., 45.

33. Ibid., 62.

34. Ibid., 90.

35. Interview with Amy Stapleton, executive director of The Methodist Fellowship of Social Action, July 30, 2006; author's notes.

36. Soelle, *The Silent Cry*, 92.

37. Nouwen, *Compassion*, 73.
38. Luke 19:42.

Chapter 3: Consumerism

1. Mark Buchanan, "Trapped in the Cult of the Next Thing," *Christianity Today*, September 6, 1999, 63–72.
2. Keynes's prescient essay "Economic Possibilities for Our Grandchildren" can be found in *Essays in Persuasion* (New York: Harcourt Brace), 1932.
3. E. D. Hirsch Jr., Joseph F. Kett, and James Trefil, eds. *The New Dictionary of Cultural Literacy*, 3rd ed. (Boston: Houghton Mifflin Co., 2002), 465. Also available online at http://www.bartleby.com/59.
4. See Neva R. Goodwin et al., eds., *The Consumer Society* (Washington, DC: Island Press, 1997), part 7.
5. See David Reisman, *The Lonely Crowd* (New Haven, CT: Yale University Press, 1953).
6. Christopher Lasch, *The Culture of Narcissism: American Life in an Age of Diminishing Expectations* (New York: W. W. Norton 1979/1991).
7. See George Katona, *Mass Consumption Society* (New York: McGraw Hill, 1964), 5–6.
8. Alan Durning, "How Much Is Enough?" in *State of the World* (Washington, DC: Worldwatch Institute, 1991), 157.
9. Alan Durning, *How Much Is Enough?* (New York: W. W. Norton, 1992), 137.
10. *Human Development Report 1998 Overview*, United Nations Development Programme (UNDP).
11. Mark 8:36.
12. See http://old.hrad.cz/president/Havel/speeches/2002/0404_uk.html.
13. Václav Havel, *The Power of the Powerless* (Armonk, NY: M. E. Sharpe, 1985), 45, 89, 90.

Chapter 4: Poisonous Inequality

1. See *Dietrich Bonhoeffer Works*, ed. Wayne Whitson Floyd Jr. et al., vol. 13, *Dietrich Bonhoeffer: London, 1933–1935*, ed. Keith Clements, trans. Isabel Best (Minneapolis: Augsburg Fortress, 2007), 402-3.
2. Simon Kuznets, "Economic Growth and Income Inequlity," *American Economic Review* 45(1995): 1–28.
3. Frank Levy and Peter Tamin, NBER working paper, March 2007; see also U.S. Census Bureau, *Household Income in the United States*, 2005.
4. This section is based especially on the insights of Jeff Faux, whose *The Global Class War* (Hoboken, NJ: John Wiley & Sons, 2006) explores the connection between "neo-liberalism" and inequality.
5. Thomas Friedman, *The Lexus and the Olive Tree* (New York: Farrar, Straus, & Giroux, 1999), chap. 5.
6. Faux, *Global Class War*, chap. 8.
7. Data of this section is from Lawrence Mishel et al., *The State of Working America, 2006/2007* (Ithaca, NY: Cornell University Press, 2007), passim.
8. The author is indebted to Robert Stivers's essay "Resistance and Economic Globalization," in *Resistance and Theological Ethics*, ed. Ronald Stone and Robert Stivers (New York: Rowman & Littlefield, 2004), 17–33.
9. John Cavanagh and Jerry Mander, eds., *Alternatives to Economic Globalization: A Better World Is Possible*, 2nd ed. (San Francisco: Berrett-Koehler), 2004.

Chapter 5: American Imperialism

1. Carl Schurz, "True Americanism" (a speech delivered in Faneuil Hall, Boston, April 18, 1859), reprinted in Merle Curti et al., eds., *American Issues: The Social Record* (Chicago: J. B. Lippincott Co., 1960), 339.

2. For more information about the U.S. military and oil, see Michael T. Klare, "Imperial Reach," *The Nation*, April 25, 2005, http://www.thenation.com/doc/20050425/klare.

3. Ben Russell, "US Warns Syria Not to Provide Haven for Wanted Iraqis," *Independent/UK*, April 14, 2003, http://www.commondreams.org/headlines03/0414-01.htm.

4. David E. Stannard, *American Holocaust: The Conquest of the New World* (New York: Oxford University Press, 1992).

5. Gaddis Smith, *The Last Years of the Monroe Doctrine* (New York: Hill & Wang, 1994); Gretchan Murphy, *Hemispheric Imaginings: The Monroe Doctrine and Narratives of U.S. Empire* (Durham, NC: Duke University Press, 2005); and Stanley Hoffman, *Chaos and Violence: What Globalization, Failed States, and Terrorism Mean for U.S. Foreign Policy* (Lanham, MD: National Book Network, 2006).

6. This topic is discussed more fully in chap. 10.

7. Occasional U.S. statements criticizing Israel's settlement policies have not been followed up by action. See Jeff Halper, *Obstacles to Peace: A Re-framing of the Palestinian-Israeli Conflict*, 3rd ed. (Jerusalem: ICAHD, 2005), 61–66.

8. Chalmers Johnson, *The Sorrows of Empire: Militarism, Secrecy, and the End of the Republic* (New York: Metropolitan Books, 2004), chaps. 4, 6.

9. See Patrick E. Tyler, "Pentagon Imagines New Enemies to Fight in Post-Cold-War Era," *New York Times*, February 17, 1992, A1. Excerpts from the document can be found at www.pbs.org, search for Defense Planning Guidance, and on the *New York Times* Web site, under "Excerpts from Pentagon's Plan: 'Prevent the Re-Emergence of a New Rival,'" March 7, 1992.

10. The full document can be found at http://www.newamericancentury.org/RebuildingAmerica'sDefenses.pdf.

11. See Federation of American Scientists, "Report of the Commission to Assess US National Security Space Management and Organization," http://www.fas.org/spp/military/commission/report.htm.

12. "Rebuilding America's Defenses," 54.

13. See Institute for Advanced Strategic and Political Studies, "A Clean Break: A New Strategy for Securing the Realm" (white paper, Institute for Advanced Strategic and Political Studies, 1996). It can be found at their Web site, www.iasps.org/strat1.htm.

14. See http://www.newamericancentury.org/iraqclintonletter.htm.

15. Acronym for "Uniting and Strengthening America by Providing Appropriate Tools Required to Intercept and Obstruct Terrorism." See Philip Shehon, "Report on USA PATRIOT ACT Alleges Civil Rights Violations, *New York Times*, July 21, 2003.

16. This writer is among those who believe that the official story of recent events in Afghanistan is seriously misleading. Its distortions are important because this story has been, and still is, the basic justification for much of our imperialist policy. An accurate account would not end our need to maintain security, but it would allow us to reduce our military and other security expenditures

and recover fiscal sanity. It would remove most of the pressure to allow torture and to deny human rights at home and abroad.

The American people have been given the impression that Al Qaeda is an expression of Arab (Muslim) anger against the United States because of its lofty ideals and moral practices. Its leader is Osama bin Laden, and we are told that it was he, operating from his base in Afghanistan, who organized the attack on the World Trade Center and the Pentagon. Al Qaeda is depicted as the world center of terrorism, defined as violence against civilians by forces opposed to their government.

A somewhat more factual picture would be as follows: Osama and those *mujahedin* he recruited, mostly Saudi Arabians, were trained and equipped by the CIA to fight against the Soviet-supported government of Afghanistan. Although by our definition now, much of what he did at that time was "terrorism," he was welcomed by Ronald Reagan as a "freedom fighter." As a Muslim enemy of the secular government of Afghanistan, he was allied also with the Taliban, who emerged victorious, and he and his associates remained in Afghanistan as welcome allies of its new government. The United States turned against the Taliban, and Osama turned against the United States. Embassy bombings in Africa were reasonably attributed to his organization.

His terrorist activities prepared the way for also attributing the September 11 attacks to him very soon after they occurred. On September 21, 2001, CNN reported that the United States had demanded that Afghanistan turn over Osama and other Al Qaeda leaders. Osama initially denied involvement in the attacks, and the Taliban declined to surrender him without evidence. The United States provided none. On September 23, Secretary Powell announced on NBC's *Meet the Press* that he was absolutely convinced that Al Qaeda was responsible for 9/11, and he indicated that the evidence would be presented "in the near future." It is this writer's opinion that such hard evidence has not yet been presented. The 9/11 commission assumed Osama's responsibility, but in their 2006 book the cochairs of the commission complain that they were not given access to any real evidence. (Thomas Kean and Lee Hamilton, *Without Precedent: The Inside Story of 9/11 Commission* [New York: Knopf, 2006], 118ff.) And although Osama has been indicted for the embassy bombings, the United States has not indicted him for 9/11 (see Dan Eggen, "Bin Laden, Most Wanted for Embassy Bombings?" *The Washington Post*, August 28, 2006, A13).

The lack of evidence, however, has not deterred the United States from using Osama's supposed involvement as the reason for much of its subsequent foreign and domestic policy, including the conquest of Afghanistan. Remarkably this conquest did not result in its announced purpose, the capture of Osama, which the United States no longer seems to treat as a priority. A supposed but nonexistent connection to Osama was part of the justification for conquering Iraq as well. Osama's freedom enables the administration to use him as a symbol of what Americans are to fear.

17. See U.S. Energy Information Administration, www.eia.doe.gov.
18. Between 1972 and 2006 the United States cast its veto 47 times to shield Israel from UN resolutions that criticized Israel and called for Israel to obey the world body. For a partial list, see Phyllis Bennis, *Burning Issues: Understanding and Misunderstanding the Middle East: A 40-Year Chronicle* (New York: Americans for Middle East Understanding, 2007), 46–49.

19. Dan Froomkin, "935 Iraq Falsehoods," *The Washington Post*, January 23, 2008, www.washingtonpost.com/wp-dyn/content/blog/2008/01/23/BL2008012301758 .html.

20. See "The Iraqi Public on the US Presence and the Future of Iraq" (Poll, Program on International Policy Attitudes, University of Maryland, September 2006), polling.sport.com.

21. Seymour Hersh, "The Iran Plans," *The New Yorker* (April 17, 2006). As of this writing, the announcement of the retirement of Admiral Fallon, who had said there would be no attack on Iran on his watch, shows that the administration is still working to remove obstacles to an attack. For those who believe that the consequences of such an attack will be truly disastrous for the world, this is frightening news. For more information see http://www.washingtonpost.com/ wp-dyn/content/blog/2008/03/12/BL2008031201898.htm?hpid=opinionsbox.

22. "The National Security Strategy of the United States of America," http://www.whitehouse.gov/nsc/nss/2002/nss.pdf.

23. We should note, however, that in "Rebuilding America's Defenses" (50), it is recognized that the policy changes called for would be difficult to achieve without "a new Pearl Harbor."

24. "The National Security Strategy of the United States of America," 27.

25. Ibid., 15–16.

26. Ibid., 7.

27. Ibid., 31.

28. Ibid., 13. .

29. Ibid., 29.

30. See Tom Regan, "Iraq Is Becoming Free Fraud Zone," *Christian Science Monitor*, April 7, 2005.

31. See, for example, Walter LeFeber, *The American Age: U.S. Foreign Policy since 1750*, 2nd ed. (New York: W. W. Norton & Co., 1990) and Stephen Kinzer, *Overthrow* (New York: Henry Holt & Co., 2006).

32. See James Risen, "How a Plot Convulsed Iran in '53 (and '79)," *The New York Times* April 16, 2000, http://www.nytimes.com/library/world/mideast/ 041600iran-cia-intro.html.

33. See, for example, Howard Zinn, *A People's History of the United States, 1492–Present* (San Francisco: HarperCollins, 2003; original ed., 1980), chaps. 22, 25.

34. World Federalists has changed its name to Citizens for Global Solutions and is less focused on global governance than before.

Chapter 6: Scientism

1. "Evolution Statement Altered," *Christian Century*, November 12, 1997, 109.

2. See especially Richard Dawkins, *The God Delusion* (London: Bantam Press, 2006).

3. This is found at the beginning of section 9 of Bacon's *Natural History*, written between 1620 and 1626.

4. Pierre Teilhard de Chardin, *The Phenomenon of Man*, trans. Bernard Walls (London: William Collins Sons, 1959; New York: Harper & Row, 1965).

5. E.g., 2004, George Ellis, applied mathematics; 2005, Charles Townes, physics; 2006, John Barrow, mathematical science.

6. Frances Crick, *Life Itself* (New York: Simon & Schuster, 1994), 88.

7. Richard Lewontin, "Billions and Billions of Demons," *New York Review of Books,* January 9, 1997, 28–32.

Chapter 7: Global Warning

1. James Lovelock, *The Ages of Gaia* (New York: W. W. Norton & Co., 1988).
2. James Lovelock, *The Revenge of Gaia* (New York: Basic Books, 2006).
3. Ibid., 140–41.
4. Peter Schwartz and Dag Randall, *An Abrupt Climate Change Scenario and Its Implications for United States National Security* (Washington DC: Environmental Media Services, 2003), 14. See also "Climate Collapse: The Pentagon's Weather Nightmare," *Fortune,* February 9, 2004; "The Sky Is Falling! Say Hollywood and, Yes, the Pentagon," *New York Times,* February 29, 2004.
5. James Hansen in *New York Review of Books,* July 13, 2006, 13.
6. Lester R. Brown, *Plan B 2.0: Rescuing a Planet under Stress and a Civilization in Trouble* (New York: W. W. Norton & Co., 2006), 187–91.
7. Ibid., 193–97. PBS program *NOVA,* April 24, 2007, on solar power is excellent. See Elizabeth Kolbert, *Field Notes from a Catastrophe* (New York: Bloomsbury Press, 2006), 44–46.
8. Ibid., 197–200.
9. Brown, *Plam B 2.0,* 49–50; James Lovelock, *The Revenge of Gaia* (New York: Basic Books, 2006), 85.
10. L. A. Martinelli and S. Filoso, "Polluting Effects of Brazil's Sugar-Ethanol Industry," *Nature* 445 (January 25, 2007): 364.
11. Jeremy Rifkin, *The Hydrogen Economy* (New York: Penguin Books, 2003), 217. On a hydrogen economy, see the special issue of *Science,* vol. 305, no. 5686 (August 13, 2004): especially 957–76, articles by Robert Coontz, Brooks Hanson, Robert F. Service, Adrian Cho, Gretchen Vogel, and John A. Turner, and the editorial by Donald Kennedy, 917.
12. See Lovelock, *Revenge of Gaia,* 73–74. Good information and some differences of opinion on the feasibility of relying on carbon sequestration can be found at the U.S. Department of Energy Web site, http://www.energy.gov/sciencetech/carbonsequestration.htm; the MIT sequestration program at http://sequestration.mit.edu/; and the Union of Concerned Scientists home page, http://www.UCSUSA.org.
13. Lovelock, *Revenge of Gaia,* 128–31.
14. Brown, *Plan B 2.0,* ch. 7.
15. Ibid., 128.
16. Bill McKibben, *Deep Economy: The Wealth of Communities and the Durable Future* (New York: Times Books, 2007), 183.
17. See Dean Freudenberger, "Food Security and Transgenetic Engineering in the Global Flood System" (position paper, Progressive Christians Uniting, April 2006). It is available from 316 W. 2nd St., Los Angeles, CA 90012. It can be ordered by e-mail at admin@pcu-la.org.
18. See the chapter on "Global Food Security" in *Progressive Christians Speak,* ed. John B. Cobb Jr. (Louisville, KY: Westminster John Knox Press, 2003).
19. Nicholas H. Stern, *The Economics of Climate Change* (Cambridge, UK: Cambridge University Press, 2007), 27.
20. George Reisman, *Capitalism: A Treatise on Economics* (Ottawa, IL: Jameson Books, 1996).
21. See www.mises.org and Reisman's Web site, www.capitalism.net.
22. See chap. 3.

23. Lynn White Jr. "The Historical Roots of Our Ecological Crisis," *Science* 10 (March 1967): 1203–17.

24. See www.protectingcreation.org.

Chapter 8: Liberation Theology

1. Ernesto Cardinal, *El evangellio en Solentiname* (San José: DEI, 1979), 2:273–76. English translation, *The Gospel of Solentiname* (Maryknoll, NY: Orbis Books, 1982).

2. Paulo Freire, *Pedagogy of the Oppressed* (New York: Continuum, 1970).

3. Ruben Alves, *A Theology of Human Hope* (Washington, DC: Corpus Books, 1969).

4. Published in English: Hugo Assmann, *Theology for a Nomad Church* (Maryknoll, NY: Orbis Books, 1974).

5. Published in English: Gustavo Gutiérrez, *A Theology of Liberation* (Maryknoll, NY: Orbis Books, 1973).

6. Published in English: Jose Porfirio Miranda, *Marx and the Bible* (Maryknoll, NY: Orbis Books, 1974).

7. Enrique Dussel's most important of his many books on Marx's thought is his three-volume commentary on Marx's *Grundrisse*, the 1858 notebooks, *La producción teórica de Marx* (Mexico City: Siglo XXI, 1985). Giulio Girardi, an Italian philosopher who has spent a lot of time in Latin America, has an abundant and influential production on the subject. Two of his most important books are *Marxismo e cristianessimo* (Assisi: Cittadella editrice, 1966) and *Sandinismo, marxismo, cristianismo: La confluencia* (Managua: Centro Antonio Valdivieso, 1986).

8. Freire, *Pedagogy.*

9. Jim Wallis makes this point by noting a saying attributed to Jesus: "'You always have the poor with you'" (Matt. 26:11).

10. See chap. 3.

11. This emphasis on the human creation of all value has led, in both capitalist and Marxist thinking, to the neglect of the natural world. As progressive Christians we call for an economics that calls attention to the value of what is provided by nature.

12. Ernesto Cardenal has written two volumes of a projected three-volume autobiography: *Vida perdida* and *La revolución perdida* (Managua: Anamá, 1998 and 2003, respectively).

13. The Spanish edition is put out by RECU in Quito, Ecuador, and the Portuguese edition by Editora Vozes in Petrópolis, Rio de Janeiro.

14. *Progressive Christians Speak: A Different Voice on Faith and Politics*, ed. John B. Cobb Jr. (Louisville, KY: Westminster John Knox Press, 2003).

15. A position paper on "Reparations" does deal with racial issues. It can be obtained from the office of Progressive Christians Uniting, 316 W. 2nd St., Los Angeles, CA 90012; and ordered by e-mail at pcc@pcu-la.org.

16. Progressive Christians Uniting, "Reparations: The Movement for Public Accountability for the African-American Holocaust" (position paper, Progressive Christians Uniting, January 2004). It is available from 316 W. 2nd St., Los Angeles, CA 90012; and ordered by e-mail at pcc@pcu-la.org.

Chapter 9: Feminist Theory

1. Rosemary Radford Ruether, *Sexism and God-Talk* (Boston: Beacon Press, 1983), 18–19.

2. Larry Ceplait, *The Public Years of Sarah and Angelina Grimké: Selected Writings, 1835–1839* (New York: Columbia University Press, 1989), 208–9.

Chapter 10: The Church and Politics

1. Marcus J. Borg, *Jesus in Contemporary Scholarship* (Valley Forge, PA: Trinity Press International, 1994), 98.
2. Augustine of Hippo, *Sermons*, ed. P. Schaff, vol. 6, no. 12, sec. 13.
3. Aquinas, *Summa theologica*, 1–2, q.12, a.2.
4. Calvin, *Commentary on Daniel*, lecture 29.
5. John Calvin, *Institutes*, IV, xx, 31, 32, citing Acts 5:29. Today, we may call such resisters "leakers" and "whistleblowers."
6. Erin Louise Palmer, "Reinterpreting Torture: Presidential Signing Statements and the Circumvention of U.S. and International Law," http://www.wel .amercan.edu/hrbrief/14/lpalmer.pdf?re=1.
7. http://www.boston.com/news/nation/articles/2006/04/30/bush_challenges_ hundreds_of_laws/. On May 4 the paper issued a clarification to the effect that it referred to 750 statutes that were provisions in 125 bills.
8. The Democrats, eyeing the 2006 election, were well aware that a majority of the public, however dissatisfied with Bush's performance in other respects, did not seem to care much about these issues of constitutional legality.
9. These statements are taken from Elizabeth Drew, "Power Grab," *New York Review of Books*, June 22, 2006, 10, 14.
10. Cato Institute, *Power Surge: The Constitutional Record of George W. Bush* (Washington, DC, 2006), 1. The unprecedented use of presidential "signing statements" to assert a theory of virtually unlimited executive authority has been widely discussed and criticized. See David S. Birdsell, "George W. Bush's Signing Statements: The Assault on Deliberation," *Rhetoric and Public Affairs* 10, no. 4 (2007): 335–60. The American Bar Association in 2006 adopted a policy opposing the misuse of this practice (*ABA Journal Report*, August 11, 2006).
11. The phrase is Randall Balmer's in *Thy Kingdom Come: How the Religious Right Distorts the Faith and Threatens America* (New York: Perseus Books, 2006).
12. Randall Balmer, "Jesus Is Not a Republican," *Chronicle of Higher Education* 52, no. 42 (June 23, 2006): B-6. The theme is repeated in Balmer's book *They Kingdom Come*.
13. The need for a new Barmen Declaration has been suggested not only by progressives but also by some conservative evangelicals (e.g., http://daveblack online.com) on somewhat different grounds.
14. Proceedings of the 21st General Council, Ottawa, 1982. World Alliance of Reformed Churches, Geneva, 1983, 177–79.
15. The Belhar Confession is posted on the Web site of the Uniting Reformed Church in Southern Africa: http://www.vgksa.org.za. Select tab "Who are we?" and "Belhar Confession."
16. Some of those progressive Christians in the United States who believe that we American Christians should now make our own call for resistance see the *Kairos* Document as a better model than the Barmen Declaration. A group of clergy in the Seattle area have recently begun work on a "new *Kairos* Document," focused on peacemaking. A first draft can be found at http://Kairos2006 .tripod.com. The Greek word *Kairos* means "moment of truth."
17. "The Kairos Document: Challenge to the Church," in *Kairos: Three Prophetic Challenges to the Church*, ed. William McAfee Brown (Grand Rapids: Wm. B. Eerdmans Publishing Co., 1990), 64.
18. See chap. 11 for discussion of this program.
19. The full text is given in the appendix.

Chapter 11: Forgiveness and Reconciliation

1. Robin Meyers, *Why the Christian Right Is Wrong* (Hoboken, NJ: Jossey-Bass, 2006).
2. Hannah Arendt, *The Human Condition* (Chicago: University of Chicago Press, 1958), 212–13.
3. Miroslav Wolf, *Exclusion and Embrace: A Theological Exploration of Identity, Otherness, and Reconciliation* (Nashville: Abingdon Press, 1996), 125, italics in the original.
4. Ibid., 126.
5. *New York Times*, April 18, 1985, cited in Donald W. Shriver, *An Ethic for Enemies: Forgiveness in Politics* (New York: Oxford University Press, 1995), 95.
6. *New York Times*, April 20, 1985, in Schriver, *An Ethic*, 96–97.
7. Ibid.
8. Shriver, *An Ethic*, 125.
9. Michael Waltzer, *Just and Unjust Wars* (New York: Basic Books), 1977.
10. Charles Harper, ed., *Impunity, An Ethical Perspective: Six Case Studies from Latin America* (Geneva: WCC Publications, 1996), 23.
11. Peter Storey, "A Different Kind of Justice: Truth and Reconciliation in South Africa," *Christian Century*, September 10–17, 1997, 788–93, at 793.
12. Ibid., 788.

Afterword

1. See Sandra Waddock, "Parallel Universes: Companies, Academics, and the Progress of Corporate Citizenship," *Business and Society Review* 109, no. 1 (2004): 5–42.
2. See Steven Lydenberg, *Corporations and the Public Interest: Guiding the Invisible Hand* (San Francisco: Berrett-Koehler, 2005).

Appendix

1. See http://warc.jalb.de/warcajsp/news_file/doc-181-1.pdf.